KV-638-216

Hacking the Xbox:

An Introduction to Reverse Engineering

Special Limited Edition

Hacking the Xbox:

An Introduction to Reverse Engineering

Special Limited Edition

Andrew "bunnie" Huang

Xenatera Press

San Diego

Published, designed and laid out by Xenatera LLC, under the trade name of Xenatera Press. For ordering and customer service, please email support@xenatera.com.

ISBN 0-974-05750-9

2nd printing.

Printed in the United States of America.

DEDICATION

For my parents, Andrew and Margaret Huang,
and for my fianceé, Nikki Justis

and

For all the hackers who have been silenced by fear of persecution:
may there be a day when we are once again free to explore
and to pursue our passion for technology.

Table of Contents

Acknowledgements

I would like to thank my dedicated and caring parents for raising me to be the person that I am today. I would also like to thank my loving fianceé, Nikki Justis, for the wonderful Christmas gift that got this whole thing started. Nikki also deserves a special thanks for helping me produce this book. She was my production staff after Wiley's lawyers decided it was too legally risky to publish this book because of the DMCA. Nikki designed the cover art, assisted with placement, and spent many long hours editing and correcting this book.

I would also like to thank the on-line hacking community for their advice and guidance, especially those who must operate anonymously for fear of persecution by government or retribution by their employer.

Lee Tien of the Electronic Frontier Foundation, Joseph Liu of the Boston College Law School and Dr. Tom Knight and Prof. Hal Abelson of the MIT Artificial Intelligence Laboratory all deserve a special thanks for helping me through the process of publishing my original paper on the Xbox security system. I never would have published if it weren't for their support and counsel.

The author is also indebted the Xbox-Linux team, Michael Steil, Milosch Meriac, Franz Lehner (thanks for all the detailed technical review!) and the amazing Andy Green (aka numbnut), for providing so much insight into the latest Xbox hacks and for providing such interesting material for the book. Mad props to you guys, keep up the great work. I would also like to thank Dan Johnson (aka SiliconIce), founder of the XboxHacker.net BBS, for starting the XboxHacker.net BBS and for his interesting material for the book, and for his very helpful technical review, advice and encouragement. Also, thanks to Gerhard Farfeleder for contributing a photograph of the Xbox-Linux team.

Thanks to Timothy Chen of Via Technologies, Inc. for contributing the P4M266 motherboard for the Xbox versus PC comparison, and for his fascinating insight into the PC industry. I would also like to thank Xilinx for their generous FPGA donations through the Xilinx University Program.

You know who you are, and you know how you helped me: xor, adq, luc, head, visor, roastbeef, kgasper, xerox, lordvictory, pixel8, El (GCN), tom from HK, and sween (Scotch!).

Prologue

README.1ST

The Xbox™ video game console from Microsoft® is an exciting piece of hardware, and not just because it can play the latest video games. The powerful and cheap Xbox has the potential to be used as a PC, an all-in-one media player, or even a web server. Unfortunately, there is a dearth of books that can teach a reader how to explore and modify modern electronic hardware such as the Xbox. Most electronics textbooks are theory-oriented and very focused, whereas real hacking requires a broad set of practical skills and knowledge. Also, the few practical books on hardware hacking that I had as inspiration as a child have long been outdated by the fast pace of technology. This book is intended to fill the need for a practical guide to understanding and reverse engineering modern computers: a handbook for a new generation of hackers.

The ultimate benefit of hacking the Xbox is its educational value, or as the saying goes, "Given a fish, eat for a day; Learn to fish, eat for a lifetime". Hence, this book focuses on introducing basic hacking techniques—soldering, reverse engineering, debugging—to novice hackers, while providing hardware references and insight that may be useful to the more seasoned hackers. The Xbox has served to educate both the security community and the hacking community: not because it is an outstanding example of security, but because the Xbox is a high profile, high volume product made by a large company whose focus charter was recently defined to be security by its chairman[1]. The Xbox experience shows that building trustable clients in a hostile user environment is hard, even for a large, well-funded company whose focus is security. One observation is that this risk and difficulty of building cheap, trustable hardware clients places an upper bound on the importance of the secret that can be trusted to such client hardware. In addition, the Xbox provides a consistent teaching example, with almost 10 million nearly identical units out there at the time of writing. The similarity of the Xbox's architecture to a vanilla PC adds even more educational value to Xbox hacking, since much of the discussion in this book also applies directly to the much broader subject of PCs.

---

[1] "Trustworthy Computing" by Bill Gates, http://www.microsoft.com/mscorp/execmail/2002/07-18twc.asp

Another interesting aspect of Xbox hacking is the underground society of hardware hackers following the Xbox. The people who hacked the Xbox and the expertise they attained will be relevant long after the Xbox has become a dusty yard sale piece. Hence, there is a conscious social focus to this book. I have included profiles of a sampling of Xbox hacking personalities. The hope is to inspire people, through role models, to pick up a screwdriver and a soldering iron and to start hacking. Instilling this sort of exploratory spirit in the younger generations will be important in the long run for preserving the pool of talented engineers that drove the technology revolution to where it is today. Many of today's engineers got their start hacking and tinkering with ham radios, telephones and computers which, back in that day, shipped with a complete set of schematics and source code. This pool of engineering talent is essential for maintaining a healthy economy and for maintaining strong national security in the computer age.

The Video Game Console Market

2002 was a year marked by turmoil, not only abroad, but also in the technology marketplace; PC sales flattened, the server business shrank, and the telecommunications market, with a few exceptions, looked dismal. Despite the bear market for technology, the video game hardware, software and accessories market had a landmark year, hitting a total dollar sales of $10.3 billion — a 10% increase over 2001.[2] This is comparable to the recording industry's sales of $13 billion in the US in 2001.

Even though the market for video games is large, running a profitable console business is a daunting challenge. Video game customers are picky, trendy, and frugal. They demand high-performance, sexy console hardware at the price of a fancy family dinner or a visit to the doctor. This combination of frugality with an expectation for high performance game hardware forces console vendors to sell their hardware at a loss. As a result, a "closed-console" business strategy is used by console vendors: the console is sold as a loss leader, and profits come from future sales of video game titles. This business strategy requires a large amount of up-front investment in console hardware and in advertising. It is the console manufacturer's responsibility to create a market for their hardware so that game developers feel comfortable investing their time and money in the platform. The Catch-22 is that nobody wants to buy a console that has few game titles. Thus, the risk of building and deploying millions of units of hardware, and the hundreds of millions of dollars of up-front losses taken on the hardware, is shouldered almost entirely by the console manufacturer. As a result, there are currently only three players in the game console business today, Sony, Nintendo and Microsoft. Of these three, Sony has a head-and-shoulders lead in the console market, while Nintendo has cornered the handheld market with its Gameboy line of products. Microsoft is the new player in the game console market. The race for second place is yet undecided. In early 2003, Gamecube sales were leading Xbox sales in Japan and Europe, while the Xbox

[2] source: NPDFunworld

maintained a sales lead over the Gamecube in huge North American market.

Crucial to the success of the closed-console business model is locking consumers into buying only approved, royalty-bearing game titles. In other words, piracy and unapproved game titles can destroy the profitability of the business. Hence, a console must employ security mechanisms that hamper game copying and unapproved game development and distribution. The failure of the Sega Dreamcast is a salient example of what happens when security mechanisms fail.

The Dreamcast was launched in Japan on November 1998. Production problems with the NEC PowerVR2 DC chip, the graphics accelerator used by the Dreamcast, limited initial shipments. The following three years were a rollercoaster ride for the Dreamcast. Popular games such as Soul Caliber, Dead or Alive 2, Resident Evil, Crazy Taxi and Shen Mue buoyed the Dreamcast's popularity, while Sony's Playstation2 launch ate away at the Dreamcast's sales and ultimately the confidence of software developers. Ironically, the Dreamcast had equivalent or superior graphics quality to early Playstation2 titles, such as Dead or Alive 2, despite the extra horsepower packed by the Playstation2. The Playstation2 is difficult to program, and took a couple of years for developers to realize the full potential of the Playstation2.

The final nail in the Dreamcast's coffin was hammered in the spring and summer of 2000. A German hacker group, Team Utopia, discovered a back door inside the Dreamcast's mask-ROM BIOS that allowed the Dreamcast to boot from a standard CD-ROM. Nominally, the Dreamcast uses a proprietary format called the "GD-ROM" for game distribution. The GD-ROM format cannot be copied using standard CD or DVD burners. However, the back door in the Dreamcast's ROM BIOS enabled pirates to eventually create monolithic CD-ROM images of video games that were bootable without any need for hardware modification. Who was going to pay for a game when it could be downloaded for free on the internet? The resulting rampant piracy diminished game sales, discouraging game developers from the console and damaging Sega's business. Six million units sold and about three years after its launch, the Dreamcast was pulled from the market. Now, Sega is exclusively in the game development business, including making games for their former competitors Sony and Nintendo as well as Microsoft.

While there are many lessons to be learned from the Dreamcast experience, this message is clear: the ability to run code from near-free sources such as CD-Rs, DVD-Rs or the network without significant hardware modifications is the kiss of death for any console business based on the closed-console model. This is a brutal problem for the Microsoft Xbox, since it is built out of standard PC hardware that was originally designed to be open and to run code loaded from numerous sources. Hence, Microsoft's fate in the console market is intimately linked to the success and robustness of the Xbox security system. The security system thus far has held up fairly well; all of the weaknesses found require at least a solderless, warranty-voiding modification to be installed. The need for hardware modifications limits the practical impact of these weaknesses, since most users are afraid to take the cover off of their appliances. However, there is an intense desire from multiple groups, legitimate and illegitimate, to get the Xbox to run code from arbitrary sources without the need for hardware modifications.

The Xbox is a victim of its own design: the choice to use standard PC hardware vastly increases the value of an "opened" Xbox to hackers and pirates alike. The Xbox is a rather satisfying target for weekend hackers and hobbyists for the same reason Microsoft adopted the PC architecture for the Xbox: existing PC programs are easily ported to the Xbox. In addition, there is a wide and deep knowledge base about PC hardware, so the learning curve for hacking the Xbox is not as steep as for other consoles. On the other hand, the Playstation2 and the Gamecube have a steep learning curve and they also have architectural limitations that hamper the porting of most PC applications. The Xbox is also a popular target for pirates because of the ease of porting legacy game emulators, and because of its high profile and ease of obtaining compatible debugging and test hardware.

Additionally, the similarity of the Xbox architecture to the PC architecture makes the Xbox a good educational vehicle. The knowledge gained in this book is applicable to a wider subject than just embedded hardware or game consoles; readers should be able to apply most of the knowledge in this book directly to PCs. In addition, there are vast documentation resources applicable to the Xbox, inherited from the PC world, that are conveniently indexed by web search engines. The ready availability of documentation assists motivated readers to build upon the knowledge contained in this book. The Xbox is also a more appealing educational example than the run-of-the-mill PC. There is also too much variation between the hardware details of PC implementations to make useful step-by-step hacking guides for the PC, whereas step-by-step guides for the Xbox are guaranteed to be accurate across millions of units that are conveniently available for purchase in almost any mall or electronics retailer.

About Hackers and Hacking

This is a book about hacking in the traditional sense: about the process and methods of exploration. Some may be surprised that this book doesn't have chapters devoted to ripping games and patching specific security checks – after all, isn't that what hacking is all about? In reality, the term "hacker" has evolved quite dramatically over the years as the public's awareness of technology has increased and as sensationalist mass-media continues to color the public's opinion of hackers.

In the beginning, a hacker was someone who worked passionately for the sake of curiosity and exploration. There were hardware hackers who took it upon themselves to remove the covers from computers to optimize their design (early computers were built out of discrete components, so they could be modified in meaningful ways with simple tools), and there were software hackers who labored to make the most compact and elegant code, since computational resources were scarce and slow. There were hackers who explored the ins and outs of the phone system, and there were hackers who explored the roofs and tunnels of buildings of university campuses. Quite often, early hackers engaged in all of these activities. Hackers would share their findings or results (hacks) with each other freely, as their reward for hacking was not financial, but satisfaction of their intellectual curiosities and the enthusiasm of their peers. As a result, hackers tended to form into meritocratic groups where membership and advancement were based entirely upon a person's ability to hack.

As technology evolved and computers became faster and more integrated, hackers found that the effort of hardware hacking was not worth the benefits. The interesting pieces of computers were becoming buried deep within hermetically sealed ceramic packages, etched into silicon structures that were difficult to see even with a good microscope. A difficult hardware hack that might double the performance of a computer was made moot within months by Moore's Law. On the other hand, software hacking was developing more of a focus on applications and less of an emphasis on algorithms or optimization. The compactness or elegance of a program was no longer directly important as memory and processor power became cheap and plentiful. Besides, compiler technology had also improved to the point where compiled code ran almost as fast as hand assembly. By the late 80's, the term "hacker" had grown to imply someone who could write volumes of C code in their sleep and create brilliant applications overnight. The old hardware hackers were either converting to software hackers, or retreating to university labs and corporations that could afford to support their expensive hobbies.[3]

The term "hacker" at that time was being increasingly associated with people who cracked passwords and programs to gain access to machines and software that was otherwise off limits. Hollywood was partly responsible for this stereotype, with a slew of movies that portrayed teenagers bringing the world to the brink of nuclear annihilation with a few keystrokes, or closet geniuses creating artificially intelligent cyber-monsters in their basement.[4] Unfortunately, the hyberbole of these movie plots was lost on the general public, and this dark impression of hackers eventually grew into a dominant part of the hacker stereotype. The inaccuracy of this stereotype contributed to the creation of a term for hackers that focus primarily upon cracking systems and programs—"crackers".

---

[3] The good news is that hardware hacking technology has been catching up with Moore's Law lately, leading to a hardware hacking renaissance. Affordable circuit board fabrication services have spring up, and the birth of the Internet has simplified the process of acquiring components. In addition, services such as the Mosis chip foundry service and FIB (focused ion beam) services have started to bring integrated circuit hacking into the realm of financial possibility for individual hardware enthusiasts.

[4] Rodney Brooks, the Director of the Artificial Intelligence lab at MIT, once said that the Hollywood idea of a crackpot inventor making an artificially intelligent being in their basement was about equivalent to someone building a 747 jumbo jet in their backyard.

Technology shapes the contemporary hacker as much as hackers have shaped technology. New generations of hackers have to work hard to penetrate the "friendly" user interfaces and the media and marketing glitz that surrounds computer technology today. Everybody uses computers and expects them to perform flawlessly and intuitively, but few really understand what's going on underneath the hood. The technology of computation has grown so complex that beginners are increasingly like parable about the seven blind men and the elephant. Some beginners will start their hacking journey by exploring the Internet. Others will start by exploring the operating system on their computer. Still others will start by looking underneath the covers of their computer. Each individual could spend a year exploring their facet, yet each will have a distinctly different view about computer technology at the end the day. The cultural rift between the young hackers and the old guard was made apparent to me when a self-proclaimed hacker hot-shot freshman at MIT scoffed, "Where are all the Windows[98] computers?...all you have are these lame Sun computers that don't even have AOL! I thought MIT would have *good* Internet access." He seemed to have no comprehension of the fact that the "lame Sun computers" were quite powerful workstations running one of the most robust operating systems in the world, and that there is Internet beyond AOL – moreover, that the MIT campus was one of the birthplaces of the Internet, with rights to more IP addresses than most ISPs and a direct connection to the backbone of the Internet.

The penetration of computer technology into every corner of everyday life intensified the stereotypes of hackers. In particular, the media's portrayal of hackers as modern-day Robin Hoods has somehow irrevocably tied hacking to aspects involving security or access to computer resources. Now, the stereotypical hacker is responsible for warez, Code Red and ping floods, while "developers" are responsible for Linux and BSD. Hackers are `31337 d00ds` that `0\/\/\/n jh00r b0x0r`, and a hardware hacker overclocks and mods their computer case with neon lights. Hacking has become trendy, and many are striving to fit the stereotype created by the media. It is very difficult today to convince people that I hacked the Xbox solely because it was there to be hacked: it was challenging, and it was new. Likewise, it is difficult for people to understand why I haven't worked on the Xbox since. After hacking the security on the Xbox, all that is left is a standard PC – which, to me, is not that interesting to work on, and definitely not worth the risk of a lawsuit from Microsoft.

The Politics of Hacking

The introduction of the Digital Millennium Copyright Act (DMCA) in 1998 took cryptography out of the hacker's domain — the law now spells out that only researchers "engaged in a legitimate course of study, is employed or is appropriately trained or experienced"[5] are allowed to investigate cryptographic methods for protecting access rights to works. As a result, Xbox hacking has been a politically charged topic. It is a battle between hackers and lawmakers to keep cryptography within the legal rights of hackers. Microsoft's laudable reaction to Xbox hackers — that is, no persecution or attempt so far to shut down Xbox hacking projects — will hopefully serve as a role model to others thinking about using the DMCA to stop hacking activities. Despite all of the Xbox hacks out there, Microsoft still enjoys robust sales of games. All of the interest and buzz generated by Xbox hacking may have increased Microsoft's sales more than piracy has hurt them. Of course, my opinions are sympathetic with the hackers, so my interpretation of the situation is colored. A more subjective and informed legal analysis of reverse engineering can be found in Chapter 12, "Caveat Hacker", by Lee Tien of the Electronic Frontier Foundation (EFF).

The most alarming aspect of the DMCA for hackers is that it embodies the fallacy that the only sources of innovation and benefit to society lie within the halls of research institutions and corporations. Suddenly, it is suddenly a crime to explore, in the comfort of your own home and hobby, the cryptographic methods used to secure access rights. Restricting the research of such technology to only established institutions disallows the possibility of technology development by unaffiliated individuals. Without the freedom to research and develop technology in your own garage, where would Bill Hewlett and Dave Packard, or of Steve Jobs and Steve Wozniak be today? Would we have Linux and netBSD if the right for hackers to express themselves freely in code was regulated? *For every copyright protection scheme that is defeated by a hacker, there is someone who learned an important lesson about how to make a better protection scheme.* To pass laws that regulate the research of technological measures that protect copyrights and the dissemination of such results is to concede that copyright technology is broken and can never be improved – that the only possible outcome of allowing common people to understand copyright control technology is the demise of the technology. I offer a counter to that mindset: some of the best peer review that I received on my Xbox hacking work did not come from the academic community. It came from individual hackers around the world — especially in foreign countries — who have been free to explore and understand access control technologies. The stricter laws in the US and the litigious nature of corporations has already negatively affected the US's standing in electronic security, and this is just the beginning.

The societal impact of the DMCA is being felt by hacker communities around the world. During the course of my work on the Xbox, I had the good fortune of meeting brilliant hackers across the globe. Hackers in America were some of the most fearful of the group, and even though they were talented engineers, they were loath to apply their skills to such problems for fear of persecution. The result is that some of the most interesting results in Xbox hacking are garnered by European and Asian hacker communities. Significantly, these results are not well known in America, as these hackers have little motivation to take the effort of sharing their findings with Americans. In fact, many foreign hackers make a conscious effort to keep their findings from leaving their communities, for various reasons including a fear of retribution by American corporations. This

[5] 17 U.S.C § 1201(g)(3), Factors in determining exemption. Of course, the meaning of "appropriately trained or experienced" is not defined. I think that the best training for applied cryptography research should involve some practical hands-on experience hacking real cryptosystems.

"brain drain" does little to strengthen America's competency in a technology as important as fair and effective digital copyright control, and in today's global economy, American corporations cannot survive pretending to do business in a vacuum.

One may point to the successful publication of my paper on the Xbox security system as an example of how the DMCA works to protect both free speech rights as well as economic interests in copyright control technology. My situation was not typical for most hackers in the US. Since I was a graduate student at the time, I had no family to worry about or significant assets to loose if I were to get involved in a lawsuit over my work. I also had the generous legal assistance of the Electronic Frontier Foundation (EFF) to help guide me through the legal minefield. The EFF helped position my paper in the most legal light possible, informing me of my rights and obligations underneath the DMCA. For example, I am required to "make a good faith effort to obtain authorization [from Microsoft] before the circumvention"[6]. Note that authorization is not required, but the good faith effort is required. The EFF helped me draft such a letter for research. I also had to fight MIT to allow my research to be published as an affiliated entity. All of the direct effort of reverse engineering the Xbox security was funded out of my own pocket, conducted in my apartment, and done after-hours on my own time. MIT initially took advantage of this fact to separate themselves from my work, forcing me to seek out the counsel of the EFF. MIT finally capitulated and allowed me to publish my paper as a student of MIT after much cajoling by sympathetic professors and after I had received a constructive, non-threatening letter from Microsoft about my research.

Freedom of speech should not require a lawyer, and free thought should not involve letters of authorization for research. I fought to publish my paper because I had nothing to loose, and because I believed in making a statement about my rights as a hacker. Unfortunately, there is a silent majority of hackers out there who have families to feed and jobs to loose, and not everyone can be so fortunate as to have the EFF helping them out.

This book you are reading is yet another example of how the DMCA has a chilling effect on free speech. Originally commisioned by the technical publisher, Wiley & Sons, this book was cancelled in the last hour over fears of lawsuits and backlash from Microsoft. Such censorship is frustrating and discouraging, and perhaps some authors would have stopped there and allowed their voice to be silenced by fear. I am taking the legal and financial risk of self-publishing this book to make a statement about my right to free and unimpeded speech as a hacker. Even this path is not free of impediments, however. The book pre-order process was suspended on its second day because the original e-commerce provider, Americart, "declined to offer [me] cart service for selling hacker materials...$15 per month doesn't pay for us to take the risk of being named in a DMCA suit."

---

[6] 17 U.S.C. § 1201(g)(2), Permissible acts of encryption research.

[7] 17 U.S.C § 1201(f), Reverse Engineering.

I must emphasize that this book does not infringe on Microsoft's copyrights, and the knowledge presented in this book cannot be directly applied to copyright circumvention. To perform an infringing act, one would have to hone their skills and apply a substantial amount of additional art and know-how aimed specifically at copyright control circumvention. To claim that this book is a circumvention tool would be tantamount to claiming that all books about circuit boards, embedded software or cryptography are also circumvention tools.

The scope of the DMCA with respect to the "fair use" of hardware is another important political topic with enormous economic repercussions. Is it illegal to modify or circumvent a cryptographically secured boot sequence for the purpose of running alternate, legitimately purchased or created, software? This question may be decided in part by the fate of Xbox hackers. A strict interpretation of the reverse engineering exemption of the DMCA[7] reveals strong arguments for making such acts of circumvention illegal. In particular, reverse engineering is only allowed for interoperability, where interoperability means "the ability of computer programs to exchange information, and of such programs mutually to use the information which has been exchanged." This definition contains two potential land mines: first, circumventing hardware-based security measures is arguably different from circumventing a program's (software) security measures. It may not be a very strong argument technically, but the clause has yet to be legally tested, to the best of my knowledge. Second, the purpose is not really to exchange information with the hardware security measures – it is to bypass the hardware security measures. The final argument against allowing the reverse engineering of the hardware security mechanisms is incidental copyright circumvention. The information gained through the process of reverse engineering can equally be applied to create copyright circumvention devices. In other words, the basic research that enables interoperability, at least in the case of the Xbox, may also be applied indirectly to those wishing to construct circumvention devices. It turns out that some very specific design flaws in the Xbox enable boot security circumvention without necessarily enabling copyright circumvention, but these flaws may be patched in the near future, bringing us face to face with original question.

There are significant economic implications if it turns out that "fair use" does not cover the reverse engineering of Xbox security for the purpose of running alternate applications. The most significant implication is that Microsoft can sell legally restricted hardware to end users, locking users into their software base. This can be used to create an unbreakable monopoly over computer hardware and software. For example, Microsoft could offer subsidies to vendors that elect to secure their hardware to run Microsoft's operating system. This financial incentive will be transferred to customers, who will be motivated to buy the discounted hardware. Once a significant portion of the installed base of hardware is locked into Microsoft's operating systems, Microsoft can set prices for their products in a competition-free market, since it would be illegal for anyone to run any other operating system on locked hardware. In reality, this scenario might be difficult for Microsoft to execute even if the DMCA did restrict the fair use of hardware, since government and civic bodies are closely monitoring

Microsoft's activities for monopolistic behavior. However, in other emerging markets, such as smart cell phones, PDAs and set-top boxes, it may not be unrealistic for a vendor to try to gain an edge over the competition through such low-ball tactics. At least, such tactics can be used to stall competition for the duration of the court proceedings, which may be long enough to cause irreparable harm to the competition's market position. Therefore, many Xbox hackers have been consciously acting to express their political beliefs through their engineering efforts.

The People Behind the Hacks

Throughout this book, I include profiles of various hackers that have agreed to be interviewed. This set of hackers is by no means the only set of hackers; in fact, it is a self-selecting group, since many hackers work in secrecy for fear persecution or because they are employed by companies with strong relations to Microsoft. The goal of these interviews is to introduce a little bit about the people behind the hacks, and to introduce their motivations and methods to promote understanding and to inspire new hackers to join our ranks.

Let me start the process by introducing myself. I'm Andrew "bunnie" Huang; most everyone calls me bunnie. At the time of writing, I was 27 years old, and I am the son of Andrew C. and Margaret Huang. I was born and raised in Kalamazoo, Michigan, but I currently live in San Diego,

Figure 0-1:
Author at his workstation.

California, with my wonderful fianceé, Nikki Justis. I recently graduated from MIT with a PhD in Electrical Engineering. One of the reasons I was selected to write this book about Xbox Hacking is because I discovered and published the first known weakness in the Microsoft Xbox's security system.

I hack in general because it is quite satisfying to know that somebody's life was made better by something I built. I feel like it is my obligation to apply my talents and return to society what it has given me. I also enjoy the challenge of exploration. I want to understand electronics as deeply as I can. Black boxes frustrate me; nothing gets my curiosity going more than a box that I'm not allowed to open or understand. As a result, I have a fiduciary interest in cryptography and security methods.

I hack *hardware* because I enjoy the aesthetics of electronics; there is something satisfying about having a tangible artifact at the end of the day, as opposed to ephemeral bits of software code. It may sound a little bit silly, but a past-time of mine is taking apart electronic devices and "reading" the circuit boards. There is also something exciting about the smell of brand new electronics equipment, fresh out of their anti-static bags; I think it is the smell of a new adventure unfolding. It is inviting like a stack of blank paper: what will I do with these blank pages? A stack of blank, white papers stand there and challenge me to fill them with useful information. This inquisitive nature stems from back in my childhood.

When I was about seven years old, my father bought an Apple][clone. He bought just the motherboard, so it didn't have a case. I still remember when he first took it out of the box – the green circuit board, the shiny chips, and all the colorful resistors and capacitors. I wanted to play with it! Curious as I was about the Apple][, I was not allowed to touch the motherboard. Of course, all this meant was that whenever my parents weren't looking, I was taking the chips out of their sockets on the motherboard and doing silly things like putting them in backwards to see what would happen. After nearly destroying the computer a few times, my parents bought me a 200-in-1 electronics experimenter kit from Radio Shack and my first electronics book, "Getting Started in Electronics" by Forrest Mims, III. These were a great introduction to electronics for me, as they satisfied by craving to play with circuits and components. My Uncle also gave me his old copy of the "Art of Electronics" by Horowitz and Hill, along with a couple of books about microprocessors. I subscribed to Byte magazine, which back in the day included regular columns about hardware projects, complete with schematics and pictures.

Eventually, I had developed enough of a sense about electronics to start understanding the schematics and the ROM listings included in the user manuals of the Apple][(I still believe that computers should ship with full schematics and source code). By the time I was in eight grade, I had developed just enough understanding to be able to build my own add-in card for the Apple][. The card had a General Instruments SPO-256 speech synthesizer that I had purchased from Radio Shack. I also added an analog to digital converter to my Apple][and wrote an application that turned my

Apple][into a talking voltmeter. I continued to build hardware, and before I was admitted to MIT I had built my own working embedded computer using an 80188 microprocessor.

During my undergraduate years at MIT, I dodged the drudgery of schoolwork by building fun little projects, such as a remote controlled light switch and music-responsive party lights for my fraternity, ZBT. It was during these years that I was first introduced to affordable prototyping services and PCB CAD tools, such as those discussed in Appendix C, "Getting Started in Board Layout". The rise of circuit board fabrication services that fit into a college student's budget is a landmark event for hardware hackers. Finally, the wire-wrap tool can be put away, and surface-mount components and complex circuits are within the reach of everyday hobbyists. Over the years, I have made a point of writing up my projects on my webpage (`http://www.xenatera.com/bunnie`) so that everyone can benefit from my experiences. Many of my projects are available with schematics, Gerber files and source code, although some of my more recent projects have been consulting jobs so I unfortunately cannot share those results with the world.

While I have your attention, I would like to set one thing straight for the record. I did not get my PhD thesis at MIT for hacking the Xbox. Hacking the Xbox was actually a diversion from my thesis that was tangentially related, but not central to my thesis topic. My thesis on supercomputers[8] focused on an architecture for efficient code and data migration. My interest in video game consoles stems from my natural curiosity about all hardware combined with the encouragement of my thesis adviser, Dr. Tom Knight. Video game consoles represent the pinnacle of performance per cost, and cost is a significant issue for supercomputers today. Hence, I was encouraged to look at all video game consoles to see what I could learn about building cost-effective hardware. The fact that the Xbox also had an interesting security system was a bonus; since government agencies have a great interest in supercomputer technology, the security of supercomputers is always a topic for consideration. In fact, a very interesting paper about building trustable computers[9] was written by my colleagues in my research group; I recommend giving it a read if you are curious about alternatives to cryptographically secured trusted computing platforms, such as Palladium and TCPA.

My best advice to aspiring hardware hackers is to be persistent and to be thorough. Significantly, persistence and thoroughness come naturally if you love what you are doing. Also, part of being a hardware hacker is being a

---

[8] The text of my PhD thesis can be found at http://www.xenatera.com/bunnie/phdthesis.pdf

[9] "A Minimal Trusted Computing Base for Dynamically Ensuring Secure Information Flow" by Jeremy Brown and Tom Knight can be found at http://www.ai.mit.edu/projects/aries/Documents/Memos/ARIES-15.pdf

pack rat. Buying new equipment is prohibitively expensive, so I accumulate broken and depreciated equipment and tools habitually, even if I don't know exactly what I might do with them, or if I can fix them. It turns out that trying to fix test equipment is a learning experience in itself, and can be quite rewarding even if the conclusion is to junk the darn thing for spare parts. Finally, to quote former Apple Evangelist and current Executive of Garage Technology Ventures Guy Kawasaki, "eat like a bird, poop like an elephant." Kawasaki points out that a hummingbird eats the equivalent of 50% of its body weight every day. Hence, eating like a bird means that you should have an endless appetite for information. Subscribe to free electronics trade magazines, browse the web (but be selective about the sites you browse – you are what you eat), go to free trade shows and sign up for every catalog and periodical you can get your hands on; take apart every piece of electronics that you own and your friends', and try to learn all you can from their design. In hardware hacking, half of your most difficult problems can be solved or made easier by just using the right selection of components or techniques. "Poop like an elephant" refers to sharing your information and discoveries with your fellow hackers. No matter how much information you digest, you can never know it all. Sharing your findings freely invites the advice and good will of fellow hackers and leads to a synergy of minds. Especially in hardware hacking where all results have a basis in tangible artifacts, hiding your techniques and results only means that other people will eventually re-invent your work without your help. On the other hand, do exercise some judgment in what you say or share; people only have so much bandwidth and they will listen more closely if you share results that are new or interesting in some way.

That being said, pick up a screwdriver, and let's start hacking!

CHAPTER 1

Voiding The Warranty

Tools of the Trade

Hardware hacking may seem daunting at first because of the sophisticated tools that are required for some projects. Fortunately, most basic projects can be accomplished with only a small investment in tools, comparable to the price of one or two video games. Appendix A, "Where to Get Equipment", contains a suggested list of starter tools and instructions on how to order these tools.

This chapter will talk about basic tools you will need for serious hardware hacking. These tools include tools to open things up, tools to attach and remove electronic components, tools to diagnose and probe circuits, and tools to design circuit boards. Of these tools, the first two can be purchased at fairly reasonable prices for good quality tools. Diagnostic and test tools such as oscilloscopes and logic analyzers are worth their weight in gold, but you'll find that these are some of the heaviest pieces of equipment and they will be a formidable investment. As for circuit board design tools, some of the best tools can come at surprisingly affordable prices.

This chapter will conclude with a step-by-step pictorial tutorial on how to open up the Xbox. More experienced hardware hackers can skip the next couple of chapters.

Tools to Open Things Up

The first step in hacking anything is getting the cover off. Most electronic appliances can be opened with just a set of Phillips and flathead screwdrivers, but the most interesting boxes will require a set of special security bits.

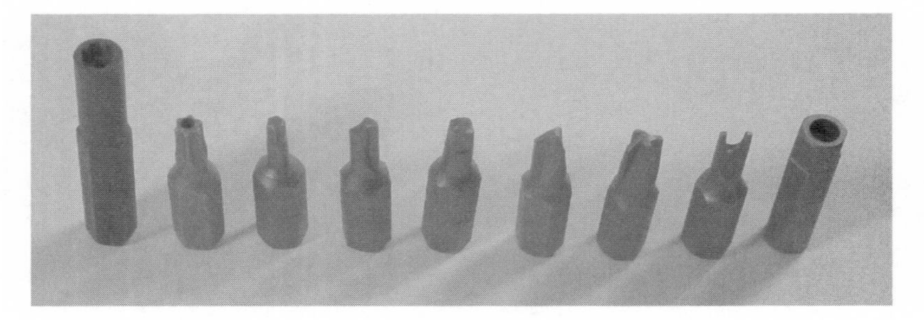

Figure 1-1
A selection of security bits. From left to right: Nintendo 4.5mm, security torx, standard torx, clutch, Robertson or square, tri-wing, torq, spanner, and security allen or hex.

Figure 1-1 is a line-up of some common security bits. Surprisingly, security bit sets are affordable and easy to obtain. MCM Electronics (`www.mcmelectronics.com`) sells a 105-piece security bit set (MCM order number 22-3495) for under twenty dollars, and a 32 piece set (MCM order number 22-1875) for under ten dollars. They are well worth the investment. Note that Nintendo security bits are sold separately. You can get the large Nintendo security bit, used in the Nintendo Gamecube, for a few dollars (MCM order number 22-1150, "4.5mm Security Bit"). A smaller version of the bit (MCM order number 22-1145, "3.8mm Security Bit") is also used in the older Nintendo systems and their game cartridges.

The Xbox uses standard torx (six-pointed star) bits of the T10, T15 and T20 size. These bits are fairly common and can be purchased at hardware stores such as Home Depot. You may also find a magnetic extension bit holder handy for reaching into a couple of tight spots around the hard drive and DVD drive in the Xbox.

Do not use excessive force when taking the cover off of any piece of equipment. If you thought you had all the screws out, but the cover is still stuck, then most likely you have either missed a screw, or there are some friction-lock tabs that you need to depress. Many times screws are hidden underneath the rubber feet on the bottom of equipment, or under a sticker label. To find screws hidden by sticker labels, firmly rub the surface of the label. You will feel a soft spot wherever there is a screw underneath. Note that breaking such a label to access the screw instantly voids the equipment's warranty. Have no fear: most equipment is designed to be serviced, so simply removing the cover rarely causes any damage.

On occasion, you will encounter a stubborn assembly that refuses to come apart. If the cover or panel flexes open around the edges or seems to have some freedom of movement, the it is possible that there is some kind of friction lock used to hold the cover on as well. Friction locks are typically tab-and-slot structures, and they are shaped so that it is much easier to insert the tab than to remove the tab. In this case, locate the tab by observing where the case seems to be stuck, and take a small flathead screwdriver and push in on the tab while gently pulling up on the case. If there are multiple tabs like this, you will need to insert a wedge of some kind, such as another screw-driver or a paperclip, to prevent the tab from re-engaging as you open the other tabs. If the cover or panel refuses to move even slightly when you apply a firm pressure, then it is possible that it is also attached with some adhesive or that it is welded shut. For example, "wall-wart" power supplies (the square black boxes that you plug directly into wall outlets) are often sealed in such a fashion. Taking such a piece of equipment apart may mean you'll never be able to get it back together into its original form.

Tools to Attach and Remove Components

Electronic components are attached to boards using a technique called soldering. In soldering, a low-melting-point alloy known as solder is heated and flowed around the metals to be joined. The solder and the metals form a local alloy. Once the joint cools, the components are electrically and mechanically connected.

The basic tools for soldering are a soldering iron, solder, flux, and desoldering braid. A pair of fine-tipped tweezers is also quite handy for jobs that involve fine-pitch components or small parts. A soldering iron is a hand-held tool that consists of a heating element and a tip; the tip is used to melt solder alloys through conduction or direct contact, in contrast to other tools that use hot gases or intense infra-red radiation. The kind of soldering iron tip required for optimal heat transfer depends upon the situation. For example, a flattened "chisel" or "conical chisel" tip will perform better than a simple pointed tip when soldering most small surface mount components. There are also many grades of soldering irons. The cheapest ones cost around ten dollars and come with large, unwieldy tips and have no temperature control; they just get as hot as they can. Better soldering irons cost more and have a sensor that actively regulates the tip's temperature. Temperature regulation makes the tool more consistent to use, and it also extends the life of the tip. Better irons also come with a wider selection of tips that can be very fine, suitable for doing the tiny compo-nents found in most electronics today. For light use, a quality direct-plug soldering iron with a good tip is sufficient. However, if you plan on building boards and really getting into hardware hacking, a hundred dollars for a quality temperature-controlled soldering iron such as the Weller WTCPT or the Weller WES50 is well worth the investment.

There is also a wide variety of solders. For most purposes, a eutectic Pb-Sn alloy solder wire with a no-clean or water-cleanable flux core is sufficient. Eutectic alloys are desirable because they go directly from a liquid phase to a homogenous solid. Kester is a major manufacturer of solders; their standard cored wire solders, Formula 245 and 331, are both pretty good. Formula 245 uses a no-clean flux, but if you like, you can use a cotton swab with some isopropyl alcohol to remove the residue. Formula 331 has a flux core that works on more materials than 245. However, with 331 you need to wash down the board with water soon after soldering, otherwise, the flux residue will become gummy and possibly interfere with circuit operation.

Many distributors sell Kester solder; for example, Kester 24-6337-8802 (25-gauge Formula 245 solder wire in a 1-lb spool) is Digi-Key (`www.digikey.com`) part number KE1410-ND. The kind of solder sold at most Radio Shacks is also quite good for soldering, although they tend to leave a sticky black residue and require cleanup with organic solvents.

Solder can also comes in a paste form, where tiny solder balls are suspended in a flux matrix. Solder paste can be very useful when attaching fine-pitched surface mount components; see Appendix B, "Soldering Techniques", for more information on how to attach fine-pitched components.

If ever a solder connection is being stubborn to form, remember that flux is the panacea for soldering woes. Always keep some flux on hand. When a joint is not forming correctly, a small drop of flux applied directly to the joint will typically fix the problem. Flux also comes in a large variety of pastes and liquids and they have different cleanup methods. A convenient flux application solution is the flux pen, such as Kester 83-1000-0951, a Formula 951 no-clean flux pen. You can purchase this flux pen from Digi-Key, part number KE1804-ND, for just a few dollars. Radio Shack also sells a flux paste in a tube, but their paste is messy and it requires clean-up.

Finally, desoldering braids are useful for cleaning up any soldering messes or mistakes you might make. A desoldering braid is a fine braided copper wire, typically laced with dry flux. Place the desoldering braid between the soldering iron and the joint you want to clean up; once the braid is hot, the excess solder on the joint will wick into the desoldering braid's capillaries. Even though the braid may be pre-fluxed, applying a drop of flux to the braid prior to use still helps the process. Chemtronics makes a nice line of desoldering braids; an example part is Chemtronics 60-3-5 "No-Clean Solder-Wick" (Digi-Key part number 60-3-5-ND).

The basic technique for soldering is discussed at the beginning of the next chapter, where you are instructed on how to install a blue LED in the Xbox's front panel.

Tools to Test and Diagnose

Electronic test equipment comes in as many forms as there are electronic products. For a beginner, the basic "must-have" tool is a digital multimeter. Digital multimeters (DMMs) have become very featureful and affordable in the past few years; a typical unit will be able to measure resistance, voltage, current, capacitance, diode polarity and continuity, for a price of around fifty dollars. Radio Shack and Jameco (`www.jameco.com`) both carry a reasonable selection of entry-level multimeters. Appendix A, "Where to Get your Hacking Gear", has a suggestion for an entry-level multimeter.

For basic modification and kit-build projects, DMMs are useful for checking for shorted connections, and for checking the basic health of a circuit before and after applying power. Continuity mode in a DMM can be helpful anytime you feel like you might have messed up a solder connection. In continuity mode, the DMM will emit a tone whenever a low-resistance path exists between the test probes. Thus, the continuity feature is useful for both verifying the integrity of a solder joint, and for checking for shorts with adjacent connections. You should not use continuity mode to check for power supply shorts, because some boards will quite normally have a sufficiently low resistance between power and ground (ten ohms or so) to trigger the continuity tone. Thus, before applying power to any newly modified or built board, use the resistance measuring mode to check and make sure that there is no dead short (zero ohms of resistance) on the power lines.

For reverse engineering and more advanced projects, the basic tools you'll need are an oscilloscope and sometimes a logic analyzer. Oscilloscopes are useful for capturing the detailed shape of electrical waveforms. One can diagnose timing, noise and interference problems with an oscilloscope. The basic defining characteristics of an oscilloscope are the number of channels or waveforms it can simultaneously display, and the maximum electrical bandwidth of the oscilloscope. High-quality oscilloscopes typically have four channels and over 500 MHz of bandwidth; discount or used oscilloscopes often have only two channels and somewhere between 20 MHz and 100 MHz of usable bandwidth. The chief limitation of all oscilloscopes is that they can only display a short segment of an electrical waveform. Logic analyzers are useful for capturing large quantities of digital data. They trade off the ability to capture waveform shape for expansive data analysis and logging capabilities. Logic analyzers are useful for diagnosing complex digital busses and circuits. The basic defining characteristics of a logic analyzer are the number of digital channels it can sample, the maximum sampling rate, and the maximum sampling depth. A typical modern logic analyzer may have several dozen channels, a sampling rate in the hundreds of megahertz, and a sampling depth of a couple megabytes. Other features found in logic analyzers are programmable trigger algorithms and the ability to detect glitches or runt pulses.

Unfortunately, the average price of a new oscilloscope or logic analyzer runs in the thousands to tens of thousands of dollars. The good news is that most projects will not require the latest and greatest in test technology, so you can get away with second-hand equipment. Swapfests are great places to pick up an old scope or analyzer for cheap; e-Bay also has some good deals from time to time. If you have to make a choice between purchasing an oscilloscope and a logic analyzer, I'd recommend getting the oscilloscope first; a logic analyzer is not nearly as versatile as an oscilloscope, and is typically more expensive than an oscilloscope. Oscilloscopes can be coaxed into capturing a limited amount of logic data, whereas a logic analyzer can never be used to measure an analog waveform. Also, it is easier to build your own home-brew logic analyzer using FPGAs and custom boards than it is trying to build an oscilloscope of comparable quality. Home-brew logic analyzers can be built to work in high-end, high-speed applications for relatively little money. Chapter 8 describes how I built a home-brew logic analyzer to eavesdrop on a critical high-speed bus in the Xbox.

In a pinch, a very simple digital trace capture device can be built with about fifty dollars in Radio Shack parts. Once, I had to capture the data on a PS/2 keyboard port, but I didn't have any test equipment, and I needed to capture the data right away. A breadboard with several bargraph LEDs wired to a set of 8-bit registers (part number 74HCT574) wired to shift data did the trick—all components that I bought at Radio Shack. The actual design is fairly simple, but because its use is very limited, I'll spare you the details. The point is that you can build your own devices for capturing digital data—something to consider before plunking down a few thousand dollars for a logic analyzer.

Tools for Design

The final set of tools to needed to round out any hacker's collection is a set of electronic design tools for PC boards and FPGAs. The subject of PC board and FPGA design is discussed in the Appendices, but it's worth mentioning here that quality versions of these tools can be acquired for almost nothing. As a result, one can design and build a complete circuit board with sophisticated reconfigureable hardware components for less than the cost of an Xbox -- this is including the cost of the design and construction tools.

PC board design used to be a very expensive proposition; tools would cost thousands of dollars and a simple board manufacturing run would cost a few hundred dollars. Today, a novice can have a simple board fabricated for a total less than seventy dollars. For PC board design tools, Altium, formerly called Protel, sells a tool called CircuitMaker2000. While I have not used CircuitMaker2000 extensively, my first impression is that it is very similar to Altium's now discontinued Protel 99SE. A 30-day free demo version can be downloaded at `http://www.circuitmaker.com`, and a free student version with restrictions is also available that is perfect for a first design project. Once you've design your first board using your free tool, you can fabricate it with a vendor such as Sierra Proto Express (`http://www.sierraprotoexpress.com`) for around thirty dollars a board at the time of writing, with a two board minimum order. As you can see, price is no longer a serious barrier, and I encourage you to try building a project or two using your own custom printed circuit boards.

FPGAs—Field Programmable Gate Arrays—are the solution for inexpensive silicon prototyping. An FPGA consists of a large array of gates and storage elements with a programmable interconnect. As a result, FPGAs can implement all kinds of digital devices, limited only by the gate and wire capacity of the FPGA. Larger FPGAs, with a capacity of several million gates, can contain entire systems, complete with microprocessors and peripherals. FPGAs are also very affordable; a 100,000 gate Xilinx Spartan II FPGA costs around twenty dollars in single quantities. And better yet, you can get unrestricted design and synthesis environments for Xilinx FPGAs for *free*! Xilinx has a free product called the "ISE WebPack", available from their website (`www.xilinx.com`), that includes features such as Verilog and VHDL synthesis, HDL testbench generation, and power-analysis software. Verilog is a C-like language for hardware design; one can think of it as a

Static Electricity: The Circuit Killer

Static electricity, also known as Electro-Static Discharge (ESD), is the bane of integrated circuits. Modern ICs are particularly sensitive to ESD; a few volts is all that is required to destroy a naked transistor. Since you do not feel static electricity discharges until the hundred or thousand-volt range, you can destroy such devices without knowing it. The good news is that most chips are built with special structures to help make them more robust to ESD. Still, it is better not to voluntarily participate in testing them. In order to neutralize static electricity on your body, always touch a grounded metallic object before touching a circuit board or a chip. The bare metal on the case of a computer that is plugged into a properly wired household outlet is a good starting point.

Wearing an antistatic wrist strap, available at almost any computer store, will minimize the risk of damaging your Xbox with ESD. The wrist strap **must** be attached to a grounded object in order for it to be effective.

In case you feel like living on the edge, working with bare feet on an uncarpeted concrete floor is also effective at keeping you grounded. Bare concrete floors are surprisingly conductive, to the point where you can get a shock or burn from prolonged contact with electronic equipment plugged into improperly wired outlets. Linoleum and hardwood floors can also be effective grounding points, depending on the kind of tile or wax used on the floor. Special conductive waxes or sprays can be applied to insure that the floor is sufficiently conductive.

strictly typed, multi-threaded C. This is great news for software hackers who would like to dabble in hardware. There are even open-source hardware design communities, such as `www.opencores.org`, where you can download the code for microprocessors and other interesting digital components, again for free.

Deconstructing the Xbox

Now that we've discussed some of the tools you'll need to hack, let's do some hacking. The first step in hacking your Xbox is opening the box. Here are the tools you will need to take the cover off of your Xbox:

- T10 and T20 Torx bits (six-pointed star shaped bits)
- A screwdriver handle for the bits
- Antistatic safety gear (see sidebar "Static Electricity: The Circuit Killer")
- Small flathead screwdriver (helpful, but not required)

Note

Before you start taking apart your Xbox, keep a few things in mind: first, there is always some risk of permanent damage when taking things apart, and taking apart the Xbox voids your warranty. Second, be sure to read through the entire section before proceeding. And third, have fun.

Step 1: Safety First

Unplug the Xbox. Leaving the Xbox plugged in will expose you to hazardous, possibly lethal, voltages.

Step 2: Remove Case Screws

Flip the Xbox upside-down and inspect the bottom. There are six screws that hold the top and bottom halves of the outer shell together, and they are all hidden underneath labels or the rubber feet. Figure 1-2 illustrates the position of all the screw locations.

Figure 1-2:
Location of the Xbox case screws. This is a view of the bottom of the Xbox.

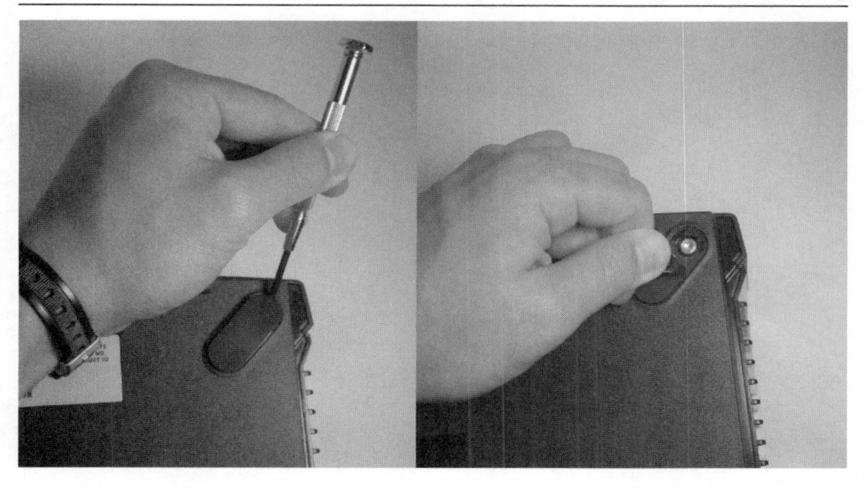

Figure 1-3:
Use a small flathead screwdriver to pry up an edge of the Xbox's rubber feet, then carefully peel them back.

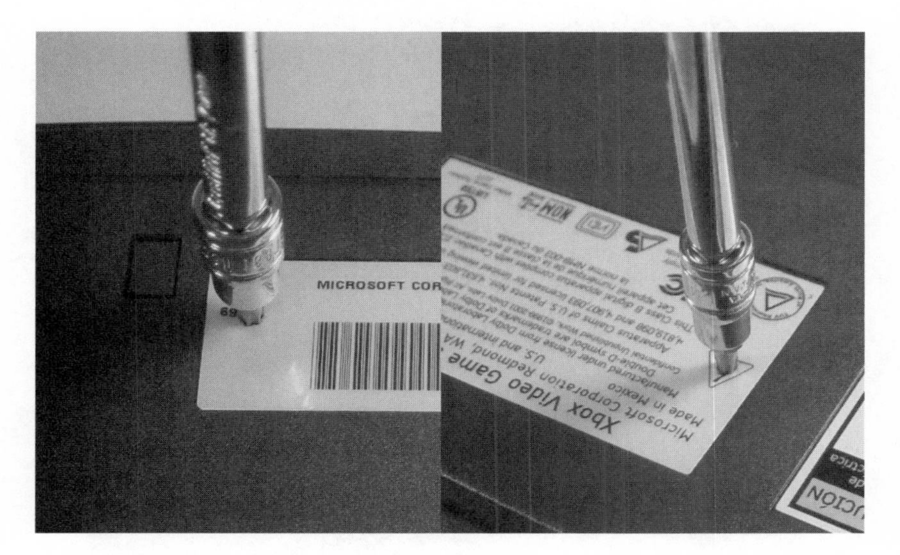

Figure 1-4:
Location of the screws hidden by the serial number label and the product certifications label.

The rubber feet are glued onto the Xbox with a strong adhesive. Removing the feet will usually require a little bit of help from a flathead screwdriver. Figure 1-3 illustrates this procedure. Once you have pried up an edge of the rubber foot, peel it back as evenly as possible so as to preserve the adhesive backing on the foot. If you are careful, you will be able to re-attach the foot later on, although after a couple of removal cycles the adhesive will lose its tack. As a replacement, you can buy rubber feet at any hardware store and attach them if you use your Xbox on a surface that is slippery or sensitive to scratching.

Use the T20 size Torx bit to remove the four screws that were underneath the rubber feet. The screws are fairly long, but their threads are short so removal should be quick.

The last two screws are hidden underneath the serial number label and the product certification label. Figure 1-4 illustrates the location of these screws. In order to locate them, firmly rub a finger over the general region where the screws should be. The label will indent slightly over the screw holes. Puncture the label with the bit and slide or rotate the bit around until it catches in the screw hole, and proceed to remove the screw. If you care about the cosmetic integrity of the labels, hold the label down while you remove the screw, otherwise the label will peel back or tear.

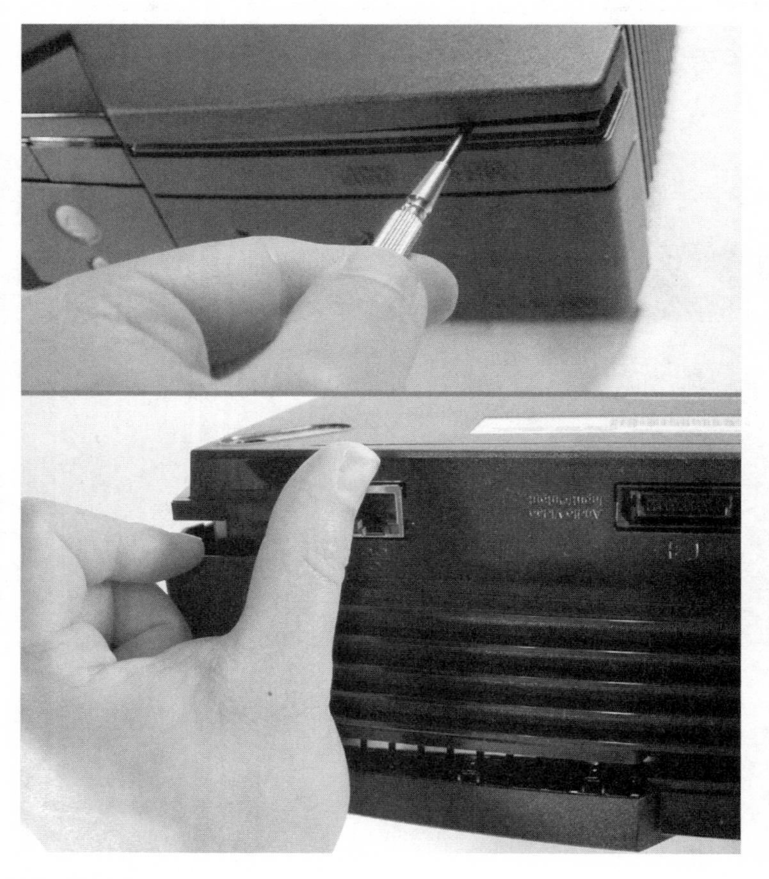

Figure 1-5:
Some places where you can pry to work open a stubborn cover.

Tip

Keep a small tray or plastic bag around to store your screws so you don't lose them. The screws that hold the Xbox together are fairly unique and you may find it difficult to purchase a suitable substitute at the local hardware store.

Step 3: Remove the Top Cover

You should have removed six identical long screws at this point. Turn the Xbox right side up, and gently grasp the box by the sides using the open palms of your hands, and attempt to lift the cover off with a gently shake. If the cover does not come off with this method, you may need to "start" the cover by prying the case with your fingers from the back. In some rare cases, you will also have to pry with a screwdriver from the front, but be careful and gentle when you do this. Figure 1-5 illustrates some of the points you can use to help remove the case.

Do not force the case cover off. If the prying methods described above yield no progress on the case cover, then it is possible that an extra screw has been added since the publication of this book. Attempt to locate the screw by feeling the labels on the back of the Xbox.

Step 4: Move the Disk Drives

Now that you're inside, you should see two drives mounted on black plastic carriers. In order to access the motherboard, you will need to *move* (not necessarily remove) the disk drives. You do not have to disconnect the drive cables, but you will need to unscrew the drive carriers.

There are three T10 Torx screws that hold down the carriers. Figure 1-6 illustrates the location of these screws. One is hidden underneath the gray IDE ribbon cable near the back of the case, and two are recessed about an inch below the surface of the drives near the front of the case. You may need a flashlight or direct overhead lighting to see the recessed screws.

The recessed screws may prove to be a bit challenging if your screwdriver does not have a magnetized bit holder, as the bit will tend to slide out as you position it over the screw. The bit is also small enough so that it can engage the space between the screw and the plastic carrier. If the drive carriers remain stiff even though you thought you have removed the screws, double-check to make sure they are actually unscrewed. You should be able to lift up the carriers slightly without undue force.

Once you have removed the screws, you will need to free the hard drive power cable, otherwise it will interfere with the removal of the drive carriers. The power cable is a black, yellow and red bundle of wires to the outside of the hard drive. The hard drive is the device on the left in Figure 1-6. It is

Figure 1-6:
Location of the three drive carrier screws. Note that the gray IDE ribbon cable is being lifted for the photograph. The box on the left is the hard drive, and the box on the right is the DVD drive.

held in a notch along the edge of the carrier. Gently work the cable free of the notch so that there is a couple inches of slack on the cable. Figure 1-7 illustrates about how much slack you should have when you are done.

Once the cable is free, you will be able to lift the hard drive out of its storage position. Lift the hard drive up and rest it over the DVD drive. With both hands, lift the DVD and hard drives out of the case, and fold them outward so they hang off to the side as shown in Figure 1-8. The cables connecting the drives should fold over easily with no resistance. Be mindful of the yellow cable coming from the back of the DVD drive; it can be easily pulled out of its socket if you are not careful.

You now have a full view of the Xbox motherboard and power supply, without having disconnected any of the drives. This arrangement will be advantageous for testing the Xbox following any hardware modifications. **Always be mindful of the power supply; it has voltages that could injure or kill you if you touch it.** Remember that the power supply is "live" as long as the Xbox is plugged in, even if the Xbox is turned off. Also note that the bottom of the hard drive carrier and the DVD drive have a secondary use as air ducting inside the Xbox. Running the Xbox with the drives off at the sides for extended periods of time could lead to your Xbox overheating. Likewise, be mindful of the large aluminum heat sinks on the

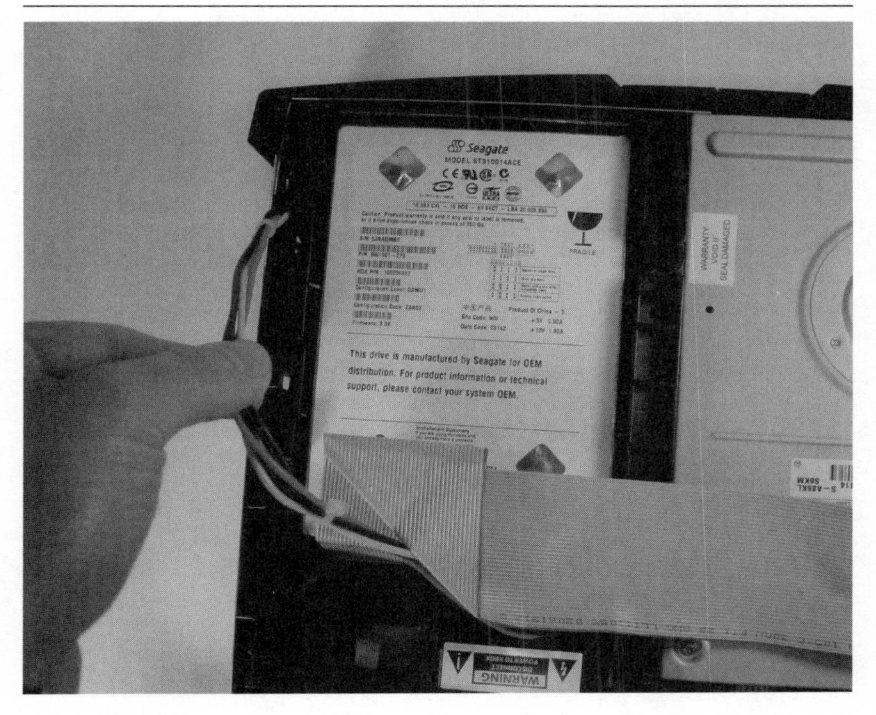

Figure 1-7:
Free the hard drive cable from its retaining notch. Once it is free, you should have a couple inches of slack on the cable.

CPU and the GPU. They can get unpleasantly hot—potentially hot enough to burn you—while the Xbox is operating.

For the project in the next chapter (replacing the LED on the front panel of the Xbox), you will not need to disconnect the hard drives, although it is preferable that you do. This will prevent you from placing undue stresses on the cables when manipulating the Xbox's case.

Step 5: Remove the Disk Drives (Optional)

In many cases, you will find it convenient and safer for the hardware to remove the disk drives entirely.

First, unplug the gray IDE ribbon cable from the Xbox motherboard. Next, unplug the yellow discrete wire cable connected the DVD drive from the motherboard. This yellow cable carries power to the DVD. It also communicates information about the state of the DVD drive's tray to the motherboard. Do not yank on any single wire in the yellow discrete wire cable, otherwise you could unseat a wire from the cable head. The preferred method of removing the cable is to grip the cable by the white connector and pull; however, if your fingers are not small enough to fit in the tight space, you can grip the entire bundle of wire and pull gently to remove the connector. Set the DVD drive aside.

Next, unplug the hard drive's power connector. You will find that the connector is very firmly seated in the hard drive. If you simply pull on the connector directly, you risk injuring yourself on the sharp edges of the case when the connector comes free of the drive. To avoid injury, use a small flathead screwdriver to gently pry the connector off of the hard drive's body. This procedure is illustrated in Figure 1-9.

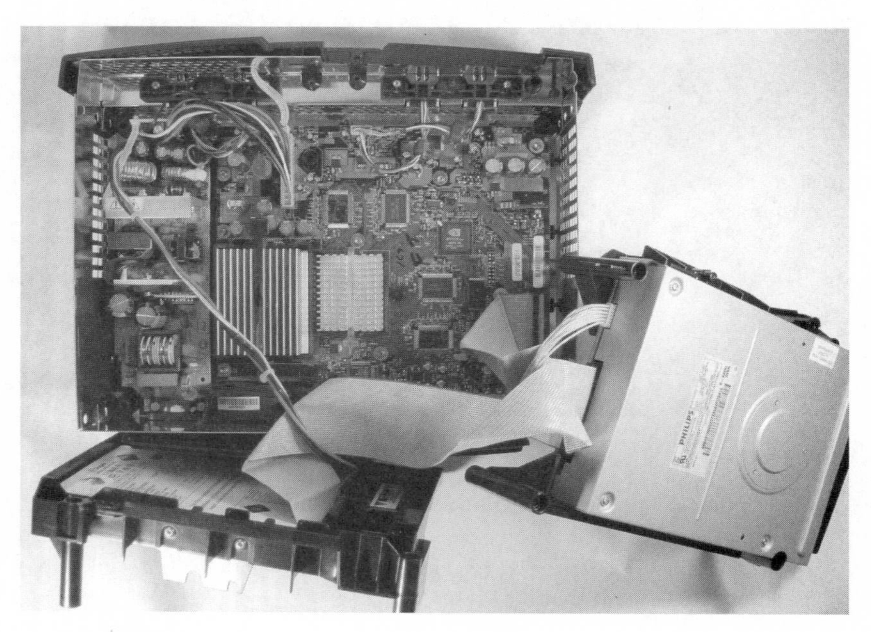

Figure 1-8:
Position of the disk drives, preserving electrical connections for testing and experimentation.

You can now entirely remove the disk drive assembly. The gray IDE ribbon cable will still span the separate drive units; you may remove them if you wish, but remember the cable's orientation so you can later re-attach the drives to the Xbox.

Re-assembling the Xbox

Now that you've taken the Xbox apart, read on to the next sections for some fun projects that you can try. When you are finished, read this section for notes on how to re-assemble your Xbox.

Before attaching anything to the Xbox, turn it upside-down and shake it gently to ensure that there are no loose screws or parts that you might have accidentally dropped into the Xbox. A loose screw will spell the end of your

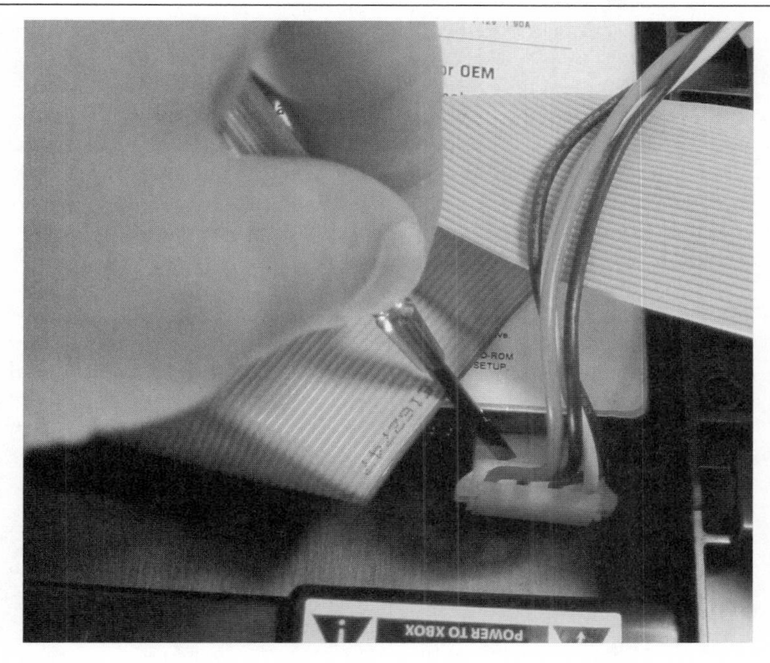

Figure 1-9:
Prying the hard drive power connector off with a flathead screwdriver.

video game console and presents a potential fire hazard, so this is a worthwhile check if you have any doubt in your mind.

The first step in re-assembling your Xbox is to re-attach the disk drives. If you followed the procedure from the previous section, your DVD drive and your hard drive should already be attached by the gray IDE ribbon cable. If they are not attached, then take the end of the cable with the fewest creases and attach it to the hard drive, and then attach the middle connector of the cable to the DVD drive. The cables will only attach in one direction; pay attention to the bump on the connector and the position of the notch on the drive connectors.

Plug the remaining free end of the gray IDE ribbon cable into the Xbox motherboard. The cable will only plug into the motherboard in one direction; note the bump in the middle of the IDE plug and the notch on the motherboard receptacle. Now, attach the yellow DVD cable to the Xbox motherboard. This cable also will plug into the motherboard connector in only one orientation, and it too has bumps on the cable and corresponding notches on the motherboard receptacle. Now, set the DVD drive into the Xbox. Check that it is flush and level by observing how the Xbox-logo DVD drive tray sits with respect to the edge of the case. It is likely that you will need to try to place the drive a couple of times before it sits just right. Use the creases in the gray IDE ribbon cable to help guide you if you are confused about the orientation of the various parts.

You're almost done. Drop the hard drive into place next to the DVD drive. Again, this drive will probably require a bit of jiggling about in order to get it to settle into place. The drive should be level with the DVD drive and flush with the edges of the metal EMI radiation shield around the Xbox case. Thread the hard drive power cable through its retaining notch in the drive tray, and plug it into the hard drive. You will need to apply a fair bit of force on the connector for a solid connection. You should feel a gentle snap when the connector is fully engaged. Finally, thread the gray IDE ribbon cable through its original retaining hook on the drive carriers.

At this point, it is a good idea to plug the Xbox in, connect it to a TV and check to make sure that the Xbox starts up properly. You can run the Xbox indefinitely with the cover off like this, as all of the cooling ducts formed by the bottom of the drive carries and the DVD drive are in place. If the drives are not properly connected to the Xbox, the console will still boot, but it will display a message about your console requiring service. Check your connections carefully if this message appears.

It is now time to screw the drives in place. You should have nine screws at this point: three short T10-drive screws for the drive carriers, and six long T20-drive screws for the case cover. Don't panic if you are missing a couple of screws, or if you have a couple extra. The Xbox will still hold together even if you're short a screw or two. Attach the screws and the case cover in the reverse order of removing them; refer to the pictures earlier in this section if you need a reminder as to where they go.

After the case cover is attached, you are ready to use your Xbox again!

Chapter 2

Thinking Inside The Box

Reverse engineering can be thought of as a very challenging yet very rewarding game. To win at reverse engineering, you need a bit of skill and a bit of luck. And like any game, to develop your skills, you just need to play, play, play.

The first step in building your skills as a hacker is to gain an intuition for the material. In the case of hardware, a good way to get a feel for things is to take the covers off of everything and try to figure out what all the components are, and what they might do. It is also helpful to order a paper catalog from a parts vendor such as Digi-Key, Jameco or Newark Electronics and just leaf through the pages in your spare time. At first, reading through a parts catalog may feel like reading a dictionary, but as you look at more and more circuit boards, you will gradually find everything making sense.

The next most powerful tool of the reverse engineer is pattern matching. All hardware engineers are constrained by the same laws of nature, and all hardware engineers use the same kinds of building blocks. Engineers also like to modularize and re-use existing designs. As a result, a single design motif can be found in many designs. Recognizing design motifs will enable you to determine the function of circuits even if you do not recognize a single part number. Likewise, one can go quite far in reverse engineering without any formal electrical engineering training.

The final tool of the reverse engineer is experimentation. When intuition and pattern matching fail to reveal the secrets of a circuit, one must resort to probing and perturbing the system and trying to deduce function based on the observed responses. While experimentation may lead to hardware failure, one can take solace in the fact that most consumer hardware is designed to be probed and tested as a requirement for manufacturing. Furthermore, in the case of the Xbox, one can take some comfort in the fact that a new Xbox is relatively inexpensive. Buying two boxes up front and treating one as the "sacrificial" box helps remove the psychological barrier one might otherwise have about performing aggressive experiments on the hardware.

This chapter will introduce you to the basics of reverse engineering, with a focus on basic techniques, such as reading circuit boards to build an intuition, and some coverage of intermediate techniques such as pattern matching and recognizing basic design motifs.

Reading a Circuit Board

The first thing you see when you take the cover off of a typical electronic device is the circuit board. Typically colored green or tan, this multilayer sandwich of copper, glass fiber and epoxy contains an exact schematic netlist within its traces. In other words, by following the traces, one can determine exactly how every component is connected. The placement of components and the layout of the traces also contains clues that can bring insight into the designer's thought process.

Circuit Board Basics

A typical circuit board consists of a few layers of patterned copper separated by thin sheets of fiberglass impregnated with epoxy. The color of a raw circuit board is whitish or tan with copper traces; however, almost all circuit boards are coated with a thin polymer called the *soldermask* that gives circuit boards their familiar green color. Molten solder does not adhere to the soldermask, so during production excess solder does not stick to the board and cause shorts. The soldermask has openings for connections to components. These openings typically have a silvery color from a thin plating of tin or solder that is applied to prevent the copper from oxidizing and to enhance solderability.

On top of the soldermask is typically a layer of white lettering referred to as the *silkscreen*. Each component on a circuit board has an outline and a unique designator on the silkscreen layer. The designator enables people to quickly associate a component on a circuit board with a component on a schematic. You can use the designator to help guess the function of a component based on the component naming scheme. Table 2-1 summarizes the component naming scheme used in the Xbox.

Tip

The Xbox motherboard includes a handy coordinate system printed along the edges of the board in the silkscreen layer. On the component side of the board, the coordinates go from A-G on the sides, and from 1-8 along the top and bottom. The reverse side of the board has coordinates M-V along the sides. Note that the letters I, O, Q, and S are skipped because they can be confused with the numbers 0, 1, and 5. Component designators on the Xbox motherboard are encoded using this coordinate system; thus, J7D1, the LPC debug port, can be found on the top side at coordinates 7D. This book will frequently use this coordinate system along with the component designators to refer to specific components.

Connections between wiring layers are made by copper-filled holes called *vias*. Since the cost of a circuit board grows with the number of layers, most consumer electronic devices are designed to keep the number of layers to a minimum. Radio receivers and audio amplifiers will typically use single-sided boards, whereas the latest PC motherboards might have up to six or eight layers. The Xbox motherboard has four layers. The top two layers are dedicated to carrying information between chips, and the inner two layers are dedicated to delivering power. The Xbox motherboard will appear opaque at first glance because the inner power layers are basically solid sheets of copper. The good news for reverse engineering is that we can trace every connection on the Xbox motherboard through casual visual inspection because all of the signals layers are outside of the opaque power layers. The Xbox design contrasts with motherboards that bury two or four signal layers inside of the power layers. Buried signal layers can make signal tracing potentially difficult. Note that the decision to bury signals inside power layers is typically not driven by security, but rather by the physics of how

Designator	Component Type
C	Capacitor
R	Resistor
U	Integrated Circuit or Transistor
L	Inductor
RP	Resistor Pack
Q	Transistor
CR	Diode
J	Connector or Jumper
RT	Resettable Fuse
Y	Crystal

Table 2-1:
Xbox component naming scheme.

electrical signals interact between circuit board layers.

Tracing a signal is fairly easy. Starting from the connection of the source component to the board, follow the copper trace. If the trace intersects with a circle, then there is a good chance that the signal continues on the opposite side of the board. If a trace ends and there is no connection to the other side of the board, then there is a good chance that the trace is connected to one of the power planes.

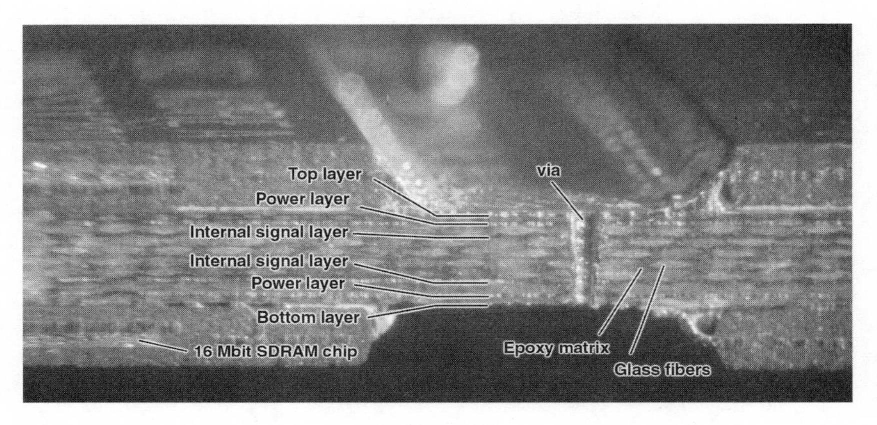

Figure 2-1:
Cross-section of a typical circuit board.

Try It

Try tracing some signals on the Xbox motherboard. On the Xbox motherboard, take a look at connector J8C1, the 40-pin IDE connector in sector 8C. Almost all of the signals from the IDE connector go to one chip, the MCPX, on the motherboard by way of some resistor packs. What might you be able to conclude about that chip? Notice how some of the traces coming from the IDE connector meander back and forth. This is a technique used to try and ensure that all wires have the same length. See the sidebar on "Why do Circuit Board Traces Meander Everywhere?" for more explanation about this technique.

Components

Now that you have a little bit of experience tracing back a signal, it is time to learn what some basic components look like.

The two major classes of components are passive and active components. Loosely speaking, passive components cannot amplify a signal, so they usually have just two leads. Sometimes multiple passive components are packaged together, so a single package of passive components will have multiple leads. Passive components include: capacitors, resistors and inductors. The most common passive components on the Xbox motherboard are capacitors. Capacitors store energy as an electric charge; in the Xbox, they are primarily used to smooth out local power fluctuations

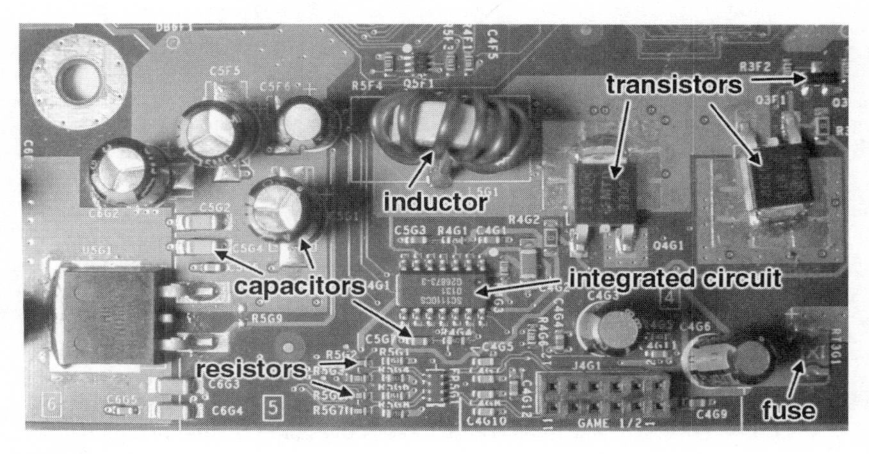

Figure 2-2:
Typical passive components in an Xbox.

Why Do Circuit Board Traces Meander Everywhere?

After looking at a few circuit boards, you will probably start noticing that the traces on the circuit board often times meander all over the place, sometimes going back and forth several times before connecting to its destination. It seems like a pointless waste when a straight trace would do the trick. However, rarely will you find a structure on a circuit board that was placed as a flighty whim by the designer. It turns out that the speed of signals in most high-end electronic devices, about ¼ the speed of light, is slow compared to the time required for a signal to arrive at its destination. For example, a signal will only travel 3 inches on a circuit board during one clock cycle in a 1 GHz processor (one clock tick at 1 GHz is a duration of 1 billionth of a second, or one nanosecond). Thus, two signals starting from the same chip will arrive at their destination at quite different times if the trace lengths are very different. To combat this, designers will put extra bends into the shorter trace so that the effective length of the trace is the same as the longer trace.

from CMOS digital logic switching, and to suppress high frequency noise.

Other large passive components found on the Xbox motherboard include inductors and resistors. The large wire-wound toroidal (donut-shaped) inductors found on the Xbox motherboard are all part of the power supply subsystem. Inductors store energy as magnetic flux. An inductor's electrical properties are complementary to that of a capacitor. Combinations of inductors and capacitors with transistor switches in between are used to build very efficient power regulators. Most of the resistors on the Xbox motherboard are used either to absorb excess energy at the termination of signal traces, or to bias a wire to a particular logic level.

There are two ways you can identify a passive device on the Xbox motherboard. The first is by the shape of the package. Package shape recognition is feasible because there are so few basic varieties of passive parts. Figure 2-2 has some pictures of the capacitors, inductors and resistors that you might see on an Xbox motherboard. The second method is to read the label next to the part on the motherboard and to infer the part's function by the reference designator using Table 2-1 as a guide.

Active components can amplify signals, and have three or more leads. The simplest active component is a transistor, with three and occasionally four leads (sometimes discrete "MOSFET" transistors have an explicit fourth "body" terminal). The most complicated active components are integrated circuits, such as CPU and memory chips, with hundreds, sometimes thousands, of leads. Integrated circuits come in a wide variety of packages,

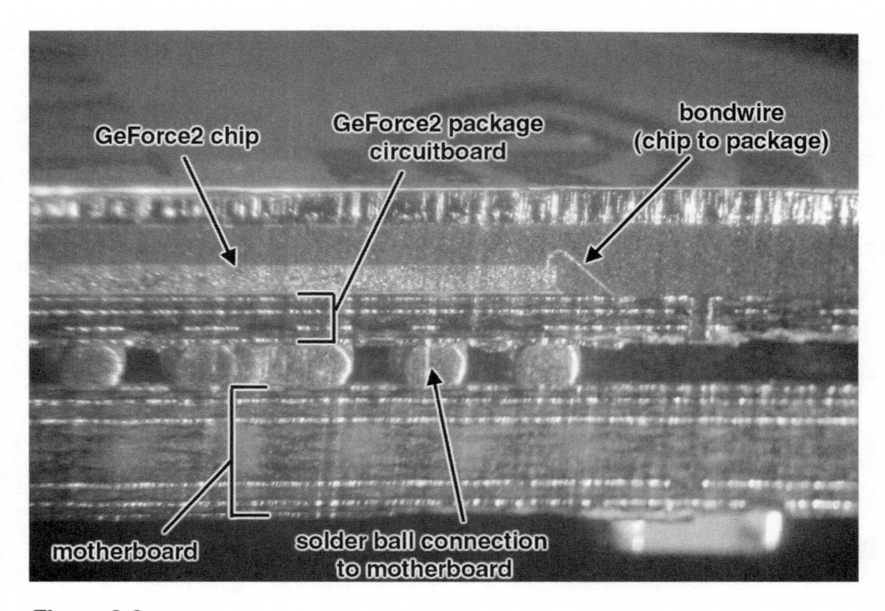

Figure 2-3:
Cross section view of a BGA packaged part (GeForce2) mounted on a motherboard.

What Are All These Resistors and Capacitors Doing on a Digital Circuit Board?

A motif you will notice on many circuit boards is a preponderance of resistors and capacitors. Capacitors are everywhere because they help keep noise to a minimum and stabilize the power supply voltages. They are required because the copper planes used to distribute power have a small amount of resistance and inductance. These small parasitics can cause big problems when a large amount of current is switched through the power supply. The exact placement and selection of capacitors is considered a bit of a black art. If you happen to knock off one of the tiny, sand-grain sized capacitors on a circuit board while working on it, chances are that you'll be able to get away without replacing it. However, given a defect of this kind, the most likely problem you will encounter are intermittent reliability problems.

While capacitors are everywhere to provide local storage of energy for all the components, the resistors are everywhere remove excess energy. Fast signals on a motherboard carry a lot of energy, and if the energy is not dissipated at the receiver in a controlled fashion with a resistor, the signal energy will reflect back to the transmitter and cause problems. The phenomenon is similar to that of sound in a gymnasium. When you speak in an empty gymnasium, there is an echo. If you speak too fast, people will be unable to understand what you say because the echo will start interfering with your speech. However, if you cover the gymnasium walls with foam, the echo will be absorbed by the foam and you can talk without interference from your echo. Resistors are like the acoustic foam you would put on walls to damp out echoes, so that circuits can talk to each other at high speeds. Unlike most capacitors, if you happen to knock off one of these resistors while playing around, you will have to replace it in order for the circuit to work properly. These "termination resistors" are often packaged four or eight to a package, so they almost look like small integrated circuits. You can distinguish resistor packs from other components because they are shiny, slightly lumpy, have a white border, and they will have a reference designator prefix of "RP" near them. When tracing a signal through a resistor pack, it is fairly safe to assume that signals flow straight through, so that a connection on one side goes straight through to the pin immediately on the other side.

and sometimes the connections are hidden underneath the package, as is the case in the Ball Grid Array (BGA) package. The graphics chip, MCPX, and CPU on the Xbox motherboard use BGA packages. Figure 2-3 is a cross section of a BGA device, revealing the hidden connections underneath.

Identifying the function of a particular integrated circuit is more challenging than identifying the function of a passive device. Functionally identical silicon can be purchased in a variety of packages that can look very different. In some cases, you can guess the function of a device by observing what the device is connected to or what the device looks like, but the most reliable method is to read the part number off of the chip and look it up on the web. Typically, parts have some kind of logo or part number prefix that identifies the manufacturer. You can then find more data on the device by visiting the manufacturer's website. In the case that you do not recognize the logo or the part number prefix, there are a few services that can help you look up part functions, listed below.

1. `www.findchips.com` is a service that can take a part number or pieces of a part number and search the inventories of many distributors for inventory matches. Most common parts will show up in FindChips, and the links provided will often lead you not only to a short description of the part, but also pricing and ordering information for the part.
2. `www.google.com` indexes everything on the web, and part numbers are no exception. Google can also be used to help find manufacturer's websites if you query on the letters in the logo plus a descriptive term such as "semiconductors". At the manufacturer's website, you will probably need to find the specialized part search engine buried in the website or go to the semiconductor products sub-page in order to do a part number lookup. The search function on the front page of a company sometimes can find part numbers, but more often indexes only useless corporate and marketing pages.
3. If neither of these services gets you there, try stripping off some of the prefixes and suffixes on the part number. In our M29F080A example, querying just the part number 29F080 will bring you to the webpages of multiple manufactures that make functionally compatible parts to the STMicroelectronics part.

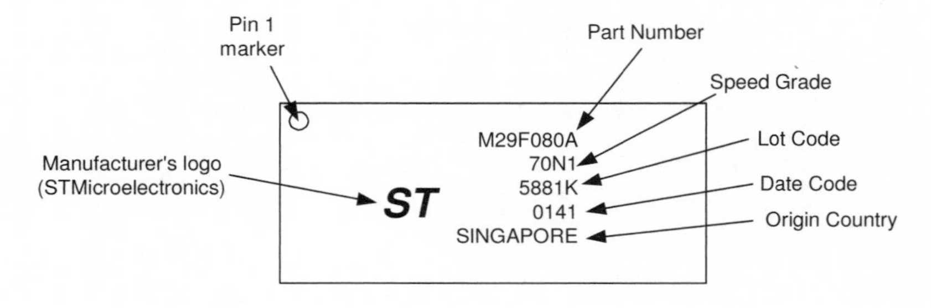

Figure 2-4:
Anatomy of a typical IC part number. The diagram is a cartoon of the chip at location U7D1 on the Xbox motherboard.

Try It

Let's try looking up an Xbox part number. Locate U7D1 on the Xbox motherboard. Figure 2-4 illustrates what you might find. The part number is typically the longest number on the chip, and it often starts with one or two alphabetic characters. Memory chips and processors also frequently have a speed grade or quality suffix after the part number. Additionally, almost all chips have a date code. Date codes are usually a four digit number of the format YY-WW, where YY is the year the chip was manufactured, and WW is the workweek. In our example, our M29F080A part was manufactured in the 41st week of 2001 in Singapore, and it has a speed grade of 70N1. The remaining number, 5881K, is a lot code that has a meaning that varies between manufacturers, but in general links a chip to a particular silicon wafer or silicon wafer lot's tracking number in the fabrication facility. The "ST" logo indicates the manufacturer of this chip is STMicroelectronics, and fortunately the website for this manufacturer can be quickly found through google or by guessing, as the URL for the company is simply www.st.com. Typing in the part number, M29F080A, into the search field on the home page brings you directly to search results that include detailed datasheets and descriptions of this part—an 8 Mbit Uniform Block Single Supply FLASH ROM.

Test Points

Almost all circuit boards in consumer electronics feature structures designed to expedite the testing of the finished board in the factory. These "test points" exist to cope with the unfortunate reality of manufacturing defects. The Xbox is no exception when it comes to test points and manufacturing defects. The bottom of the Xbox motherboard is populated with hundreds of test points—tiny silvery circles—that allow a contact probe to access almost every interesting signal within the Xbox. These test points are a welcome gift to reverse engineers and to people who wish to modify their hardware, because they provide easy access to signals that might otherwise require a microscope and a steady hand.

A set of test points are probed all at once on the manufacturing line with a piece of equipment called a "bed of nails tester". Aptly named, the bed of nails tester consists of hundreds of spring-loaded "pogo pin" structures. A motherboard is aligned to the testbed and clamped down with either mechanical plungers or a vacuum chuck. Similarly, you can use pogo-pins to make your own solderless modifications to an Xbox motherboard by leveraging the test points. You will need to build your own circuit boards (see Appendix), but the result will be a board that you just have to screw down to install—*no soldering required!*

Xbox Architecture

Before diving into the pattern matching examples, we will need a pattern reference. Let's take this opportunity and study the Xbox internal architecture as the pattern reference, and eventually compare the Xbox architecture to a PC and to another video game console.

High-Level Organization

The Xbox has a Pentium-III class processor running at 733 MHz as its CPU. The "S-Spec" number on the CPU is closest to that of a Mobile Celeron. The CPU is connected via a standard P6 133 MHz Front Side Bus (FSB) to a graphics processing unit (GPU) plus northbridge combo chip called the NV2A by nVidia. Its closest PC relative is the nForce IGP chip by nVidia. Since the northbridge logic and the GPU are combined into a single

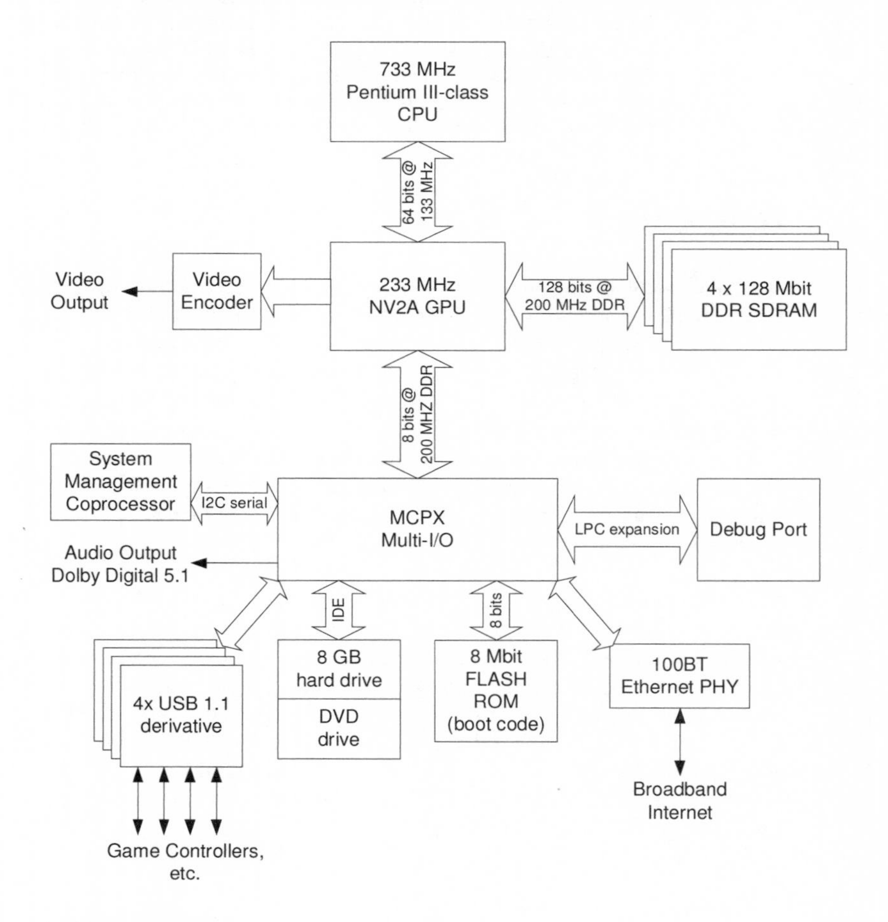

Figure 2-5:
High level architectural view of the Xbox.

chip, the CPU and graphics processors can share a common bank of memory. This is called a "unified memory architecture" (UMA). Compared to a traditional split video/main memory architecture, a UMA costs less to build because it eliminates the dedicated video memory. However, UMA has lower performance in certain situations because UMA introduces memory access contention between the main processor and the graphics processor. In order to alleviate some of this contention, the system memory is frequently split into multiple banks. The nForce IGP, for example, splits the memory into two banks that can be independently accessed by both the GPU and the CPU through a switching network.

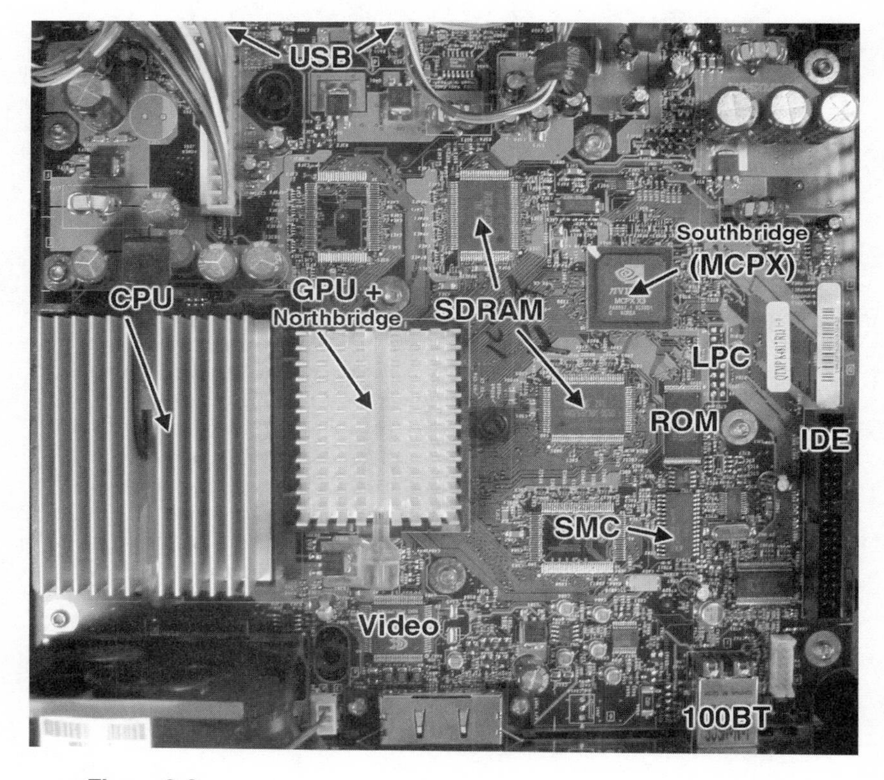

Figure 2-6:
Photograph of an Xbox motherboard with the major components labelled.

The GPU is connected to a kitchen-sink chip called the "MCPX" via a fast, narrow bus called a HyperTransport bus. The MCPX combines a southbridge chip plus almost all of the Xbox peripherals, including USB controllers, a legacy boot ROM interface, a Dolby digital audio processor, a mass storage IDE controller, an ethernet controller, and interfaces to system management functions.

The connectivity of all the major blocks that compose an Xbox are illustrated in Figure 2-5, and Figure 2-6 illustrates the location of these blocks on an actual Xbox motherboard.

Functional Details

The following sections present a cursory overview of the pieces that constitute the Xbox architecture. Attention has been taken to the details that are necessary for understanding how to reverse engineer the Xbox security mechanisms.

CPU

The CPU (Central Processing Unit) is the computational heart of a conventional computer. The subject of CPU architecture deserves an entire book alone, so we will cover just the material required to understand how to reverse engineer the Xbox. In particular, we will investigate how to gain control of the Xbox CPU.

A CPU reads sequences of instructions stored in memory—programs—that tell the CPU to perform various computations or to make decisions based on available data. The instructions are stored in memory as numbers called *opcodes*. Opcodes take *operands* as arguments. Programmers use alphabetic mnemonics when writing low-level machine code so they don't have to remember hundreds of opcode numbers. For example, a kind of byte-wide subtraction instruction has the opcode `0010.1000` (binary) or `0x28` (hexadecimal) and the mnemonic "`SUB`". The requisite subtraction opcode varies depending upon the source and width of the subtraction data. Keeping track of all of the opcode to operand rules is overwhelming, so the process of translating mnemonics and operands to instruction numbers is accomplished with a program called an *assembler*. Likewise, the process of translating instruction numbers back into mnemonics is done with a disassembler. Significantly, most programs are not written in assembly language; a higher-level language, such as C, is typically employed. These high-level languages are translated into machine instructions using compilers. Automatic decompilation of machine instructions back into a high-level language can be difficult because of the process of compilation—especially optimized compilation—discards much of the high-level structural information contained in the original source code.

The processor keeps track of which instruction is being executed with an *instruction pointer* (IP). An IP is also referred to as a *program counter* (PC) in some contexts. IPs typically advance through a program one instruction at a time, unless a branch instruction is encountered. A branch instruction gives the program an opportunity to make a decision by inspecting data inside the CPU and jumping to a new location based on the outcome of the inspection. *Understanding the movement of the instruction pointer is a central part of reverse engineering an Xbox.* Being able to manipulate the IP is tantamount to having control of what the Xbox can and cannot do. The security measures implemented in the Xbox software architecture attempt to guarantee that the IP is always executing only Microsoft-approved code by always cryptographically verifying a piece of code for authenticity before running it.

Binary and Hexadecimal Numbers

Digital circuits use 1's and 0's to represent numbers. This binary, or "base-2", notation is a reflection of the way electrical signals are used to represent numbers: two ranges of voltage levels are used to define one logic state or the other. It is possible to build electrical systems that represent information using more than two voltage levels, but only at the cost of power and complexity. Modern modems, for example, use multiple voltage levels and phase information to represent multiple bits of data in a single time unit.

Number composition and arithmetic in binary follows the same rules as our familiar decimal ("base-10") representation. In decimal, 0's are used as placeholders to remember when a digit has overflowed. For example, 1 more than 9 leads to an overflow because there is no single digit bigger than 9. Hence, the number 10 records that we had one overflow of the right-most decimal location. Likewise, in binary, 1 more than 1 is 10, since the largest single digit in binary is 1.

Thus, in decimal, the value of a four-digit decimal number $d_4d_3d_2d_1$ can be broken down as:

$$d_4 * 10^3 + d_3 * 10^2 + d_2 * 10^1 + d_1 * 10^0 = d_4 * 1000 + d_3 * 100 + d_2 * 10 + d_1 * 1$$

Likewise, a four-digit binary number $b_4b_3b_2b_1$ can be broken down as:

$$b_4 * 2^3 + b_3 * 2^2 + b_2 * 2^1 + b_1 * 2^0 = b_4 * 8 + b_3 * 4 + b_2 * 2 + b_1 * 1$$

For example, the number 1010 = 1*8 + 0*4 + 1*2 + 0*1 = 10 decimal.

Keeping track of numbers in straight binary can become cumbersome quickly; for example, to represent decimal 968, you need ten binary digits. To save on screen space, binary numbers are converted to octal or hexadecimal. The octal format, or "base-8", was popular in the early days of computers, but has since become a rarity. Hexadecimal, or "base-16", is the de-facto numbering system. There are 16 digits in hexadecimal, so the hex digits that correspond to decimal numbers 10 through 15 are represented by the letters A through F. Table 2-2 summarizes the conversion between binary, decimal and hexadecimal for the first 16 positive integers.

In order to differentiate hexadecimal numbers from decimal numbers, many people use the C language convention where 0x[number] represents a hexadecimal number, and [number] is implicitly a decimal number. Binary numbers have no similar standard to draw from in C, so some people use the Verilog standard, [digits]'b[number], where [digits] is the number of digits in the binary number. The suffix "b" after a string of 1's and 0's, such as 1010.1100.1110b is also used to denote a binary number. Notice how a "." was used to group the binary digits into sets of four; this assists in mentally translating the binary number into hexadecimal: 0xACE.

continued...

Binary and Hexadecimal Numbers, continued...

Bin	Dec	Hex	Bin	Dec	Hex
0000	0	0	1000	8	8
0001	1	1	1001	9	9
0010	2	2	1010	10	A
0011	3	3	1011	11	B
0100	4	4	1100	12	C
0101	5	5	1101	13	D
0110	6	6	1110	14	E
0111	7	7	1111	15	F

Table 2-2:
Binary, decimal and hexadecimal conversion table.

The heart of a CPU is a tiny, but very fast, memory called the register file. Multiple pieces of data can be written into and read out of a register file each processor clock cycle. Data from the register file is fed into an execution unit called the arithmetic logic unit (ALU). The function computed by the ALU is controlled by instructions fetched from memory. After the data has been processed by the ALU, it can either be written back into the register file, or stored into memory.

One important performance feature of almost every modern CPU is a memory access accelerator called a *cache*. Caches are small, fast memories that store copies of data and instruction snippets that are likely to be used in the near future by the CPU core. Caches are slower than register files but faster than main memory; likewise, caches store more data than a register file, but store less data than main memory. One important feature of the Xbox CPU cache to be aware of is that it is a writeback cache. Writeback caches allow copies of data stored inside the CPU to be out of sync with what exists in main memory. This timing difference can complicate attempts to trace CPU execution by observing external memory traffic alone. The cache memory can also be leveraged by security routines to hide intermediate computation result from someone observing the memory bus.

Northbridges and Southbridges

The terms Northbridge and Southbridge are vernacular specific to the PC architecture. They refer to the two basic support chips that are found in virtually every PC. A Northbridge chip connects the CPU to main memory as well as any high-performance expansion busses, such as AGP and PCI. A Southbridge chip hangs off of the Northbridge chip and contains all of the extra peripherals that are found in a typical PC—parallel, serial, USB, mouse, keyboard, IDE controllers, audio codecs, and more. Dividing the PC architecture into these three main modules—CPU, Northbridge and Southbridge—enables PC designers to mix and match different kinds of memory architectures with a diverse selection of processors and peripherals.

The connection between the Northbridge and the Southbridge chipsets varies from chipset to chipset. In the case of the Xbox, a high performance, narrow parallel bus called HyperTransport is employed as the connection between the functional equivalent of the Northbridge and Southbridge chips. The bus is only 8 bits wide in each of two directions, but the bus is clocked at 200 MHz and data is sampled on each clock edge so the effective peak transfer rate is 400 Mbytes/second in each direction. A Northbridge chip is connected to a CPU via a bus called the Front Side Bus (FSB). In the case of the Xbox, the FSB is a 64-bit 133 MHz bus that uses AGTL+ logic levels.

Knowing and understanding the kinds of connections between chips is crucial in reverse engineering because the kind of connection will dictate how difficult it is to intercept data going between various components. The details of the relatively easier bus to tap, the HyperTransport bus, are discussed in chapter 8, "Reverse Engineering Xbox Security".

In the Xbox, the Southbridge is a chip designed by nVidia called the MCPX, and it is a derivative of the nVidia nForce MCP Multimedia and Communications Processor. The Northbridge chip was also designed by nVidia, and it is called the NV2A GPU. Both the Northbridge and Southbridge chips were manufactured by TSMC (Taiwan Semiconductor Manufacturing Corporation). The NV2A combines both a GPU (Graphics Processing Unit) and the traditional memory and expansion bus controllers found in most Northbridge chips. As explained previously, combining the graphics processor and the Northbridge allows system designers to merge the graphics memory into main memory, at some performance penalty.

RAM

The Xbox motherboard employs 64 Megabytes of DDR SDRAM for the main memory. DDR SDRAM stands for Double Data-Rate Synchronous Dynamic Random Access Memory. By combining synchronization and DDR techniques, the aggregate bandwidth of the Xbox main memory achieves 6.4 Gigabytes/second.

A RAM is basically a table of information that is indexed by the CPU. Each location in RAM has a unique index number called its address, and as the name "random access" implies, there are no restrictions on the order of data access in a RAM.[1]

[1] Actually, SDRAMs can have a few restrictions on memory access patterns (such as page modes and burst modes) for performance reasons. The "random" moniker is intended to differentiate RAMs from First-In, First-Out (FIFO) and Last-In, First-Out (LIFO) style memories where data is accessed using a strict set of ordering rules.

The term "dynamic" is applied to RAM that has to be constantly refreshed in order to preserve the integrity of data. For example, the RAM used in the Xbox must have every location read out and written back about thirty times a second. The performance penalty is not as bad as it sounds, as special hardware is built into modern DRAM chips that help optimize the process.

The "synchronous" prefix means that inside the DRAM, the procedure for data access is broken down into a series of steps. Each of these steps are independent and can occur in parallel, so that multiple data requests can be in-flight simultaneously. An external timing signal, known as a clock, is used to synchronize the movement of data access requests through the various steps inside the DRAM. As a result, data access requests flow through each step like water through a pipe, and this technique is also known as pipelining. Synchronous DRAMs have higher bandwidth throughput than their predecessors, because pipelining allows multiple requests to be processed at once. However, the time required from when an access is first issued to an SDRAM to when the data finally appears on the output—the access latency—is not improved by pipelining.

The term "Double Data Rate" refers to the way synchronous data is transferred relative to the synchronizing clock. A clock waveform consists of a repeating pattern of high and low signals. In traditional systems, data is only transferred on the low-to-high transition of a clock waveform. In a DDR system, data is transferred on both the low-to-high and the high-to-low transitions. Thus, for the same clock frequency, twice the amount of data can be transferred. The performance mnemonic quoted by DDR SDRAM vendors, such as DDR266, refers to the transfer rate, so the actual clock speed is ½ the performance mnemonic, or 133 MHz in this case.

ROM

Every computer needs to have some kind of persistent or non-volatile memory for storing the start-up, or boot, program. The DDR SDRAM discussed above does not work for this application because all data in a DDR SDRAM is lost when the power is removed. Current versions of the Xbox use a FLASH ROM instead to store data that has to persist even when the power is turned off. ROM stands for Read-Only Memory, and FLASH refers to a specific style of storage element that is electronically reprogrammable. FLASH style memories are convenient in PCs because they can be reprogrammed by the end user to fix mistakes in the boot code. However, in the Xbox, FLASH ROM programming by the end user is purposely disabled. The write signal required for programming is disconnected by leaving out the jumper located on the back of the Xbox motherboard at component location R7R4 (see the sidebar titled "Enabling FLASH ROM Programming Hardware" for more information). In the case of the Xbox, the reprogrammability of FLASH is primarily leveraged as a convenience for Microsoft during development and production. It is quite likely that in a few months, the Xbox will use cheaper hard-wired "mask ROMs" once Microsoft believes it is ready to etch its boot program and kernel in stone (or silicon, as the case may be).

Enabling FLASH ROM Programming Hardware

Patching the signal that was disconnected by Microsoft in order to prevent in-system FLASH ROM programming is a fairly simple procedure. The FLASH ROM write signal was disconnected by omitting a single resistor, component number R7R4, located on the bottom side of the Xbox motherboard at sector 7R. You can solder a piece of wire between the two silver pads of the resistor, or you could even simply bridge the pads with a large amount of solder. Note, even though FLASH ROM programming is enabled in the hardware by this patch, you still do not have a program that actually does the reprogramming. Running such a program is a much greater challenge due to the cryptographic software security system put in place by Microsoft.

The boot ROM is pivotal in reverse engineering any computer, because it contains critical code that is responsible for initializing the whole system. In the case of the Xbox, the boot FLASH ROM plays an even more crucial role because it is partially responsible for implementing the tight software security system. The exact role of the FLASH ROM in the security system will be explained later, but the important thing to remember for now is that the FLASH ROM controls the initialization of the hardware in the Xbox and also contains the initial operating system kernel image.

Odds and Ends

The Xbox features a small 8-bit coprocessor called the System Management Controller (SMC). The SMC is a complete miniature computer with RAM, ROM and a processor in a single package. The processor inside the SMC uses the PIC (Peripheral Interface Controller) architecture, originally developed at Harvard university around 1975 and adapted by General Instruments for commercial sale. Arizona Microchip Technology (now called Microchip Technology, `www.microchip.com`) acquired the PIC product line in 1985 and has been selling it ever since. The SMC can be found in sector 7B on the Xbox, and its reference designator is U7B2. The SMC monitors the power button on the front of the Xbox, so the SMC must run even when the CPU is turned off. As a result, the Xbox power supply has a low-current 3.3V "standby" power line that is always active when the Xbox is plugged in. The SMC is also responsible for controlling the lights around the power button on the Xbox, and it controls the DVD eject mechanism as well. Finally, the SMC has a function that monitors the health of the CPU, and reboots the CPU in case it crashes. The SMC monitoring function must be disabled if you wish to run your own operating system on the Xbox. The SMC talks to the CPU via the MCPX through a 1-bit serial interface known as I2C.

Another important feature of the Xbox is the LPC debug port. The LPC debug port is a 4-bit wide bus that runs at 33 MHz. LPC stands for "Low Pin Count", and it was originally devised as a method for connecting a large number of slow legacy devices, such as keyboards, serial ports, parallel ports and boot ROMs, to the Southbridge chip via a simple intermediate translation chip. The debug port is provided on the Xbox presumably for manufacturing test purposes by Microsoft's hardware contractor. When the Xbox nears its final stages in production, the LPC debug port is used to load a boot program that performs tests, diagnostics and burn-in on the Xbox motherboard. The LPC debug port is discussed in more detail in chapter 11, but the important thing to know for now is that one can force the Xbox to read its initial boot ROM image through the LPC debug port by connecting an LPC-compliant ROM device and shorting one of the data pins (D0) on the FLASH ROM to particular voltage (zero volts). This is perhaps the easiest method for forcing the Xbox to boot your own code—given that you know how to get around the secret boot code that secures the Xbox.

Pattern Matching

Now that we are familiar with the Xbox architecture, we have a reference point for perhaps one of the most powerful reverse engineering tools—pattern matching. Being able to make educated guesses about the function of various parts by simply observing their connectivity, placement and shape is the first step in becoming a crack reverse engineer. To demonstrate the power of pattern matching, we will compare the Xbox motherboard to a PC motherboard and to a Nintendo Gamecube motherboard.

Learning a lot of patterns is the best way of becoming a good pattern matcher. I take apart every piece of equipment that I buy, and I pore over the circuit boards to try and learn what other designers know by "reading" the circuit board. Every circuit board tells a story about its design process; rarely will one encounter a peculiar circuit feature that does not have some intended purpose.

Caution

When taking apart any piece of electronic equipment, be sure to first unplug it and wait a minute for the charge on the large capacitors in the power supply to dissipate. Also be sure to use appropriate static electricity control measures described in chapter 1!

Comparison: Xbox Versus the PC

The similarity of an Xbox to a PC is a boon to hackers, since the PC platform is very well documented. Every part in an Xbox has an analog in a typical PC, so almost any high-level question can be answered by just reading about a similar PC part. Thus, it pays to take a closer look at the similarities between the Xbox motherboard and a standard PC motherboard. Another benefit is that much of the information in this book will apply directly to PCs, so you can easily apply what you will learn from hacking the Xbox to a large number of situations.

The Xbox's closest relatives are systems based on chipsets that use a unified memory architecture, such as nVidia's nForce or Via Technology's ProSavageDDR. The architectural diagram presented in the previous section was derived by reading through the published specifications of the Xbox and reading through material available on nVidia's website about the nForce chipset. In this section, we will compare the Xbox to the Via Technology ProSavageDDR-based P4M266 motherboard. The Xbox is compared here with a non-nVidia chipset motherboard to emphasize the broad similarities of the Xbox to PCs.

Figure 2-7:
Via P4M266 motherboard with integrated graphics.

Figure 2-7 shows a picture of a PC motherboard, the Via P4M266. Even though the chipset is manufactured by a different vendor, the similarities between the P4M266 and the Xbox are striking. Almost all of the material covered in the previous section applies to this PC motherboard. The primary differences are a few miscellaneous ports and connectors, and the presence of PCI and AGP high-performance expansion ports. The Via P4M266 also lacks an explicit LPC debug connector, since all of the legacy peripherals are directly realized by an LPC multi-I/O chip.

Contrast: Xbox Versus the Gamecube

The Nintendo Gamecube is an interesting comparison against the Xbox. The Gamecube is a machine designed for the same purpose as the Xbox—gaming—but with a very different design philosophy in mind. The Xbox and the Gamecube both use the same gross architecture—a CPU, a graphics coprocessor, some memory, and some support chips—but the similarities end there. The Gamecube design demonstrates an exacting attention to detail and cost. The Gamecube motherboard is small and simple, the component count is kept to a minimum, and the heat sinking and thermal design is very simple. The clean, straight layout of most of the PCB traces on the Gamecube motherboard reflects the fact that almost every IC is custom-designed specifically for the Gamecube. As a result, the Gamecube is a much more economical platform to build than the Xbox.

One can recognize the gross organization of the Gamecube by inferring each chip's function from the basic marketing information Nintendo provides. Further details about the architecture of the Gamecube are difficult to infer, because it uses so many custom components that have no counterpart in a standard PC. By the pattern of the traces on the motherboard, one would be lead to believe that the large chip in the center of the board, the "Flipper" chip, is the equivalent of an integrated graphics Northbridge chip in a PC. This is almost correct. A key difference is that even though the Flipper chip combines both a memory controller and a graphics controller into a single package, the graphics function still has its own dedicated memory, built inside the same chip. This kind of organization allows a very high performance memory to be used by the graphics engine, with the trade-off of the memory being a bit smaller than if off-chip memories were used. The smaller size of the on-chip memory is compensated in part by the use of extremely fast off-chip memory.

The Gamecube does not use DDR SDRAM like the Xbox does; instead, it uses what is called a 1-T SRAM. 1-T SRAMs are DRAM memories that emulate a very fast type of memory known as the Static RAM (SRAM). SRAMs have much lower random access latencies than DRAMs, and they also do not require each memory cell to be refreshed 30 times a second like DRAM does. The actual magic behind how DRAM can masquerade as fast SRAM is fairly complicated and is beyond the scope of this book, but you can find more information at the 1-T SRAM manufacturer's website, `www.mosys.com`. The Gamecube also has yet another piece of memory, known as ARAM, that is slower than the 1-T SRAM memory, and is used

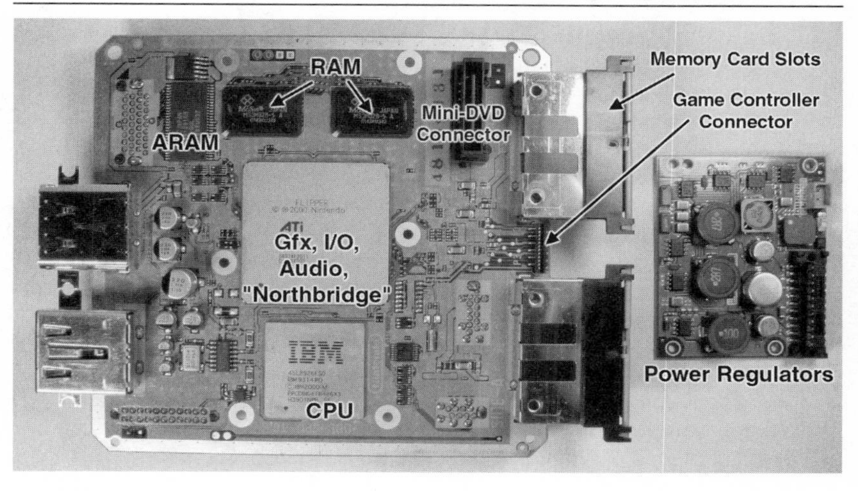

Figure 2-8:
Gamecube motherboard plus its power regulator card. The motherboard is about half the size of the Xbox motherboard.

to store things like audio samples that do not require high-bandwidth accesses. Having a disparate memory architecture means that the Gamecube can squeeze a more consistent amount of performance out of each subsystem, something important in keeping frame lag to a minimum. The trade-off, however, is that the Gamecube can be more difficult to program, and mismanagement of the multiple pieces of memory can lead to performance problems.

Another important distinction between the Gamecube and the Xbox is that the Gamecube consumes much less power than an Xbox. Power consumption may seem unimportant at first, since both consoles are designed to be plugged into a wall outlet, but the Gamecube's lower power envelope requires fewer heat transfer components and smaller power supplies to be used, saving on cost. Figure 2-8 includes a picture of the Gamecube power regulator for reference; the power regulator is a fraction of the volume of the Xbox power supply plus the local switching regulators on the Xbox motherboard. To be fair, note that the Gamecube does have a small external AC to DC converter, while the Xbox takes wall power directly into the console. Furthermore, electronic components degrade much faster at elevated temperatures, as described by the rule of Arrhenius. For example, a 10 degree Celsius operating temperature increase roughly doubles the failure rate of a component. By this token, the Gamecube should be more reliable over the years than the Xbox since the Gamecube puts out less heat, and because the Gamecube's thermal management system is as good as, if not better, than the Xbox's.

Finally, it is interesting to note that the Gamecube uses proprietary I/O interfaces everywhere. The game disk format is a mini-DVD format, and the DVD reader connects to the motherboard through a proprietary connector. Using a smaller DVD media allows Nintendo to reduce the latency of data seeks, which means shorter game loading times. The game controllers and memory cards also use a proprietary signaling format. Everything in the Gamecube is somewhat similar to our familiar PC, but nothing was directly incorporated into the design unchanged.

In addition to optimizing the manufacturability and cost of the Gamecube, the use of mostly proprietary chips and standards makes the console much more difficult to reverse engineer than the Xbox. For example, note that in Figure 2-8, there is no obvious ROM chip in the Gamecube. Thus, in order to even start looking at Gamecube code, one has to hunt down and extract a ROM hidden somewhere in one of the chips on the motherboard! This is one of the rare times where security through obscurity works. Even if there were no security at all on the Gamecube, the cost and effort of trying to burn your own code onto Nintendo's custom DVD format is just not worth it for the individual enthusiast.

CHAPTER 3

Installing a Blue LED

Now that you have taken the cover off of your Xbox, it is time to do a couple of starter projects. The next chapters walk you through some elementary modifications and repairs that you can perform on your Xbox. These projects are designed and written for readers who have little or no experience with hardware hacking. More advanced topics on the Xbox can be found in later chapters.

In this chapter, you will be instructed on how to replace the normally green LED in the Xbox front panel with a blue LED. This project requires minimal soldering. Most of the effort is in removing the front panel and the LED circuit assembly. Let's get started!

Note

A stock Xbox uses a green/red combo LED, but the red LED is only used to indicate error conditions. The procedure described in this chapter will convert your Xbox front panel indicator into a blue-only LED. The proper substitute would be a blue/red combo LED (T-1, 3mm diameter lens). However they are difficult to find, so the instructions here do not use them. The instructions will give the necessary background knowledge for you to improvise and incorporate your own LED solution if you are so inclined.

What You'll Need

The following is a list of the equipment that you'll need to complete this project:

- Low-wattage soldering iron with a fine point tip
- Solder
- Flux and soldering iron tip cleaner (optional)
- Small flathead screwdriver
- T-10 bit Torx driver
- Two low voltage (3 volt) blue LEDs in a T-1 (3 mm) case
- Masking tape for holding parts in place during soldering

You can substitute any color LED that you like, but it must turn on at a voltage of around 3 volts and have a T-1 style case. Pay attention when buying your LEDs, because many blue and white LEDs are rated to work only at 5 volts. The LED used in this text is a Lumex SSL-LX3044USBC. You can buy it through Digi-Key (`www.digikey.com`). The Digi-Key part number is 67-1747-ND, and for the budget-conscious, Digi-Key can send the LEDs via United States Postal service's first class mail. Note that there is a $5 handling fee for orders through Digi-Key that are less than $25.

If the minimum order restriction is a problem for you, Mouser Electronics (`www.mouser.com`) also has a line of blue LEDs, and they have no minimum order. An example part is the Kingbright blue LED in a T-1 case with a water clear lens; the Mouser stock number is 604-L7104PBC/H for the brighter, slightly higher voltage version, or 604-L7104QB/D for a version that operates at a lower voltage but with a lower rated brightness.

You can also use a bi-color LED if you would like to maintain the error condition LED functionality as well. The Xbox requires a common-cathode bi-color LED in a T-1 case with three leads. Unfortunately, bi-color LEDs with a blue element in the smaller T-1 case are very difficult to find.

Removing The Xbox Front Panel

The Xbox front panel is a molded piece of ABS plastic that is held in place with four T-10 torx screws and three molded friction locks. The electronics in the front panel connect to the Xbox motherboard through a single nine-wire connector that winds its way through a hole in the metal electromagnetic interference shield.

Open the Xbox as instructed in Chapter 1. Lift and move the hard drive and the DVD drive up and toward the back of the box just enough to expose the front edge of the Xbox motherboard. You should not have to undo

Figure 3-1:

Position the disk drives so that the front edge of the motherboard is exposed.

any of the disk drive cables. Figure 3-1 illustrates how your Xbox should look after these steps.

Note

Older Xbox models will have a vertically mounted PC board near the front of the Xbox. This PC board can be removed by grasping the board and pulling it out of its socket. You may find that removing the vertically mounted PC board is helpful when trying to release the middle friction lock of the front panel. Do not forget to replace the PC board when you are done!

Remove the four screws that hold the front panel assembly in place. The location of these screws is illustrated in Figure 3-2.

Detach the front panel wire connector from the Xbox motherboard as illustrated in Figure 3-3. A firm, steady force is all the connector should require. Do not jerk the connector out, because you may damage the wires.

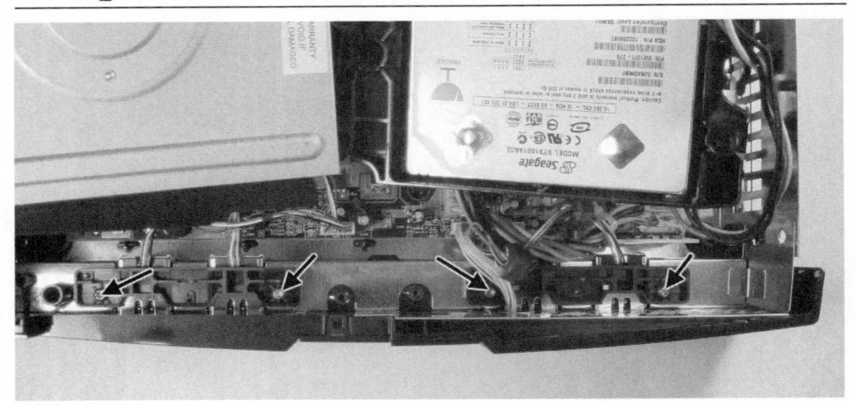

Figure 3-2:
Location of the four retaining screws on the front panel assembly

Now for the tricky part: the friction locks. A friction lock is a hook made out of plastic that holds parts together. The hook is shaped so that it is easy to insert, but difficult to extract. Releasing a friction lock typically requires some

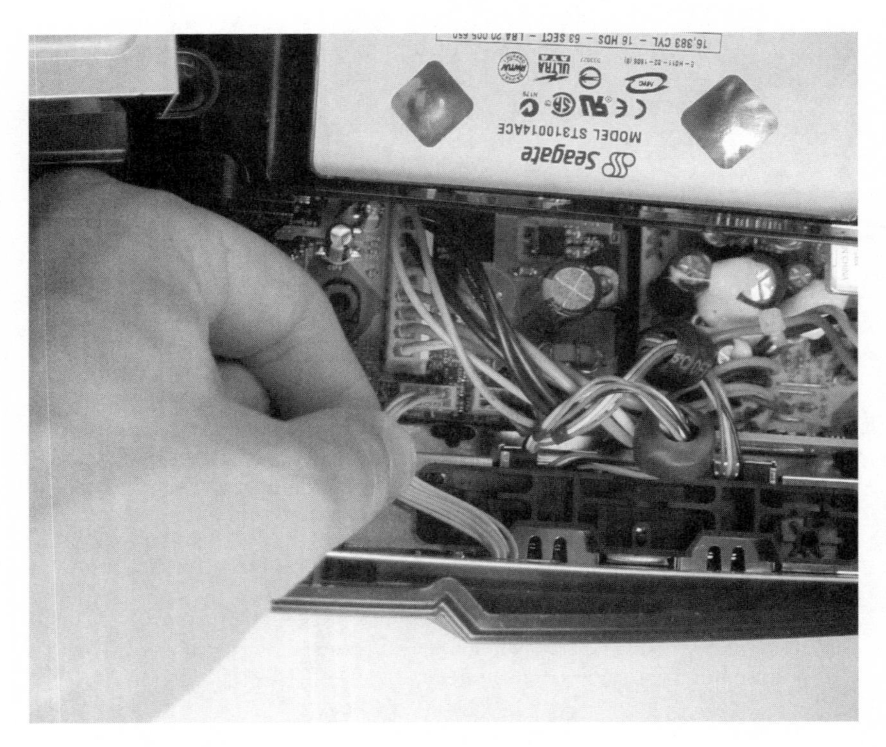

Figure 3-3:
Detach the front panel wire connector from the Xbox motherboard.

kind of bending or pushing on the plastic. There are three friction locks that hold the front panel in place: one on either edge of the front panel, and one in the middle poking through the metal electromagnetic interference shield. First, loosen the friction locks on the edge using a thin-bladed flathead screwdriver as illustrated in Figure 3-4. These locks are very tight, and you may have to release it in sections, starting with the top section. Insert the screwdriver tip into the space along the side between the panel and the main case body, and pry until you feel a slight give. Remove the screwdriver and repeat the process near the bottom of the case. You may need to try several

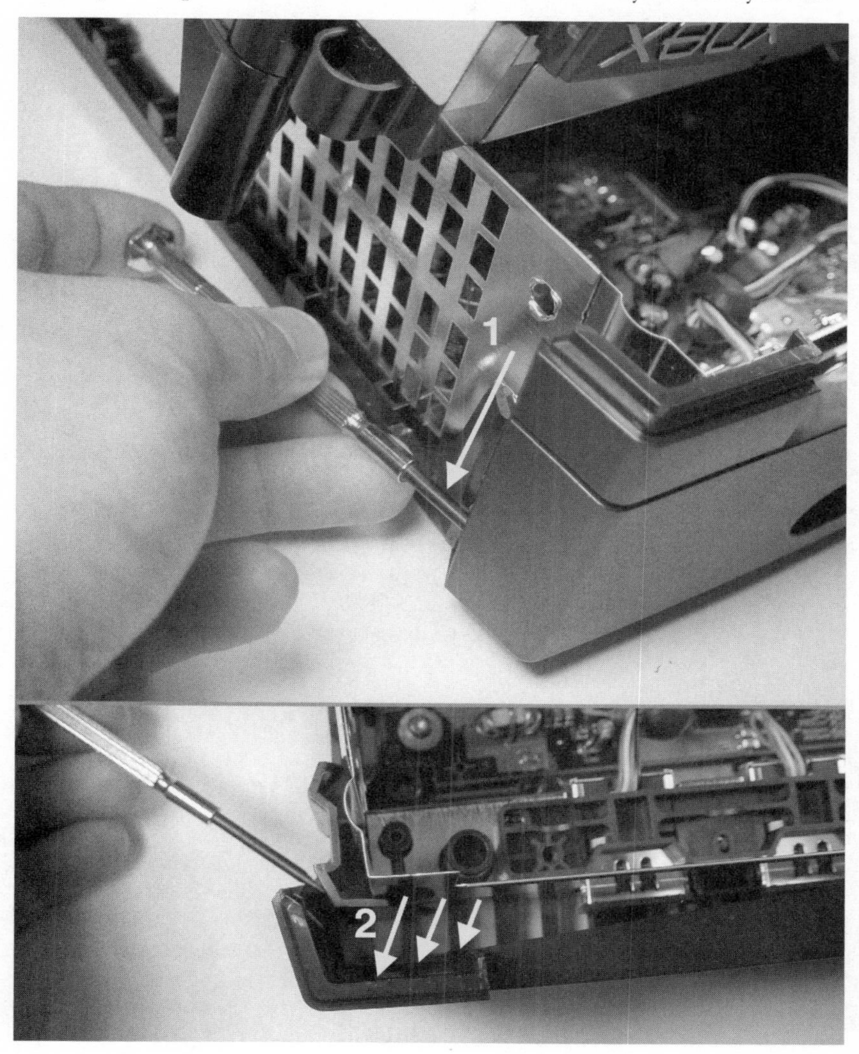

Figure 3-4:

Loosen the edge friction locks with a flathead screwdriver. 1 – Start working from the top and move down; 2 – once the panel is free, it should bend outward from the case.

times before the lock is free. Do not apply excess force to the case, as you could crack or nick the plastic. When the edge of the front panel is free, you will be able to flex it away from the case.

Repeat this process for both edges.

Once both edges are free, pull up on the middle friction lock, and the front panel should pop off. The location of the middle friction lock is illustrated in Figure 3-5.

Once the front panel is free, thread the front panel wire connector through the hole in the metal electromagnetic interference shield and lay the panel flat on a table with the outer face down.

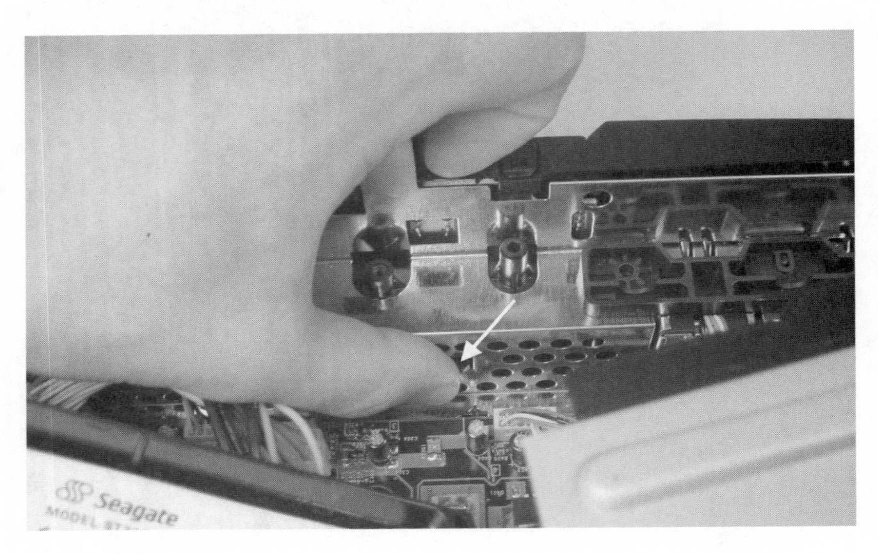

Figure 3-5:
The thumb is pressing on the middle friction lock.

Removing the Front Panel Circuit Board

The front panel assembly of the Xbox contains a small circuit board, held in place with a single friction-lock retaining clip. The location of this clip is illustrated in Figure 3-6. Use a finger or a screwdriver to push down on the friction lock and pull the front panel circuit board assembly out of its cradle.

Lay the circuit board assembly onto a table with the green side down. You should see two clear LEDs and two flat push-button switches.

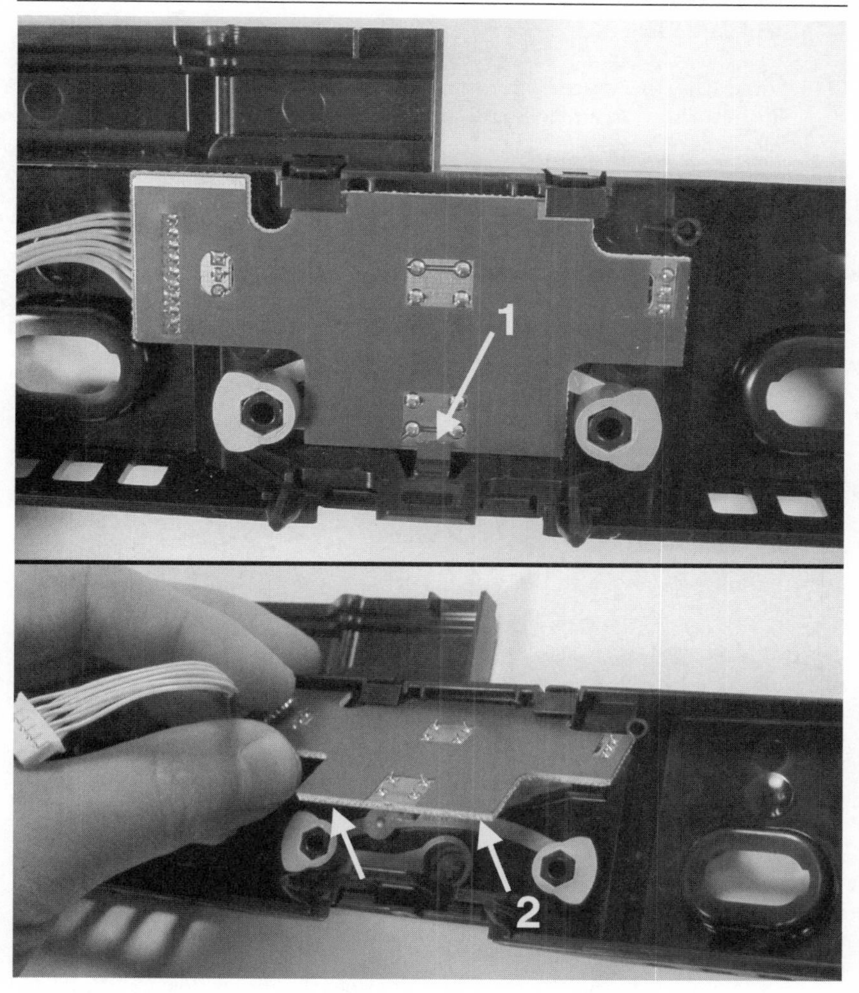

Figure 3-6:

Lift the printed circuit assembly out of the front panel. 1 - push down on the friction lock tab, using a screwdriver if necessary; 2 - lift the assembly out of the front panel.

Installing the Blue LED

Now that the circuit card assembly has been removed, it is time to install the blue LED. This will require some soldering, so plug your soldering iron in and let it heat up. Keep in mind that it is important to use a soldering iron with a fine tip and to use soldering iron tip cleaner to condition the tip before using it. See Appendix A, "Where To get Your Hacking Gear", if you need any of these items; you can equip yourself for just a little more than the cost of a video game.

Remove both of the existing LEDs with a flush-cutting wire cutter. Preserve as much of the metal legs coming out of the LEDs as possible. You will use these metal legs to attach your blue LED later on. Figure 3-7 illustrates how the circuit board should look when you are finished.

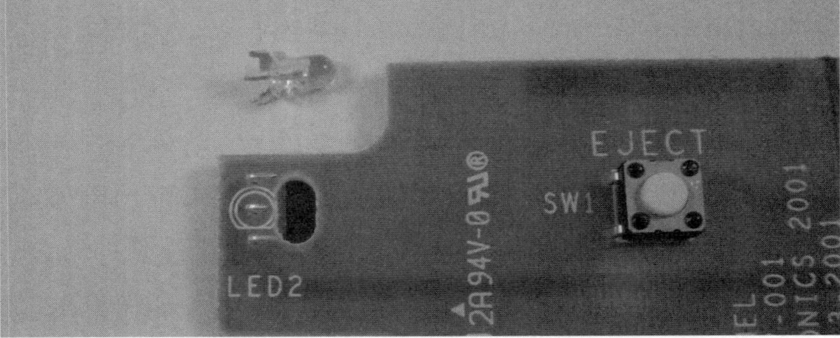

Figure 3-7:
Cut the existing LEDs off of the circuit card assembly. Top - cut the LED as close to the case as possible; Bottom - the LED removed. Remove both LEDs with this procedure.

To assist with soldering, tape the circuit board down to a flat surface with a piece of masking tape, so that the board does not move. Position the blue LEDs so that their legs touch the metal stubs of the old LEDs on the circuit board assembly. Figure 3-8 shows how to identify the polarity of an LED and their proper orientation on the circuit card assembly. See the sidebar on an Anatomy of an LED if you feel unsure about how to identify the polarity of an LED. Tape the lens portion of the LEDs in place with masking tape so they do not roll around while you solder them. You will need to bend or cut the legs of the LED that will be installed on the right hand side of the board because the yellow wire connector will be in the way.

Warning

Pay careful attention to an LED's polarity. If you install an LED backwards, no light will be emitted. See the sidebar on the Anatomy of an LED if you are unsure how to identify the polarity of an LED.

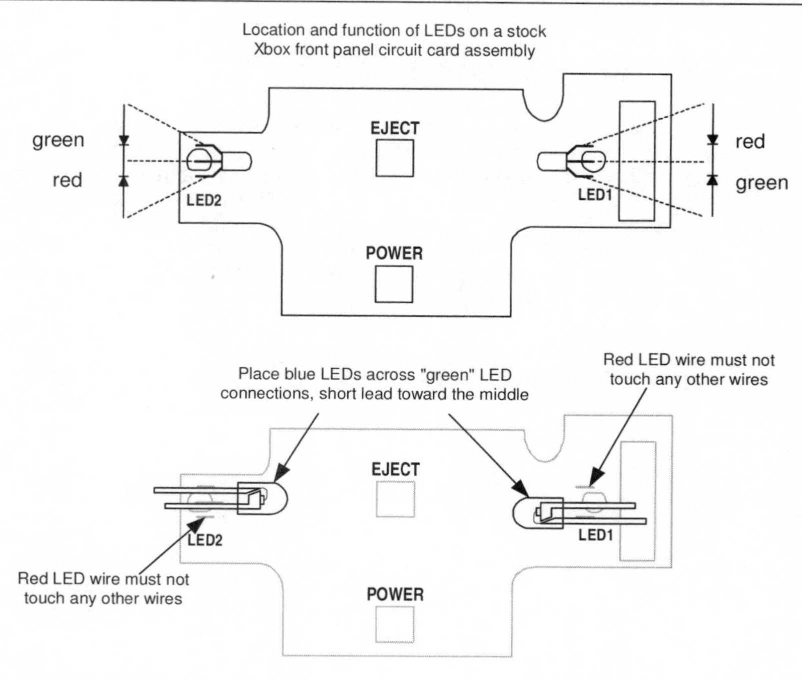

Figure 3-8:
Placement of the blue LEDs on the front panel circuit board assembly. Note the anti-symmetry of the LED colors on each side of the circuit board.

Figure 3-8 also illustrates the polarity and function of the stock Xbox LEDs. Adventurous readers are encouraged to improvise and install multiple LEDs or surface-mount LED packages to try and get more colors and functionality. It is possible to install LEDs that are slightly larger than the T-1 package used in the Xbox by first sanding down the edges of the LED.

Once you have double-checked the LED polarities and verified that the short lead on both LEDs is abutting the remains of the original LED's center lead, solder the LEDs in place. Figure 3-10 shows the LEDs being soldered in place. If you have never soldered before, you may find it helpful to read Appendix B, "Soldering Techniques" before proceeding.

Before using the soldering iron, melt a little bit of solder wire to verify that the tip is sufficiently hot. The solder wire should melt instantly if the tip is hot enough. If the soldering iron is too cold, you will not be able to form a good joint and you run the risk of damaging the circuit board.

Hold the hot iron tip against the blue LED's lead and push the lead into the metal stub on the circuit card assembly. While the lead is heated, apply a touch of solder wire to the point where the blue LED lead meets the metal stub. The molten solder's surface tension should cause the solder to wet the

The Anatomy of an LED

LEDs, or Light Emitting Diodes, are polarized devices. In other words, diodes only allow current in one direction which means that they will not work when put in backwards. Figure 3-9 illustrates the anatomy of an LED. The shorter lead on the side of the LED package with a small flat is called the "cathode". The cathode must be connected to a potential more negative than the other lead, the "anode", in order for the LED to function.

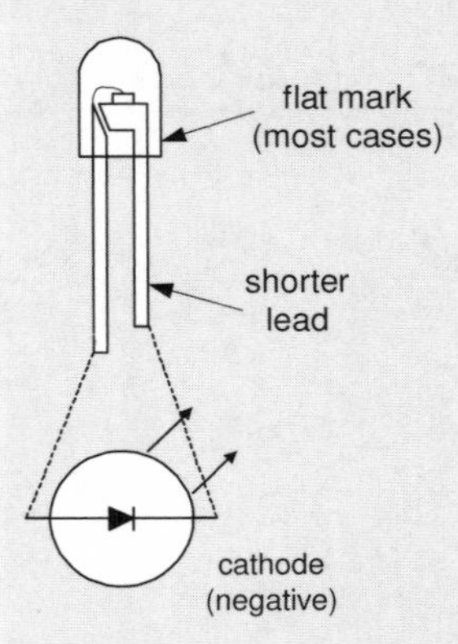

Figure 3-9:
The anatomy of an LED.

Note, that LEDs characteristically require a different amount of forward voltage to turn on. Red LEDs typically require 1.7 volts, green LEDS require about 2.1 volts, and blue LEDs require 3.5 volts and up. Early blue LEDs required almost 5 volts of forward voltage, but advances in technology have decreased their voltage making them easier to integrate into battery-powered and low voltage electronics. When shopping for an LED for this project, be observant of the required forward voltage. If you install a 5 volt blue LED, its light output will be very dim, since the maximum forward voltage generated by the Xbox drivers is around 3 volts.

blue LED's leads and the metal stub on the circuit board assembly. If this does not happen, remove the iron and apply a little bit of flux to the joint, and try again. Do not hold the soldering iron tip against the metal stub for extended periods of time, it will melt the solder that holds the stub in place. You will know that the stub's solder joint to the board has melted, when the stub starts to sway freely. If this happens, hold the soldering iron tip against the board and slowly drag the soldering iron tip away. Dragging the tip will prevent the stub from getting pulled out of the board with the iron. Wait for the stub to coo,l and bend the stub back into position.

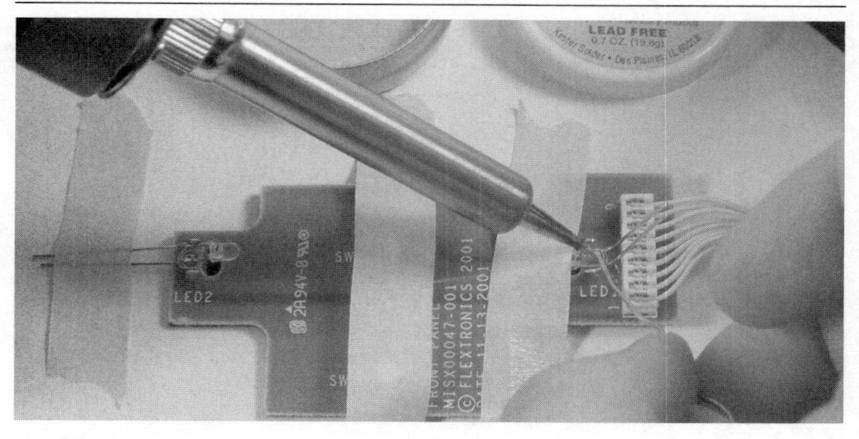

Figure 3-10:
Soldering the LEDs in place. Note how the board and the LEDs are taped in place using masking tape.

Once you have soldered all four connections on the two LEDs, clip off the excess LED leads as short as you can without cutting the metal stubs. The finished board should look similar to Figure 3-11.

Figure 3-11:
Finished board assembly.

Re-Assembling the Front Panel

Snap the circuit card assembly back into the front panel by aligning the top edges underneath the retaining clamps and pushing the card into the friction lock.

Now, take the full front panel assembly and mate it to the Xbox. First, feed the wire connector through the original oval-shaped hole through the electromagnetic interference shield. Then, push the front panel into the Xbox, and all three friction locks should snap into place.

Re-attach the front panel wire connector to the Xbox motherboard. The connector has a shape that only allows you to insert it in one direction. However, the plastic used in the connector molding is soft and you could insert the connector backwards if you push hard enough, possibly causing irreversible damage tot he connector. You can verify the correct orientation of the connector by lining up the missing pin on the board receptacle to the missing wire on the connector header, as illustrated in Figure 3-12.

Figure 3-12:
Orientation features of the front panel wire connector. The arrows indicate the position of the empty polarizing pin.

If you have an older Xbox, re-attach the vertical circuit board assembly by pushing it into its sockets. This circuit board is the interface card for the Xbox game controllers, so you'll definitely want that installed correctly.

Now, you are ready to test your newly modified front panel assembly. Replace the disk drives in their bays and verify that their power cable and ribbon cable connections are secure. Plug the Xbox in, and you should be treated to a blue glow coming from the Xbox front panel.

If you don't see what you expect, do not panic. The next section, Debugging, goes over some of the possible problem scenarios and their solutions.

Once you are satisfied with the modification of your Xbox, turn the Xbox off and replace the four retaining screws on the front panel assembly. You will need to remove the disk drives again to access the screw holes. Replace the disk drives, power up the Xbox one more time to verify that everything is working fine, and then re-assemble the rest of the Xbox as described in Chapter 1.

Debugging

Sometimes things go wrong. In my experience, something going wrong is more often the case than not. The most important thing to remember if something doesn't work is, "don't panic!". Keep your wits together, make observations about what is going wrong, and try to hypothesize the cause the malfunction. For your reference, Table 3-1 contains a list of common problems and their possible causes. Appendix E, "Debugging: Hints and Tips", contains a more in-depth discussion about debugging techniques.

Problem	Possible Cause
Xbox does not turn on.	• Front panel wire connector not properly inserted. • Xbox not plugged in. • Front panel wire connector damaged, or front panel circuit card assembly damaged.
Xbox turns on and functions properly, but no light comes out of the LEDs or only half of the light circle around the eject button is lit.	• One or more LED installed backwards. • One or more LEDs installed on the red LED's metal stubs, instead of the green LED's metal stubs. Verify this by turning on the Xbox without the video cable plugged in. This will cause the Xbox to send a flashing signal to both the red and the green LEDs.
Xbox turns on and sequences through initial animation, but the console indicates that it needs service.	• Hard drive or DVD connectors have come loose. Verify that the gray ribbon cable header is fully inserted into each drive and that the power connector for each drive is fully inserted. • On older Xbox models, check that the vertical game controller interface board was re-installed properly.
Xbox turns on, but game controllers do not respond.	• On older Xbox models, check that the vertical game controller interface board was re-installed properly.
Xbox turns on but DVD does not eject.	• Verify that the wire connector between the front panel and the Xbox motherboard is properly inserted. • Verify that the DVD power connector is properly inserted.

Table 3-1:
Debugging guide for installing a blue LED.

CHAPTER 4

Building a USB Adapter

Cable building is a compulsory part of hardware hacking. Many modifications and experiments performed on pieces of hardware will require a custom cable to adapt your existing connectors into what you need. In this chapter, you will learn how to build a USB adapter cable for the Xbox, something not available in most retail outlets (although select on-line vendors, such as Lik-Sang (`www.lik-sang.com`), do carry this item). A USB adapter allows standard USB hubs, keyboards and mice to be connected to the Xbox for the purpose of running Linux. This chapter presents the basics of robust cable building in a tutorial fashion; experienced hardware hackers should feel free to skim or skip this chapter.

Starting Materials

This project requires the following materials:

- One Xbox game controller break-away cable replacement or game controller extension cable. A picture of these cables is shown in Figure 4-1.
- One USB type A extension cord or a USB type A female socket. A picture of a USB type A female socket is shown in Figure 4-2.
- A soldering iron, solder and flux.
- A diagonal wire cutter and a wire stripper.
- Electrical tape.
- (Optional) 3/8” heat shrink tubing and hot-glue.
- (Optional) Third hand soldering aid

The step-by-step description in this Chapter uses a break-away replacement cable, available at any video game retailer, and the USB extension cord. If you want to use something different, check out the Xbox Hardware

Figure 4-1:
Left, an Xbox game controller extension cable. Right, an Xbox breakaway cable.

Figure 4-2:
USB type A female connector.

Reference Appendix for the pinouts of the various connectors employed by the Xbox.

Strategy

When building the Xbox USB adapter cable, the basic idea is to cut the Xbox break-away cable and the USB extension cable in half and to join the proper ends of the two cables together. Fortunately, there is a standard wiring code for USB-compliant cables. Red is +5V power, black is Ground, White is Data (-) and Green is Data (+). In order to join the cables together, all that needs to be done is to connect wires of like colors together. Note that the Xbox cable will have an extra yellow wire that carries a copy of the composite video sync signal for use in light-gun type game interfaces. This extra yellow wire can be safely ignored. This Chapter will walk you through the process of connecting the wires and sealing the cable step-by-step.

Warning

Some USB cable manufacturers will not comply with the standard USB wiring code. The most common deviation is reversing the white and green wires, although on rare occasion the color code is outright ignored. It is always a good idea to verify that your USB extension cable actually complies with the USB color code using a continuity meter.

Implementation

First, cut the Xbox break-away cable near (about 2”) the Xbox connector end, and cut the USB extension cable near the female connector end. Discard the male half of the USB extension cable and the half of the Xbox cable with the smaller connector.

Next, use the diagonal cutters to cut 1/2” slits into the insulation of each cable, as illustrated in frame 1 of Figure 4-3. Peel the insulation back to reveal the wires. The wires will be protected by a braided metal shield and a some metal foil. Peel the metal braiding and foil back, and cut off the excess insulation and shielding. Strip the ends of the red, green, white and black wires so that about 1/8” of bare conductor is showing. Do not strip the yellow wire in the Xbox break-away cable. Dip the bare ends of the conductors into some solder flux. Figure 4-3 illustrates this process.

If you are concerned about the robustness or safety of the adapter cable assembly, slip a 1-1/4” segment of heat shrink tubing onto one of the cables. This tubing will later be slipped over the bare solder joints and filled with hot glue to make a robust connection. The shielding is not mandatory, but the cable will not be as robust without the heat shrink reinforcement; in particular, the cable will be susceptible to breakage if subjected to repeated bending or strain.

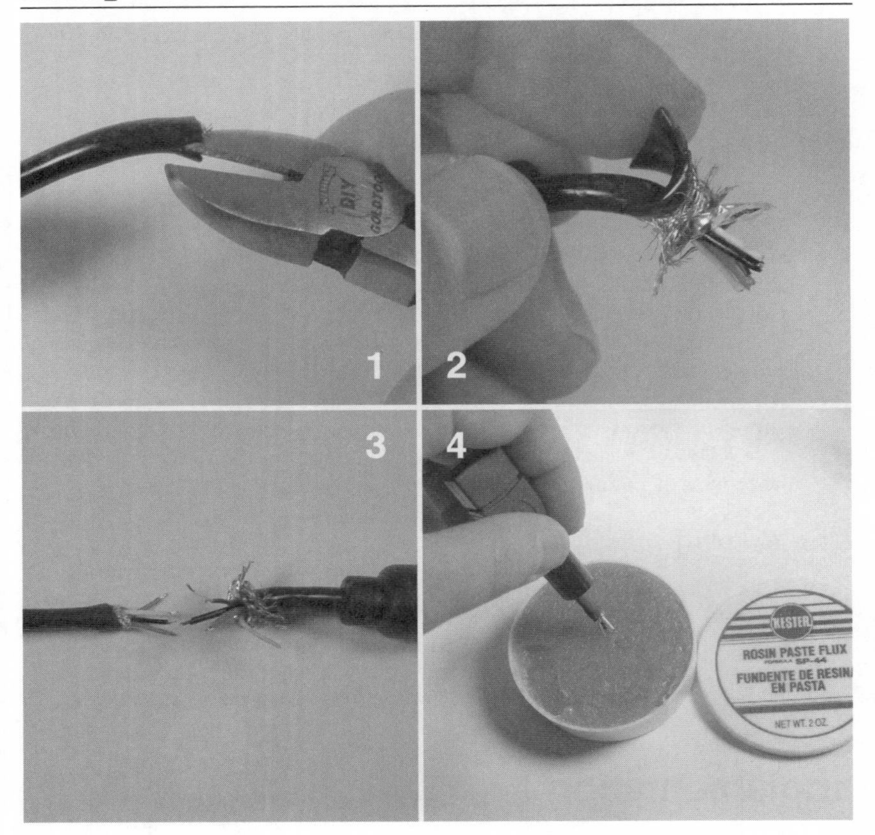

Figure 4-3:

(1) Cut slits into the insulation of the cables and (2) Peel the insulation back to reveal the wires and shielding inside. (3) Cut off the excess shielding and insulation, and strip 1/8" off the end of the wires. Note how the yellow wire in the Xbox connector cable (right) is not stripped. (4) Dip the stripped wire ends in soldering flux.

Continue the cable building process by soldering together wires of like colors, as shown in Figure 4-4. Have a friend help you hold the cables in place while you solder them, or use a "third hand" tool (Jameco order number 26690) with alligator clips to hold the cable in place. All of the solder joints should look smooth and shiny. Give a firm tug on each joint to verify that the solder connection is good. Wrap a small piece of electrical tape around the open joints to prevent the exposed joints from shorting together. **Test the cable** before proceeding to the next step where the joints will be **permanently** encased.

Once the cable has been tested and confirmed to be good, it is time to put a robust casing around the solder joints for mechanical reinforcement, as shown in Figure 4-5. Place a couple of small dabs of hot glue over the open solder joints to hold them in place so they do not short against each other. Slip the heat shrink tubing over the solder joints. Fill both sides of the

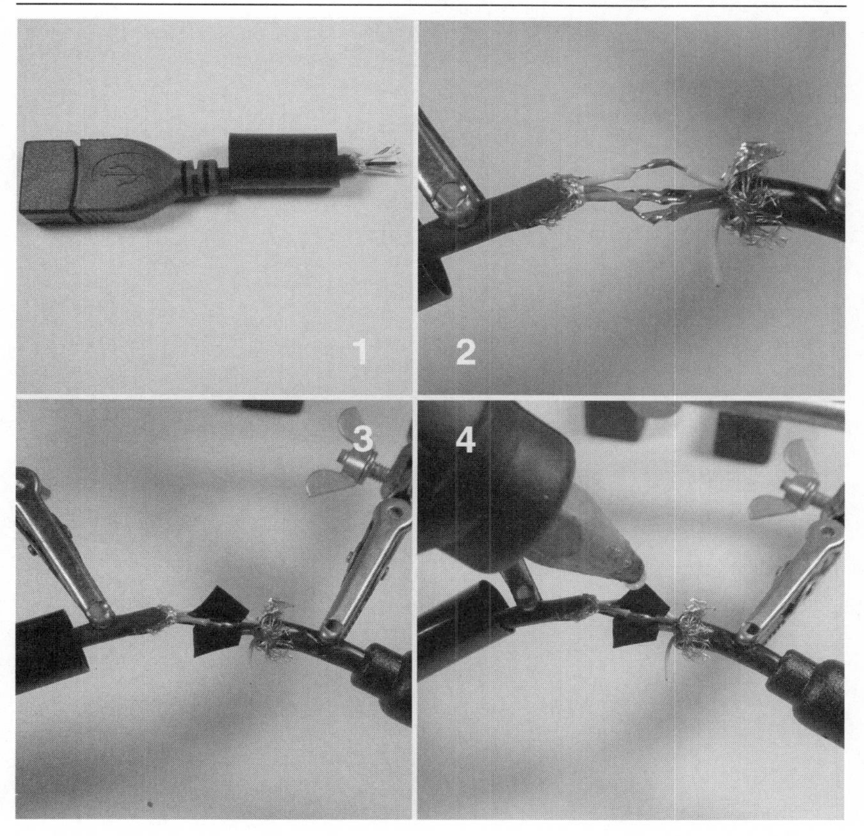

Figure 4-4:

(1) Slip a piece of heat shrink tubing over the cable before soldering. (2) Solder the wires together, like color to like color. (3) Wrap the wires in electrical tape to prevent shorting. Test the cable. (4) Apply small dabs of hot glue to the tested cable to hold the electrical tape and wires in place for the next step.

tubing with hot glue. The tubing will shrink from the heat of the glue and form a solid, permanent conformal case over the joint. The hot glue acts as a strain relief for the joint as well, thus the cable will be robust under most normal operating circumstances.

Although the cable is fully operable without the hot glue and heat shrink tubing treatment, you can still improve the connection's stability if you do not have these items handy. Electrical tape can be wrapped carefully around the individual joints as a makeshift mechanical reinforcement.

Now that you have finished your USB to Xbox game port adapter, chapters 11 and 12 describe some of the steps necessary to install Linux on the Xbox so you can use your new adapter.

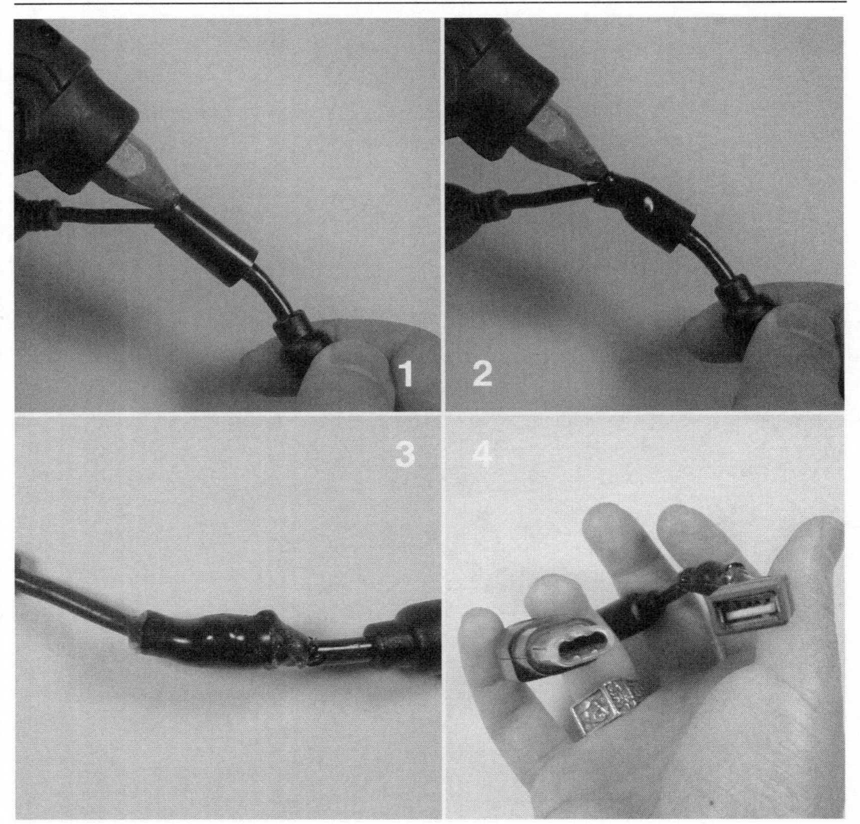

Figure 4-5:

(1) Slide the heat shrink tubing over the joint, and begin filling the tube with hot glue. (2) The hot glue will cause the heat shrink tubing to collapse. (3) The end product is a permanent conformal casing that will stand up against most abuse. (4) A picture of the final product, showing the Xbox and USB cable ends.

CHAPTER 5

Replacing a Broken Power Supply

In the unfortunate (and surprisingly common) event that an Xbox breaks after its 3 month warranty period, the only official method for getting it fixed is to pay Microsoft for the repair bill. Even the simplest fixes can cost over a hundred dollars, or about half the original purchase price of the console. As a result, I have received numerous emails from people asking how to fix broken power supplies and hard drives. Unfortunately, replacing a broken hard drive requires defeating the Xbox security system, since a unique key is used to lock Xbox motherboards to a particular hard drive. Installing a new hard drive would require a modchip that can reprogram or bypass the hard drive lock. Furthermore, a copy of the factory-installed Xbox software is required, something that is illegal to distribute or copy even for repair purposes. Therefore, the topic of Xbox hard drive replacement is too dicey to be discussed in this text. Readers are encouraged to search on-line for any of the numerous FAQs about replacing hard drives. On the other hand, the power supply used in the Xbox is very similar to that used in a standard PC. There are many websites where you can purchase exact replacement Xbox power supplies, such as Llama.com (`www.llama.com/xbox/Repairs/repairs.htm`), XboxRepair.com (`www.xboxrepair.com`), and Firefly-HK (`www.firefly-hk.com`), or you can attempt to build one yourself out of a standard PC power supply!

Considering the frequency of power supply failures, we will show how to adapt a standard PC ATX power supply for the Xbox. The approach described in this section requires no soldering, at the expense of having to flip an extra switch to power on the Xbox. Appendix C, "Getting Into PCB Layout", describes a simple project that you can build to have the convenience of no additional power switches. Of course, it is easier to purchase an exact replacement power supply for the Xbox and use parts of the procedure presented in this chapter to help you with the installation. However, there is less educational value in doing a direct replacement than in doing an adaptation. If you decide to adapt the ATX power supply for use with the Xbox, you will learn how to make crimp cables as well as learn a little bit about electronics theory and about how the Xbox works.

Another reason for adapting a standard PC ATX power supply to the Xbox is to provide extra power to the console. The OEM (original equipment manufacturer) or "stock" Xbox power supply puts out just barely enough power to meet the Xbox's demands. Connecting extra drives or fans to an otherwise unmodified Xbox can overload the OEM Xbox power supply and cause it to burn out.

Note that at the time of writing, a new hardware revision of the Xbox (known as "v1.2" in the Xbox hacking community) was released that *appears* to have a standard ATX power supply connector, instead of the proprietary Xbox power supply connector described later in this chapter. Check to make sure that your Xbox power supply connector matches the connector described in this chapter before proceeding with the adaptation procedure. The Xbox power supply connector assumed in this chapter has twelve pins in a single row, whereas the newer Xbox power supply connector has twenty pins arranged in two rows of ten. Also note that even though the latest Xbox hardware revision has an ATX-like connector, it does not necessarily mean that it is electrically compatible with a standard ATX power supply. It would be prudent to measure the voltages on the power connector and compare them to the ATX specification (`www.formfactors.org/developer/specs/atx/atx2_1.pdf`) before attempting to mate a standard ATX power supply to an Xbox with the new ATX-like connector.

Caution

Replacing a power supply potentially exposes you to hazardous voltages. Before removing the power supply, always unplug the Xbox from the wall outlet and wait a minute for stored charges to dissipate. In addition, improper installation of the replacement power supply could result in permanent, even explosive, damage to the console. Only perform this procedure if you are sure that the power supply is discharged and off, and if you are willing to take the risk of potentially further damaging your console.

Diagnosing a Broken Power Supply

If your Xbox is experiencing problems powering up, first you must diagnose the problem and locate the source of failure. It does no good to replace a power supply when the fault is actually within the console or in the wall outlet. Perform these diagnostic steps to verify that the Xbox power supply is in fact the culprit, and not something else.

1. Verify that the power outlet is functional by plugging a lamp into the outlet. Use a 100 watt lamp minimum to accurately

simulate the load of the Xbox.

2. Visually inspect the power cord for kinks and cuts.

3. Verify that the power cord plug is firmly seated in the Xbox power receptacle, and the Xbox still does not turn on despite these checks.

4. Visually inspect the inside of the Xbox for char marks or ruptured capacitors. If char marks are visible on the motherboard, then you may have to replace the Xbox motherboard (i.e., buy a new Xbox). If there are char marks on the power supply, then most likely the power supply was damaged and you may begin replacing the power supply. Keep in mind that a power supply failure may also damage the motherboard, so there is still a chance that the Xbox will not work after the power supply is replaced.

5. Verify that the main power supply connector is firmly seated, and that the front panel circuit assembly connector is firmly seated. The location of the front panel circuit assembly connector is illustrated in chapter 3, "Installing a Blue LED", Figure 3-3. The power switch for the Xbox is connected to the motherboard through the front panel circuit assembly connector.

6. Verify that the 3.3V standby voltage (3.3VSB) is within specification using a voltmeter. Take this measurement when the Xbox is off but still plugged in. Measure 3.3VSB by probing the sixth wire in the power supply connector from the end closest to the front panel, and any of the black wires on the power connector. You can measure power supply voltages by inserting the tips of a voltmeter probe into the free space between the power wires and the power connector. There is a metal collar around the power wires inside the motherboard power connector's body. If the value of 3.3VSB is not between 3.14 to 3.47 volts, then you may need to replace the power supply.

7. Press the power button on the Xbox to turn it "on" (presumably, if the power supply is broken the Xbox won't do much). If the power supply makes noises or if it smokes, unplug the box and proceed with replacing the power supply. If the box seems dead, measure each of the primary voltages coming from the power supply. The yellow wire should have a voltage between 11.4 to 12.6 volts; the red wire should have between 4.8 to 5.25 volts; and the orange wire should have between 3.14 to 3.47 volts. All of these voltages are referenced with respect to the black wire. Also, check that the voltage on the Power OK signal (located at pin 12, the pin farthest from the front panel) is above 3.1 volts.

If everything in the checklist above checks through, then it is quite unlikely that the problem is with your power supply. Further things to check are the electrical and mechanical integrity of the power switch (see Chapter 3 for how to remove the board with the power switch) and the functionality of the motherboard. However, if you did observe indications of a failed power supply, read on.

Replacing the Power Supply

The overall strategy for replacing the Xbox power supply is to adapt a standard PC ATX power supply for use in the Xbox. Here is the equipment necessary to replace the Xbox power supply:

- **A standard ATX power supply.** Please note, a 1-U power supply will fit within the footprint of the Xbox case, but it will probably be a little bit too tall to close the case.
- **(Optional) An ATX motherboard power cable extension.** Power cable extensions can be purchased through numerous vendors, including PC Power and Cooling `www.pcpowerandcooling.com`). Modifying the extension cable for the Xbox instead of the ATX power supply's cable allows you to re-use the power supply in a standard PC once you are ready to toss your Xbox.
- **A crimping tool.** The Molex universal crimping tool (Digi-Key part number WM9999-ND) is highly recommended, but it is a little bit expensive (about $35). A cheaper crimping tool, such as the Jameco 159265, can be purchased for about a third the price but it is more frustrating to use and you may have to use solder on the crimps to achieve the desired connection strength.
- **One 12 position 0.156" pitch connector housing** (i.e. Digi-Key part number WM2313-ND) ***or*** **two stacking 6 position 0.156" pitch connector housings** (i.e. Jameco part number 104731). This housing is used for the Xbox power connector replacement.
- **Thirteen crimp terminals for the 0.156" pitch power connector** (i.e. Digi-Key part number WM2313-ND or Jameco part number 78318).
- **Two 1N4001 or better silicon rectifier diodes in a DO-41 package** (i.e. Digi-Key part number 1N4001DICT-ND or Jameco part number 35975).
- **A wire stripper.** Any wire stripper that can handle 18 gauge wire will do.
- **A wire cutter.** Any diagonal wire cutter will do.
- **Electrical tape.**

Using Diodes to Drop Voltages

The Xbox requires a +3.3V standby supply voltage, but an ATX power supply only outputs a +5V standby supply voltage. The "correct" solution to this problem would be to use a voltage regulator that precisely converts +5V into +3.3V, but the goal of this hack is to be able to replace the power supply with a minimal amount of soldering.

The alternate solution is to use two diodes are used to reduce a +5 volt supply down to a "close enough" +3.6 volt supply. We can do this because the voltage across a forward conducting diode is logarithmically proportional to the current through the diode. In other words, for most currents, the voltage across a diode is almost constant. It turns out that silicon diodes almost uniformly have a forward voltage drop of about 0.7 volts, so two of them in series will drop 1.4 volts.

The diodes used in this hack, the 1N4001, are only capable of conducting 1 ampere of current, so don't use this trick in other applications that require a large amount of current. Fortunately, the stand-by supply for the Xbox only needs to draw a tiny amount of current so burning out the diodes is not a concern.

As a final note, the voltage dropped by a diode fluctuates slightly with the amount of current through the diode, so do not use this trick in applications that require precisely regulated voltages. In the Xbox application, we are running the voltage a little bit on the high side, but fortunately the digital logic powered off of this supply can tolerate this condition.

Strategy

The interface for a standard ATX power supply is very similar to that of an Xbox's power supply. The Xbox requires +3.3V, +5V, +12V, a +3.3V standby supply, as well as two control signals, "power OK" and "power on". The power OK signal indicates that the power output from the power supply is stable and properly regulated, and the Power On signal is a control signal from the Xbox that turns the power supply on and off. A typical ATX supply has +3.3V, +5V and +12V outputs with enough juice to run an Xbox, and it also has a power OK signal that is compatible with the Xbox motherboard. However, an ATX power supply generates a +5V standby voltage instead of a +3.3V standby voltage, and the Power On signal has an inverted polarity from the Xbox. Both of these incompatibilities can be addressed in a manner that requires no soldering. Two diodes in series are used to reduce the +5V standby voltage down to a voltage of a little less than +3.6V. The Power On signal to the ATX power supply defaults to "on", so it will remain unconnected, making the power supply always on even if the console is off. This isn't problematic for the console's electronics, but it might be aesthetically disconcerting. Appendix C, "Getting Into PCB Layout", describes a sample design that you can implement to avoid these incompatibilities in a more graceful manner. However, the design outlined in the Appendix will require you to invest some effort in the form of soldering and board design.

Procedure

The procedure for replacing the Xbox power supply is divided into two parts:

1. Modifying the standard ATX power cable to be an Xbox power cable.
2. Removing the old power supply and installing the new one.

Building the Xbox Power Cable

Start by cutting off the existing ATX power supply's motherboard connector as shown in Figure 5-1. You may elect to perform this modification using an ATX motherboard power extension cable, so you can preserve the ATX power connector on the power supply for future use. The procedure is identical for both options, but the pictures in this chapter are taken using the ATX motherboard extension cable.

Now, attach crimp terminals to the following wires ten of the ATX cable, as shown in Figure 5-2:

- One yellow wire
- Three red wires
- One orange wire
- Four black wires
- One gray wire

If you are using a cheaper crimp tool, you may have trouble making a sufficiently strong crimp connection. In this case finish the connection by soldering the crimp terminal onto the wire. Use a copious amount of heat when soldering, or else the solder will not fully penetrate the wire and the crimp terminal. The soldering iron should be in contact with the joint for about five seconds before and after applying the solder.

On the violet wire (the +5V standby wire), attach two diodes in series between the end of the wire and the crimp terminal. The procedure as shown in Figure 5-3 uses portions of crimp terminals for connecting the diodes, so no soldering is required. Note that diodes are polarized devices: they will not conduct electricity if they are installed backwards. The diodes should be installed with their cathodes (the end with the band painted on them) toward the motherboard.

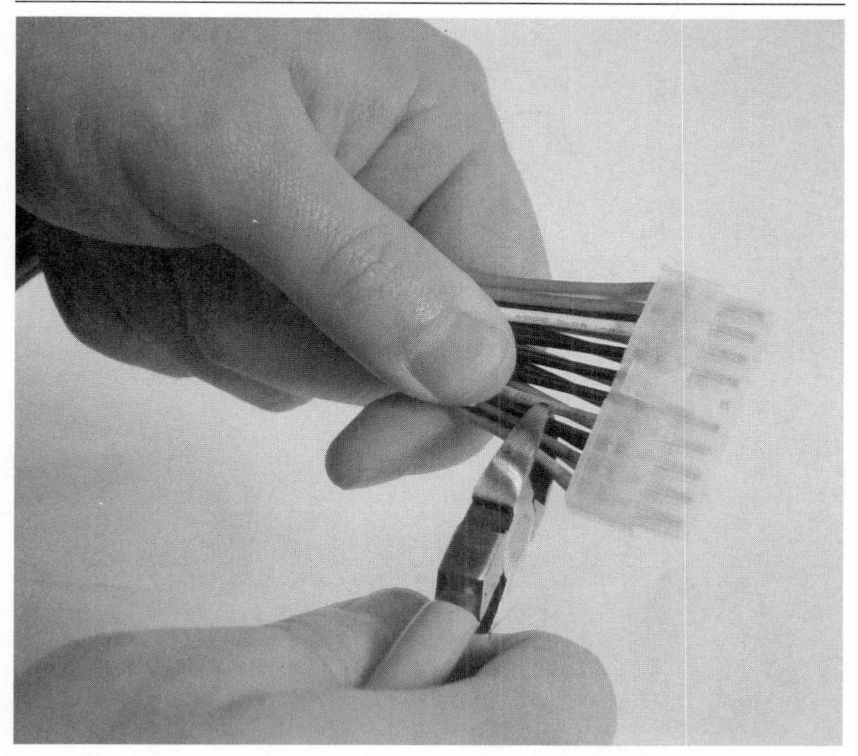

Figure 5-1:
Cut the connector off of the ATX power supply cable.

Next, wrap all of the unused wires on the ATX cable with electrical tape to prevent any accidental shorts that will damage the power supply and possibly the Xbox. Be sure to also wrap the diodes with electrical tape as well. This procedure is illustrated in Figure 5-4.

Finally, insert the finished crimp terminals into the 0.156" connector housing. The crimp terminals will lock into place inside the housing when they are fully and properly inserted. Figure 5-5 illustrates the process of inserting the crimp terminals into the connector housing. Insert the wires in the order specified in Table 5-1. Some vendors do not sell the larger 12 position connector housing. In this case, use two 6 position connector housings, and pay special attention to the ordering you choose for stacking the connectors. Also, note the location of pin 1 with respect to the polarizing lip of the connector. Pin 1 is located at the top of the connector when the polarizing lip is on the left and you are viewing the connector from the side that wires are inserted (the top view). Since it is very easy to invert the connector or get this backward in some way, use the existing Xbox connector as a reference. The yellow, red, orange and black wires should all line up when compared against each other.

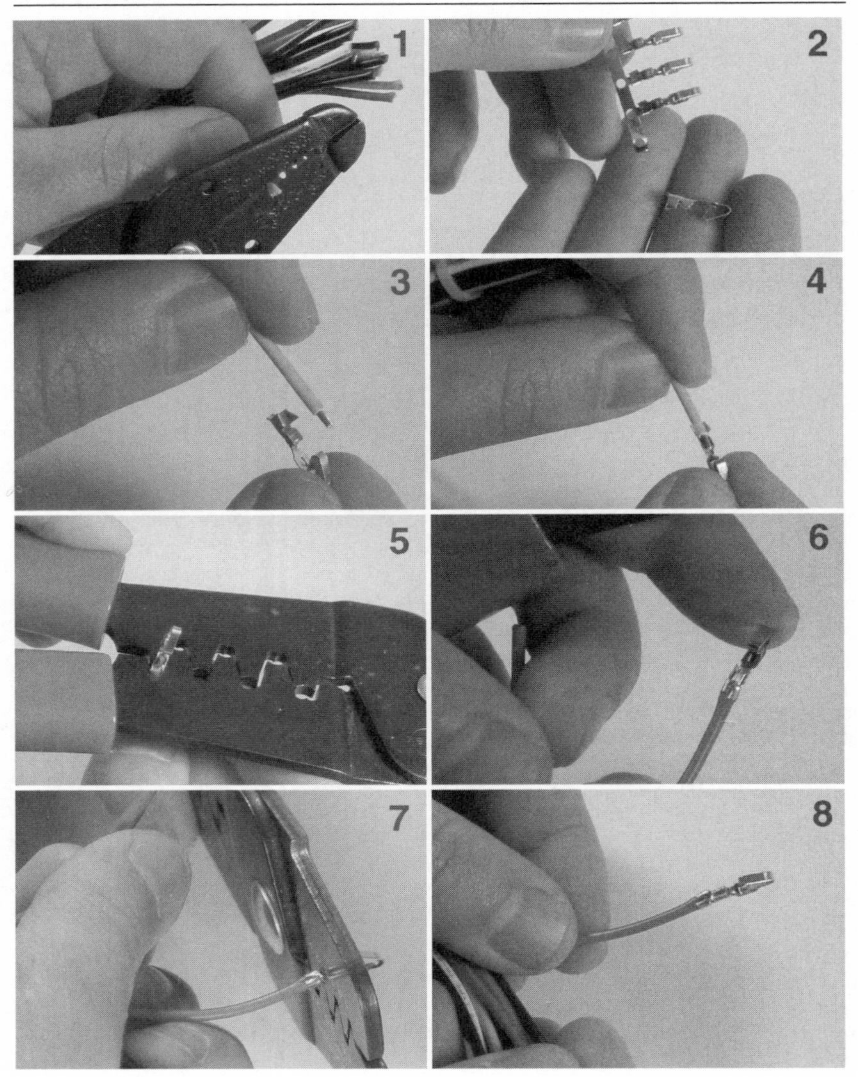

Figure 5-2:

Attaching a crimp terminal to the end of a wire. (1) Strip about 1/8" of insulation off the end of the wire. (2) Remove a virgin crimp terminal from the retaining strip, if necessary. (3,4) Insert the wire into the crimp terminal, such that 1/16" of insulation is sitting between the longer pair of crimp fingers. (5) Crimp the insulation portion (longer pair) of the crimp fingers. (6) Shows wire with just the insulation portion crimped. (7) Crimp the conductor portion of the crimp fingers. (8) Finished crimp terminal. The conductor crimp terminals should be folded in tightly on the bare wire for good contact. Test the crimp connection by firmly pulling on the terminal end.

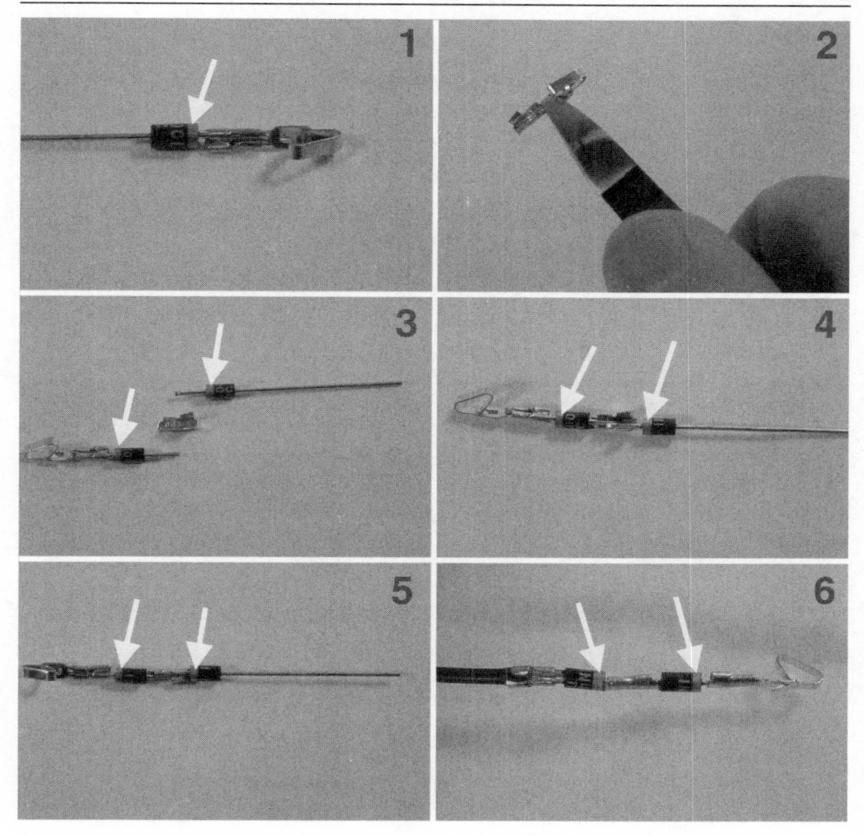

Figure 5-3:
Attach two diodes in series between the end of the violet wire and the crimp terminal that goes into the power connector. Arrows indicate the proper orientation of the polarizing line painted on the end of the diode. This procedure will consume a total of three crimp terminals. (1) Attach one diode to a crimp terminal with the polarizing band near the crimp terminal. (2) Cut a crimp terminal in half to remove the leaf contact. (3,4) Position the diodes within the crimp portion of the severed connector, noting the polarity of the diodes. (5) Diodes shown after crimping. (6) Attach the diodes to the end of the violet wire using the same procedure with a second severed crimp terminal.

Double check your work after completing the assembly of the power supply cable, as any error could result in permanent, irreparable damage to the console. Figure 5-6 illustrates what the finished connector assembly should look like. You may wish to use a cable tie, if available, to bundle the unused wires so they do not get in the way and accidentally short or become damaged.

Figure 5-4:
Wrap the unused wires and the diodes in electrical tape to prevent accidental shorting.

Pin	Color
1	Yellow
2	Red
3	Red
4	Red
5	Orange
6	Diodes + Violet
7	Black
8	Black
9	Black
10	Black
11	Empty
12	Gray

rib

Table 5-1:
Wiring table for connecting ATX power supply cable to Xbox power connector (view from wire entry side, polarizing rib is on the left).

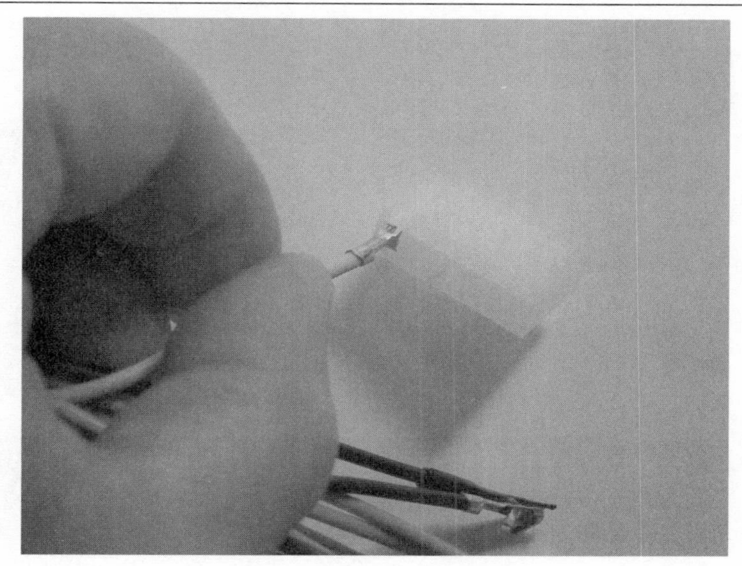

Figure 5-5:
Inserting a crimp connector into the connector header.

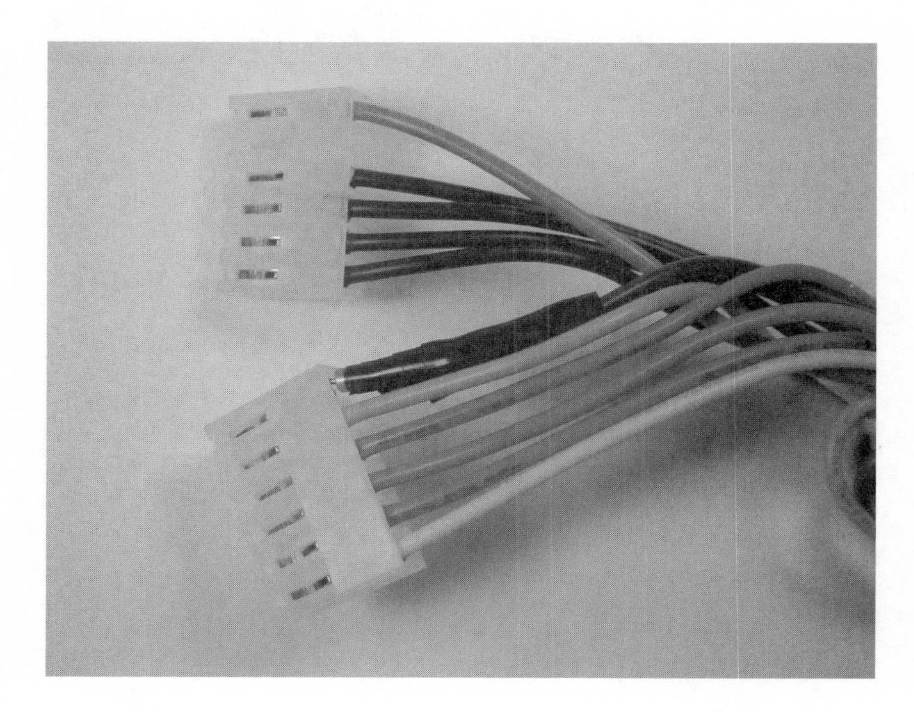

Figure 5-6:
Final cable assembly.

Figure 5-7:
Location of the two power supply mounting screws.

Installing the Replacement Power Supply

Now that we've prepared a replacement power supply, we must swap out the old, broken supply for the replacement supply. Remove the top of the Xbox case as described in Chapter 1, "Voiding the Warranty". Detach the hard drive power connector and lift the hard drive out of the case. Once again, you should not need to detach the gray IDE ribbon cable connected to the hard drive.

At this point, verify that the Xbox is unplugged and that it has had an opportunity to sit for at least a minute to dissipate any stored charge in the power supply. Working on the Xbox while plugged in, or soon after it has been unplugged, is extremely hazardous. The Xbox will deliver a nasty, possibly lethal, shock if you touch any part of the power supply with your bare hands before the power supply has dissipated its stored charge.

Unplug the Xbox power supply connector by grasping the full bundle of power wires and pulling firmly on the cable while holding the box down with the other hand. Mind the sharp metal edges of the case and heat sinks when removing the cable.

Remove the two T-10 torx screws that hold the Xbox power supply in place. Figure 5-7 illustrates the location of these screws.

Lift the power supply out of the Xbox case by first raising the end of the power supply closer to the front of the Xbox.

Compare the cable you created against the Xbox power supply cable, paying attention to line up the polarizing ribs in the same orientation. The red, yellow, orange and black wires should line up between the two connectors. This check will help ensure that you do not damage the Xbox through a wiring error on the cable.

Plug your ATX power supply cable assembly into the Xbox power connector. The yellow wire should be lined up with the pin closest to the front of the Xbox. Keep in mind that there is nothing to protect you from inserting the power cable offset by one or two pins. If you see a bare pin on the power connector, then you have inserted the cable by a one pin offset. Double check for this condition, it could lead to permanent damage of the Xbox hardware and/or the power supply.

Plug the Xbox hard drive into one of the ATX power supply's disk drive power connectors. The hard drive uses an identical connector to the standard PC disk drive power connector so no modification is necessary.

Verify by visual inspection that no wires are shorted against the case or caught in the blades of the cooling fans. Now, you are ready to power on the Xbox.

Operating with the Replacement Power Supply

Most ATX power supplies come with a power switch on the supply. Set the power switch to the off position. Plug the ATX power supply in, and then turn the power switch to the on position. At this point, the ATX power supply will apply power to Xbox, even though the Xbox's system controller thinks the box is powered off. As a result, the cooling fans inside the Xbox will be spinning. Now, press the power switch on the front of the Xbox. The Xbox should power on normally at this point. Congratulations!

Figure 5-8:
1U slimline ATX power supply connected to the Xbox using the modified ATX power supply extension cable.

Caution

Some Xbox versions are missing a heatsink fan for the GPU. If your Xbox motherboard does not have a fan mounted directly on one of the chips, then you have such an Xbox. Xboxes that lack a heatsink fan for the GPU are prone to overheating under certain conditions, and must be operated with the disk drives installed over the motherboard for reliable long-term operation. The undersides of the disk drives form an air ducting system that guides air over the GPU heatsink from the main Xbox case fan. Note that your ATX power supply cable will prevent the disk drives from installing flush with the case, and this is not a major cause for concern with respect to airflow ducting.

When you are ready to turn the Xbox off, you can simply flip the power switch on the ATX power supply, or you can use the power switch on the front of the Xbox to power the Xbox off first, and then turn off the ATX power supply.

Debugging Tips

If the Xbox did not power on properly after replacing the power supply, test your power supply cable using the checklist in the section at the beginning of this chapter called "Diagnosing a Broken Power Supply". The most likely problem you will encounter is a bad crimp connection or poorly/improperly attached diodes. A bad crimp connection may also lead to intermittent operation where the Xbox powers on but crashes frequently.

If the Xbox powers on, but halts during the power on sequence for some reason, refer to Table 3-1 in the section titled "Debugging" at the end of chapter 3 for a list of possible problems and their causes. Appendix E, "Debugging: Hints and Tips", contains a more in-depth discussion about debugging techniques and methodology.

If the Xbox works properly but crashes occasionally, then you may have an Xbox that has no heatsink fan over the GPU. See the "Caution" note on the facing page describing this problem. You may need to add an extra fan or enhance the existing ducting system with a piece of paper and some sticky tape to remedy this problem.

Chapter 6

The Best Xbox Game: Security Hacking

The next step beyond modifying and tweaking the Xbox hardware is taking control of the Xbox hardware. Unfortunately, gaining control of the hardware is not as easy as one might think. The designers of the Xbox put a great deal of thought into securing the hardware against sophisticated software attacks as well as most simple hardware attacks. The Xbox's security mechanisms are an artifact of the Xbox's digital rights management architecture. Note that in principle, applying hardware to "fair-use" purposes, such as running your own homebrew programs, should not be illegal. However, the relationship between fair use, secured hardware, and the relatively new copyright control circumvention laws is still unclear. Chapter 12, "Caveat Hacker", discusses the legal issues of hacking in more detail.

There are many ways around the Xbox's security measures. In this chapter and in chapter 8, "Reverse Engineering Xbox Security", I will tell the story about my adventures mapping out the Xbox security system. I write not only about the successes, but also about the failures I encountered, so that you can learn from my experiences. Chapter 9, "Sneaking in the Backdoor", explains some approaches taken by others to get around the Xbox's security measures. Chapter 7, "A Brief Primer on Security", provides the background necessary to appreciate chapters 8 and 9.

First Encounters with a Paranoid Design

When the Xbox was announced in the Spring of 2000, excitement rippled throughout the hardware enthusiast community. The cause for this excitement was not just the gaming potential of the Xbox, but rather the potential of the Xbox to be used as a high performance, network-enabled x86-architecture PC at the affordable price of $300. Price cuts a few months after its introduction have since dropped the cost of an Xbox to below $200. The similarity of the Xbox to an x86 PC meant that a huge base of existing applications and expertise could, in theory, be easily ported to the console.

My first look inside an Xbox was in late November 2001 when my girlfriend (now fianceé) gave it to me as an early Christmas gift. I immediately got down to business. In order to take control of the Xbox hardware, the first task is to extract the boot ROM and analyzing its contents; recall from the discussion on Xbox architecture in Chapter 2 that the boot ROM of the Xbox contains all of the code for establishing the Xbox's operating environment.

To Snarf a ROM

The type of ROM used in the Xbox is an electrically erasable and programmable variety known as FLASH ROM. FLASH ROM typically comes in one of a few package types, and the Xbox uses one of the most popular packages, the TSOP (Thin Small Outline Package). It is located in sector U7 on the top side of the Xbox motherboard, and the reference designator for the part is U7D1. The TSOP package is very recognizable because it is one of the few chip packages that is rectangular and has pins only on the *narrow* edges of the package. Most other packages put pins on the long edge or all edges to maximize connectivity, but FLASH ROM has relatively low I/O requirements per silicon area. A quick check on the base part number, 29F080, with a Web search engine verifies that this part is indeed an 8 Mbit FLASH ROM.

There are a few techniques that one can use to read out ("snarf") the contents of the FLASH ROM. The no-solder approach is to buy a test clip that snaps onto the FLASH ROM, and read out its contents by powering up and controlling the ROM through the test clip, while the rest of the Xbox is powered off. A suitable test clip for this purpose can be purchased from Emulation Technology, `www.emulationtechnology.com`. The test clip override approach has a few problems with it, the biggest being the possibility of permanently damaging chips connected to the FLASH ROM that are not receiving power through the test clip. However, in the specific case of the Xbox, this does not seem to be a problem and those who attempted this approach did meet with success[1]. I did not initially take this approach as I did not want to risk damaging the motherboard, and because I could not afford the $300 test clip required for the job.

Another ingenious approach is to solder wires to the test points around the FLASH ROM to eavesdrop on the Xbox as it reads the ROM's contents. Eavesdropping can be accomplished by either connecting the wires to a

---

[1] Andy Green has an excellent page that documents his experiences with the test clip approach at `http://www.warmcat.com/milksop/milksop.html`

custom board that can interface with the ROM, or by using a logic analyzer to capture the data as it is accessed by the Xbox CPU. The latter approach was used with success as well, and in fact some back doors in the Xbox boot sequence were discovered as a consequence of this methodology[2]. I chose not use this approach either, as I did not have a logic analyzer at the time when I got my first Xbox, and because soldering all the wires down can be very tedious, difficult and error-prone. My approach was more traditional: just remove the FLASH ROM and drop it into a ROM reader. I also placed a socket on the motherboard, so that future removals and programmings of the ROM would be very quick and reliable.

Figure 6-1:
Removing the Xbox FLASH ROM using a tweezer-style soldering iron.

Removing the FLASH ROM in a manner that preserves the integrity of its fine-pitched pins is a task that is simple if you have the right tools, and nearly impossible with the wrong tools. The key is to heat all of the pins of the FLASH ROM simultaneously; once uniform heating is achieved, the FLASH ROM will fall right off the motherboard. Clearly, the standard pencil-style soldering iron is not going to be able to heat all of the pins

[2] Visor has written up his experiences with the logic analyzer snooping approach at `http://www.xboxhacker.net/visor/aXventure1.txt`

simultaneously. The proper tool for the job are "tongs" or "tweezer" style soldering irons as shown in Figure 6-1 below. These soldering irons have two heating elements, so it can heat both sides of the chip simultaneously. Furthermore, the soldering iron must have a paddle-tip that is wide enough to heat the length of the chip all at once. A soldering iron with these types of features can cost quite a bit (hundreds of dollars), but it is a worthwhile investment as it comes in handy in all kinds of situations. I use an Ersa SMT Unit 60A soldering iron that I bought for a good discount on the floor of a tradeshow, and it quickly paid for itself through the few board assembly jobs that I picked up on the side while finishing my degree. A more affordable iron by Xytronic can be purchased through Jameco (#168410) for about $70, but I have not used it so I cannot vouch for its quality. Another budget approach that is very simple and straightforward is to use a desoldering alloy, as described in Appendix B, Soldering Techniques. Note that a suitable socket for the ROM[3] is relatively cheap—under $20—although installing the socket does require a steady hand and an optical magnifying device of some kind.

Once the ROM is removed and its pins cleaned and inspected, the ROM's contents can be read out in a ROM reader. Of course ROM readers can be purchased, but it is always a good learning experience to build your own ROM reader. You can read up a little bit on ROM programmers that I've built at my website, `http://www.xenatera.com/bunnie`. My original Flashburner[4] programmer is a simple device that is easier to understand and build than its second revision[5], but it is less powerful. However, if your goal is to read out ROMs as quickly as possible, just purchase a ROM reader outright. A good ROM reader is an essential tool in any serious hardware hacker's toolbox. Needham's Electronics (`http://www.needhams.com`) makes a great line of ROM programmers/readers that fit a wide span of budgets.

An Encounter with Microsoft

After extracting the ROM contents, the next step is to share its contents with fellow hackers for analysis. Or is it? Within twelve hours of posting the contents of the ROM to my website, I received a call from an engineer at Microsoft politely requesting that I remove their copyrighted content from my website. Of course, I immediately removed their content from my website; I should have known better before posting it in the first place. This first brush with Microsoft was a sobering warning that reverse engineering the Xbox was not going to be like any other home appliance reverse engineering project. There are laws that protect aspects of reverse engineering, and a vast body of copyright law that protects the intellectual property (IP) owner. Collaborative reverse engineering of the Xbox while respecting

---

[3] Emulation Technologies (`http://www.emulation.com`) makes a wide line of affordable sockets for purposes just like these. The specific model for the Xbox is the S-TS-SM-040-A.

[4] `http://www.xenatera.com/bunnie/proj/flashburn/fb.html`

[5] `http://www.xenatera.com/bunnie/proj/fb2/`

Microsoft's rights is a legal minefield.

On one hand, Microsoft should be able to invest in a product and take a risk in hopes of a profit. However, profitability is not guaranteed by law. For example, selling the consoles at a huge loss, as Microsoft has done, in hopes of selling software to make up the difference ("loss leader") is a risky proposition, and there is no guarantee by law that Microsoft has to come out ahead in the end. On the other hand, we as hackers have the right to tinker ("fair use") with hardware purchased with our own hard-earned cash, and if Microsoft wants to basically sell PCs at a huge discount to us, that's fine. Whether or not we purchase enough games (around ten or more) to compensate for Microsoft's losses on the Xbox is entirely up to Microsoft's business and marketing strategy. In my eyes, Microsoft's large loss-to-revenue ratio is a bit of an anomaly in this industry. Sony and Nintendo roughly break-even on the cost of their console hardware. Also, cell phone providers often sell their phones at a loss comparable to that of the Xbox, but require the subscriber to enter a contract to ensure that the cost of the phone is recouped; breaking the contract implies termination fees. Perhaps this is a reflection of Microsoft's confidence in the Xbox Live business model.

Somewhere in the middle of all of this is the interplay of cryptographic copyright protection mechanisms and the right to fair use. It turns out that the Xbox makes extensive use of cryptography to enforce copy protections as well as console usage policies, which brings us to the Digital Millennium Copyright Act of 1998 (DMCA), a relatively new, untested body of law. With little established court precedent and plenty of gray area in between the letters of the law, you as a hacker must assess the potential liabilities that you could face. Chapter 12, "Caveat Hacker", explores in greater detail the legal issues of hacking in the new millennium.

Analyzing the ROM Contents

Rebuffed by Microsoft, but ROM contents still in hand, I proceeded to analyze the ROM contents. One would expect that the boot ROM contains a hardware initialization procedure, followed by instructions that load up the operating system, and possibly the operating system code itself. But where to start? The program inside the ROM can be thought of as a ball of yarn: once you find the starting point of the thread, it is just a matter of perseverance to unwind the ball of yarn to its core. Fortunately, the starting point of the Xbox's Pentium processor is very well documented by Intel. On power-up, the processor starts running code at a special hard-wired location, called the *reset vector*. This reset vector is at address `0xFFFF.FFF0`, near the top of memory. Let's look at the data contained at this location (in hexadecimal):

```
0xFFFF.FFF0 EBC6 8BFF 1800 D8FF FFFF 80C2 04B0 02EE
```

The first two bytes, `EBC6`, are a jump instruction to location `0xFFFF.FFB8`. The first byte, `EB`, is the specific opcode for a "jump, short, relative, displacement relative to next instruction"; the second byte, C6, is the 8-bit signed offset of the jump. In other words, the first thing the processor does is jump to another location—something every boot program does, since you only have 16 bytes of runway in the reset vector before you fall off the high end of memory. Since this is typical code for a reset vector, it is okay to reprint the code here for educational purposes.

The next chunk of code is a piece that initializes the processor's GDT (Global Descriptor Table) and IDT (Interrupt Descriptor Table) state. The GDT and IDT set up the processor's memory management scheme and interrupt handling scheme. You do not need to understand exactly what these registers do, but if you are curious, Intel's "IA-32 Intel Architecture

```
// key initialization routine
 unsigned char K[256]; // 0xFFFFC80 in flash
 unsigned char S[256]; // 0x10000 in SDRAM

 for( i = 0; i < 256; i++ ) {
   S[i] = i;
 }
 j = 0;
 for( i = 0; i < 256; i++ ) {
   // RC-4 would do j = (j + K[i] + S[i]) % 256
   j = (j + K[i] + S[j]) % 256;
   // swap S[i], S[j]
   temp = S[i];
   S[i] = S[j];
   S[j] = temp;
 }

 // decryption routine
 unsigned char cipherText[16384]; // 0xFFFFA000 in FLASH
 unsigned char plainText[16384];  // 0x400000   in SDRAM

 for( index = 0x4000, i = 0, k = 0; index > 0; index– ) {
   // xbox version
   t = (S[i] ^ cipherText[k]) % 256;
   plainText[k] = t;

   // swap( S[i], S[t] );
   temp = S[i];
   S[i] = S[t];
   S[t] = temp;

   i = (i + 1) % 256;
   k++;
 }
```

Listing 6-1:
Decompilation of the dummy cipher found in the FLASH ROM

Software Developer's Manual, Volume 3: System Programming Guide" explains the function of these registers in detail. This manual is available off of Intel's developer website, `http://developer.intel.com`.

After setting up these registers, the processor gets kicked into protected mode and jumps to `0xFFFF.FE00`—a region exactly 512 bytes below the top of memory—and this is where things start to get interesting. After a short snippet of code that sets up the segment registers, a program called a *jam table interpreter* (also known as the X-Code interpreter in the Xbox community) is executed. A "jam table" is industry vernacular for a table of values that contains opcodes for reads, writes and simple decision operations, used in the context of hardware initializations. Hundreds of operations are required to initialize a typical PC, and jam tables help cope with this complexity without bloating the core initialization code base. Using jam tables also helps make initialization more flexible and capable of dealing with user-configurable hardware parameters, such as the type and amount of memory installed. In the case of the Xbox, the jam table interpreter starts fetching jam table opcodes from a location near the bottom of the FLASH ROM. Keep in mind that the opcodes implemented by the jam table interpreter are quite powerful; one can write and read data from any location in the Xbox using jam table opcodes.

After the terminal opcode is executed by the jam table interpreter, the processor clears the MTRRs (Memory Type Range Registers, used to declare the cacheability of various regions of memory) and starts to decrypt a 16 kB region of memory starting at `0xFFFF.A000`. There cipher used to decrypt this region of memory looks very similar to RC-4, but has some subtle differences. Listing 6-1 shows the cipher reverse-engineered into C code, with the help of a tool called IDA Pro by Data Rescue corporation (more about this tool in the next couple of chapters).

The data decrypted by this cipher is actually a block of code that gets executed at the end of the decryption process, but something goes very wrong here.

The decrypted code is garbage. It doesn't work.

Furthermore, the jam table opcodes seem to be corrupted. This phenomenon was corroborated by other hackers working on the problem, thus ruling out a code translation error. Clearly, there is more to the Xbox than meets the eye. Theories and rumors started to emerge to explain this strange behavior. Some of the popular theories included:

- **Address and/or data line scrambling.** Somewhere, the address or data lines were being inverted or permuted with some 1:1 mapping function. The scrambling function could be programmed into the chipset as part of the initialization procedure, so that the initial boot block would read like plaintext while the rest of the data would be scrambled.

Memory Address Decoding Tricks

A number of tricks exist that can be used to make regions of memory appear different in some way than their physical representation would indicate. The two tricks relevant to the analysis of the Xbox boot sequence are *aliasing* and *overlaying.*

Memory locations are aliased when two addresses refer to the same memory location, typically accomplished by ignoring a few address bits. To illustrate aliasing, consider a system using a 3-bit address. There are only $2^3 = 8$ unique locations addressable in a 3-bit system: 000, 001, 010, 011, 100, 101, 110 and 111. Now suppose that you have a memory with four locations; it requires only two bits to distinguish each of the four locations: 00, 01, 10 and 11. If you use our 3-bit address scheme to talk to this four-location memory, one of the address bits must be ignored. If the highest bit is ignored, then address 000 and 100 will both map to location 00 in memory. In other words, location 00 is *aliased* to addresses 000 and 100.

Memory overlaying is a technique where out-of-band information is used to select between different banks of memory. Let's suppose that we wish to have a bank of secret memory. To do this, we insert a selector between our public and secret memories, and the CPU. This selector can choose to present the CPU with data from either the secret memory or the public memory, as indicated in Figure 6-2. As a result, the program that controls the address selector also controls who has access to the secret block. If the computer starts up running code located in the secret bank of memory, a program in the secret code region can use this mechanism to hide itself by setting the selector to point at public memory before running programs located in public memory.

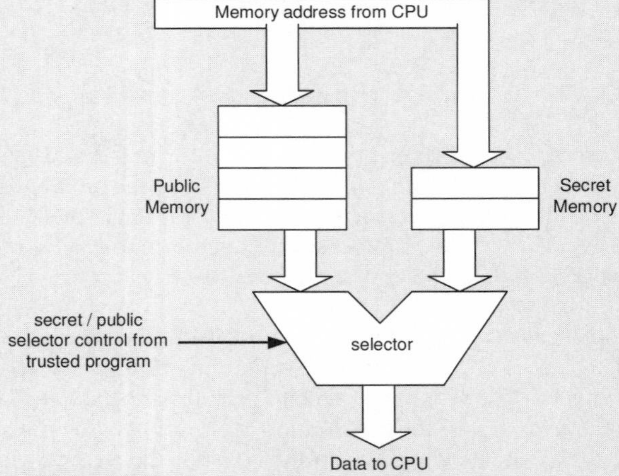

Figure 6-2:
Memory overlaying to hide secret regions.

- **Secondary crypto processor.** Another processor on the Xbox was actually handling the Xbox's initialization, and the boot code in the ROM is bogus.
- **Boot code contained in the processor.** The processor is actually initialized by a chunk of code sitting on the processor die, and the boot code in the ROM is bogus.
- **Boot code contained in the chipset.** The processor functions identically to a standard Pentium, but the chipset contains boot code that overrides the bogus code inside the ROM.

For almost all of these theories, the only way to prove or disprove them is to perform experiments on the hardware. For example, in order to ensure that the SMC (System Management Controller, an 8-bit self-contained processor that is always on when the Xbox is plugged in) played no role in the secure boot sequence of the machine, hackers captured traces of the waveforms on all of the SMC's pins and analyzed them against the expected sequence of events if the SMC were to play a crucial role in machine initialization.

A crucial observation from a fellow hacker was that the Xbox booted perfectly even when the reset vector code at `0xFFFF.FFF0` was changed. One would expect that if the first instruction executed by the processor at `0xFFFF.FFF0` were corrupted, then the machine would crash. Rather, the machine operated flawlessly. This observation was verified by a set of experiments where various parts of the FLASH ROM were intentionally corrupted. The results were that corrupting surprisingly large regions of the FLASH ROM had no effect on the booting of the Xbox. In particular, the entire boot initialization sequence from `0xFFFF.FE00` to `0xFFFF.FFFF` could be nulled out and the Xbox would boot just fine.

This finding alone gave strong support to the theory of a bogus boot block in FLASH ROM. The question remained, however, about where the real boot code was stored. There were three options: in a secondary crypto-processor, in the processor, and in the chipset. The secondary crypto-processor theory was discounted on the basis that there were no chips on the motherboard that were powerful enough or active enough at boot time to play the role of a crypto processor. Storing the boot block in the processor was also deemed a less likely option than storing the boot block in the chipset. The rationale for this analysis is based on the economics of building chips. A Pentium III processor is very complex with many hand-crafted blocks, and modifying the silicon to include a secure boot block would require significant engineering resources as well as an up-front investment of about a quarter of a million dollars just for masks alone to produce the custom silicon. In addition, it was rumored that Microsoft had originally chosen an AMD processor for the Xbox, and switched to Intel at the last minute. If custom blocks were integrated into the processor core, Microsoft could not have switched between CPU vendors so easily. On the other hand, nVidia's chipsets are designed modularly using silicon compilers, so it is technically easier to add warts like a secure boot block. Furthermore, the chipset in the Xbox is a custom build of the nForce made just for

Microsoft, tailored specifically for an Intel front-side bus (FSB). As a result, the cost of adding a secure boot block could be rolled into the engineering resources and the mask sets already allocated to such a project.

Operating under the theory that the real boot code is located in a secret ROM overly in the chipset, the challenges remaining were to figure in which chip (Northbridge or Southbridge) the code was stored, and how to extract this secret ROM. A few strategies for extracting the secret ROM presented themselves:

- **Use the JTAG "boundary scan" feature** on the Pentium to try and capture the initial boot code. JTAG is a diagnostic bus that allows users to read and set the state of every pin on a chip through a special serial port. It is a very powerful and versatile debugging tool.
- **Probe the processor FSB (Front Side Bus)** to try and capture the boot code as it enters the processor.
- **Install a memory sniffer** to try and capture the decrypted data stream as it is written into memory.
- **Use microscopy** to read out the contents of the secure boot area from the chip surface.
- **Probe the bus between the Southbridge and the Northbridge** chips to try and capture the boot code being sent to the processor by the chipset. This would only work if the boot data is stored somewhere in the Southbridge chip.

None of these theories were trivial to test, so the Xbox hacking effort slowly ground down to a halt as frustrated hackers gave up on trying to cryptanalyze the FLASH ROM image. I would have been one of the quitters (after all, I had a doctoral thesis to finish *and* write in just a few months) if it weren't for the community of determined hackers feeding me encouragement. Over Christmas break in December 2001, I kept in touch with my

Figure 6-3:
Missing JTAG via. Note how the filled in copper region (lighter area) has a hole where a via used to be. This is the result of a last-minute change to the board layout without recalculation of the fill regions.

hacker friends via IRC channels and web fora. Hackers from all over the world and all walks of life pervaded the Xbox hacking IRC channel, and I enjoyed learning from them and chatting with them about their various experiences, both technical and personal.

Even though I was determined to spend all of January writing my PhD thesis[6] and avoiding Xbox hacking, I was still pulled in by the intriguingly complex security employed by the Xbox. As time went on, the need for a hardware guy to join the small group of hardcore hackers hanging out on the IRC channel became increasingly clear. By the end of January, the reports I was hearing about the Xbox security scheme were too interesting ignore. I purchased a second Xbox and I started removing all of its key parts using a hot air gun. Stripping down the Xbox served many purposes. First, removing the chips exposed all of the traces and connections on the Xbox so that I could easily follow the connections between chips using the continuity test mode on my multimeter. Second, I was able to drop all of the interesting chips into a hot acid bath and remove their plastic encapsulation for analysis under a microscope. Finally, buying an Xbox and totally ripping it apart gave me a sort of peace of mind when it comes to probing and modifying a working Xbox. Reverse engineering is like gardening. Planting a garden is much more challenging if you're trying to keep your hands and knees clean, so you might as well get over it and start rolling in the dirt.

The results of the Xbox tear-down revealed some of the measures that Microsoft took to secure the box against hardware hackers. For example, the first thing I checked was the JTAG connections on the Pentium CPU. All of the JTAG signals were conveniently routed to a set of easy-to-tap resistors near the processor, except for one, the `TRST#` signal. `TRST#` plays a critical role in initializing the JTAG interface. Interestingly, `TRST#` was tied to the internal ground plane, in a difficult to access area, permanently deactivating the JTAG mechanism. Inspection of the Xbox motherboard revealed hints that the `TRST#` signal was stripped out at the last minute. The biggest hint of a missing via is a hole in a power trace perfectly sized for a via near a cluster of vias dedicated to JTAG signals, as illustrated in Figure 6-3.

Another blow to the JTAG approach for extracting the secret ROM is the fact that Intel's JTAG scan codes are proprietary. Reverse engineering the codes to a level where I could use them for extracting the secret boot data was a major project on its own.

Giving up on the JTAG approach, the next method for extracting the secret ROM was to strip the packaging off of the CPU, GPU and MCPX and to inspect the bare die with a microscope and search for any candidate ROM structures. Package removal or "decapsulation" was accomplished by bathing the chips fuming hot sulfuric acid. I don't recommend trying this approach at home; one time I spilled the toxic, corrosive solution all over myself and

[6] For those interested in supercomputer architecture, data and thread migration, fault tolerance, high speed low-latency networks, or massively multithreaded machines, check out my thesis at `http://www.xenatera.com/bunnie/phdthesis.pdf`.

thankfully, my protective gear was consumed instead of my skin. Fuming sulfuric consumes organic material faster than a burning flame. Fuming nitric, also very toxic and dangerous, can also be used. While I have not tried it myself, reports indicate that fuming nitric is more effective at removing the epoxy encapsulation, especially in situations where selective package removal is desired.

The manual inspection approach using a traditional visible light microscope had some hope; however, the technique is limited by the physics of light. Not even the best visible microscopy technology can resolve a 150 nm transistor, since the shortest wavelength of light is 450 nm (corresponding to the color blue). I was hoping the secret code would be stored on the chips using a traditional array ROM structure, with the metal lines defining a 1 or a 0 etched into the top metal layers which can be identified with an optical microscope. The use of a hard-wired ROM structure is motivated by cost: FLASH ROMs and fuse-based PROMs require extra processing and manufacturing steps that can add significant cost to the system, whereas the use of top metal layers would be motivated by risk management on the designer's part. Top metal layers are the coarsest layers (so coarse that an optical microscope has a chance at resolving features), and are thus the cheapest layers to change in case there is a bug in the ROM code. Also, during initial bring-up, the top layer is the easiest to cut and jumper using a chip repair machine knows as a FIB (focused ion beam) machine. Unfortunately, a quick glance at the chip under the microscope revealed no such structures.

At this point, the only remaining option for extracting the secret R M was to probe the live Xbox hardware, in an effort to capture the code durin loading into the Xbox processor. Eavesdropping for code upstream of the Southbridge chip and the FLASH ROM meant probing either the Front Side bus, the Northbridge-Southbridge bus, or the main memory bus. The trade-offs of executing these probing approaches will be discussed in Chapter 8, after a short introduction to basic security concepts in the next chapter.

CHAPTER 7

A Brief Primer on Security

Hacking the Xbox requires security hacking in addition to hardware and firmware hacking, as discovered in the last chapter. We will go over some of the possible motivations behind adding sophisticated security to something as mundane as a gaming machine, and then we will dive into the basic principals and algorithms necessary to understand and appreciating the Xbox's security mechanisms.

Who Needs Security, Anyways?

The video game console, a toy for most people: low cost, consumer electronics. Why is it that Microsoft went through such pains to secure their system? In the game of security hacking, quite frequently understanding the motive of the securer will be helpful in finding weaknesses that you can exploit.

Cryptography is not security. Cryptography is a means to an end for security, but real security involves the entire system architecture, including the end users. As Kevin Mitnick said in a recent Slashdot interview, "...security is not a product that can be purchased off the shelf, but consists of policies, people, processes, and technology"[1]. I believe that security is *fundamentally* a social concept. In practice, you can open your windows and leave the front door locked and people won't just walk in through your window or pick your doorlock, even though both are relatively easy tasks. Locked doors and open windows works because a locked door is mostly a symbolic measure; it forces an intruder to make a conscious act of violation in order to enter a house, and that alone is enough of a line to separate criminals from well-doers. Sony's Playstation console has a good example of front-door lock

[1] http://interviews.slashdot.org/article.pl?sid=03/02/04/2233250&mode=nocomment&tid=103&tid=123&tid=172.

security. The mechanism used to copy-protect their games is simple, involves no cryptography, and is easily overridden with easily installed, inexpensive hardware modifications. Despite this, sales numbers indicate that purchasing Playstation games has not gone out of style; the front-door lock is working.

Microsoft employs a variation of front-door lock style security. Video games for the Xbox are distributed using the (so far) uncopyable DVD-9 format, a single-sided, dual layer media format. User-writeable DVDs, on the other hand, are always in DVD-5 format, a single-sided, single layer media format. DVD-9 capable burners are not likely to be available soon due to the difficulty in making a writing system capable of burning one layer without affecting the integrity of the other layer. Thus, by distributing security data between the two layers of a DVD-9 disk and requiring a game executable to come from DVD-9 media, Microsoft has a fairly effective front-door lock on its video games. By judiciously requiring the DVD-9 format, Microsoft has pretty much forced any potential game copier into a realm where some kind of hardware modification is necessary.

Why then would Microsoft risk investing in such a complex security scheme on the Xbox? Is Microsoft's main motivation really to quell piracy? It is quite possible that in fact the primary reason for the rest of the Xbox security system—the secure boot sectors, signed executables, trust relationships and encrypted/authenticated network protocols—lies not in anti-piracy measures.

One possible motivation for all the security is to prevent the use of the Xbox console for any purpose other than gaming. The Xbox console is in the unique position of being an almost 100% stock PC. Unlike the Gamecube and the Playstation2, there is an enormous body of software that seems like it should just run on the Xbox, given the right BIOS programming. To make matters worse, Microsoft loses much more money on its console hardware than its competitors. Some estimate that its losses may be as high as $200 per console, assuming the most recent retail price of $199. Hence, it is in Microsoft's interest to try and ensure that it is not selling subsidized GNU/Linux boxes. However, even this is probably not Microsoft's main goal. The Xbox's 64 MB of main memory, lack of a keyboard or mouse out of the box, and a fairly slow processor by today's standards makes it less appealing than, for example, the $200 Microtel PC available at Walmart as of late 2002. In addition, Microsoft has deep pockets; if the Xbox gained market traction and outsold Sony's Playstation2, Microsoft would only have to stomach a few billion dollars of up-front loss—relatively small in comparison to the roughly $40 billion cash-pile on which Microsoft sits. Thus, it is quite possible that the critical mission of Xbox security is not to prevent alternative console uses or to deter piracy.

Perhaps the real reason for the complex security of the Xbox is to ensure the success of Xbox Live, Microsoft's on-line gaming service. Microsoft's marketing hype and PR statements indicate that it is betting on the success of Xbox Live to drive hardware sales. Furthermore, Xbox Live is a subscription service, and one year from its launch users will have to pay a monthly fee. If Microsoft can get its subscribers hooked on Xbox Live, then all of a sudden the Xbox business looks quite profitable, even if a substantial amount of money is lost up-front on the hardware. The trick is, of course, getting Xbox users hooked on Xbox Live. Billed as the "Disneyland of on-line gaming", the goal of Xbox Live is to provide a well-executed and fair gaming experience. Central to the value proposition of Xbox Live that there are no cheaters. In order to ensure that nobody is cheating, users must be forced to authenticate themselves against a registry maintained by Xbox Live, and their game state must be kept secure and unmodifiable. In addition, game software must be unpatched. Even more crucial is the fact that you only need a few cheaters to ruin the gaming experience of an entire user base. All of a sudden, the front-door security protections offered by the DVD-9 format seem inadequate. The odds are against you if you betting the success of a business on the morality and honor of a user base of millions of twenty-something hardcore male gamers with a reasonable amount of computer savvy distributed throughout. The hardware must be trustable, network connections secure, and executables signed and sealed.

The statement that the hardware must be trustable bears repeating. Given an untrustable user base, the only way to establish a trust relationship with clients is if a seed of trust exists in every piece of hardware. Hence, Microsoft must include in every client a piece of tamper-proof hardware that enables some kind of attestation. Attestation is the ability to prove that some piece of data, such as a player's identity or game state, is in fact generated by software and hardware that is untainted. The tamper-proof hardware does not have to implement the attestation function directly, but it must at least ensure that the system is in a trustable state before attestation. There are many ways to ensure that hardware is trustable. The brute-force method is to make the entire piece of hardware physically secure. Automated Teller Machines are prime examples of hardware that is physically secure. Sealed in thick sheet metal and covered with intrusion sensors, it is difficult to physically penetrate and modify the hardware of an ATM. While effective, this is an impractical and expensive solution for a video game console.

A more economical solution is to use a small piece of trusted tamper-proof hardware that can make "measurements" on the rest of the system. These sorts of measurements are typically accomplished through the use of a cryptographic hash function. If all of these trust measurements conform with the expected values, then one might be able to conclude that the entire system is trustable. I say might because this scheme is vulnerable to man-in-the-middle attacks where a hacker sends spoofed valid data in response to a measurement query. Man-in-the-middle attacks refer to a general class of attacks where an adversary can freely modify and control the information being passed between two parties. Because of the man-in-the-middle weakness, it does not make sense to use an extremely sophisticated tamper-proof module to make the system measurements. A single packaged silicon chip is probably good enough, as it is typically easier to intercept and spoof the measurement data going past on a printed circuit board than it is to penetrate the epoxy package of a chip and modify the chip's circuitry.

The trust measurement system can be implemented using a measure-once approach. Starting with the processor cold-boot sequence, every piece of code is measured for trust before execution. If the processor never executes untrusted code, then what is there not to trust? This scheme requires a very simple tamper-proof hardware module—a tamper-proof ROM that stores the cold-boot code, a "seed" of trust. The type of cryptography used for the measurement and verification process is typically a combination of hashes and public-key cryptography. Public-key cryptography is preferred for this application because the private key required to generate a valid code segment is a secret kept by only the hardware vendor. Again, this scheme is vulnerable to many kinds of man-in-the-middle attacks, as well as pure cryptographic attacks and attacks on the implementation of the system.

A Brief Primer on Cryptography

> **ci·pher** (*n*): **1 a**: ZERO **b**: one that has no weight, worth, or influence : NONENTITY. **2 a**: a method of transforming text in order to conceal its meaning — compare to CODE [2]

Ciphers provide no security on their own. More specifically, ciphers only provide security if the key is secure, if the algorithm is strong, and if there are no back doors into the system. If someone hands you a CD-ROM encrypted with a strong cipher and locks you in a padded room with a supercomputer, the sun will probably go supernova before you can decrypt the CD-ROM. On the other hand, if you could observe and probe the machine as it was working to encrypt the CD-ROM, the encryption is moot. You could get the enciphering key by eavesdropping the keyboard. Or, you could dump the contents of the computer's memory and obtain the plaintext without knowing the key. The situation with the Xbox is similar to the latter. Ultimately, the Xbox must access and run the programs presented to it on valid disks. Furthermore, the Pentium CPU used in the Xbox cannot tell the difference between an authorized instruction and an unauthorized instruction. Finally, the user has full access to probe and modify the Xbox hardware. Thus, even if the Xbox uses strong ciphers, it is questionable if the keys are secure and that there are no back doors into the system. This section will briefly describe the kinds of cryptographic algorithms used in the Xbox. We will focus on the practical implications and implementation issues of these algorithms. You will need this kind of understanding of these algorithms in order to appreciate the available attacks on the Xbox security system. I make no pretense of addressing the theoretical aspects of cryptography; those are beyond me and beyond the scope of the book. I refer interested readers to Bruce Schneier's excellent book, *Applied Cryptography*, by Wiley publishers; most of my knowledge in cryptography comes from that book. Readers who are already familiar with cryptography should be able to skim or skip the remainder of this chapter.

---

[2] Merriam-Webster OnLine Dictionary (`www.webster.com`).

Classes of Cryptographic Algorithms

There are a few important classes of cryptographic algorithms used in the Xbox. These are

- Hashes
- Symmetric ciphers
- Public key ciphers

Hashes come in several varieties. Hashes of the cryptographic variety are used to summarize or "digest" a large amount of data. The summary is a number of fixed length, typically around 100 to 200 bits long, while the source data can be of almost any size. The most important property of a hash is that it is a one-way computation. In other words, it is easy to compute the hash, but it is very difficult (see the sidebar on Very Difficult Problems to understand exactly what this means) to derive sequences of data whose hash digest are identical or to determine anything about the original data from the hash. The strength of a hash against finding two sequences of data that hash to the same value is referred to as its "collision resistance", and in general, a good n-bit hash requires about $2^{n/2}$ random data sequences to be hashed and compared in order to cause a collision. Since hashes are designed to be very easy to compute and very collision-resistant, they are often used to detect if any bit has been changed in large regions of secure data. For many applications, it is sufficient include just an encrypted hash of a message in lieu of expending the computational effort to encrypt the whole message.

Symmetric ciphers are algorithms that have encryption and decryption keys that can be easily derived from one another. Most of the time, the encryption and decryption keys are the same. Symmetric ciphers use a *mixing function* to combine a *key schedule* with data that has been processed by some *cryptographic function*. This mixing may be repeated several times over a single block of data as in a block cipher, or it may occur once as in a stream cipher. All of the basic functions in a symmetric cipher are computationally simple, so symmetric ciphers are the preferred method for encrypting bulk data.

Typical examples of mixing functions are XORs, modular additions and modular multiplications. The simplest function, XOR, has the property that any number XOR itself is zero. The XOR operation is often denoted with a $\oplus$ symbol. The XOR operation also has all the usual properties of arithmetic (commutative, associative, distributive, etc.), so

$$(A \oplus B) \oplus B = A \oplus (B \oplus B) = A \oplus 0 = A$$

Thus, if A were a message and B were a key, $(A \oplus B)$ would be the ciphertext, and the plaintext can be recovered by simply performing an XOR with B again.

A key schedule is an algorithm that takes a relatively short key and expands its information over a long series of bits. Key schedules are used to help diffuse the key data over a larger block of data so the relationship between the ciphertext and the key is obscured.

A typical cryptographic function as used in a symmetric block cipher consists of a set of carefully designed substitutions, permutations, compressions and expansions. These functions serve to confuse and diffuse the plaintext. Subtle changes in any piece of a cryptographic function typically have a profound effect on the security of a cipher.

The fact that the encryption and decryption keys are closely related in a symmetric cipher makes them difficult to use in certain security applications. For example, if I wish to distribute an encrypted document to a mailing list, everyone on the mailing list must also effectively know my encryption key if they can read the document. In addition, initiating contact with a remote party is difficult, because at some point I have to transmit a key to them. Someone observing the transmission medium could steal the key and read, forge, and modify all subsequent messages.

Public key ciphers are algorithms that use a different key for encryption and decryption. They are also referred to as asymmetric ciphers for this reason. The big advantage of public key ciphers is that one of the keys can be kept a

Very Difficult Problems

Cryptographic functions are all based on mathematical algorithms whose results are easy to compute given all the operands, but whose operands are very difficult to compute given just the result. The security of a cryptographic function is precisely the difficulty of computing these operands given just the results. Let us take a moment and explore what it means to be very difficult.

Consider the symmetric cipher AES. It uses a 128-bit key, and so far, it is strong against all known analytical cryptographic attacks, such as differential and linear cryptanalysis. When I say it is strong against analysis X, I mean that it will require at least as many operations to recover the key or plaintext using a brute-force search as it would using analysis X. A brute-force search is when I take a very fast computer and try every one of the 2^{128} possible keys in order to recover the original data. Most cryptographic algorithms in common use today are strong against all known cryptanalysis techniques, so the important number to understand is how hard is a brute-force attack. As it turns out, older algorithms such as DES, a 56-bit cipher is not a very difficult problem. It is fairly easy to build a machine using FPGAs (Field Programmable Gate Arrays) that can crack keys at an economy of about 2^{22} keys/second/dollar (2^{22} is about four million). Note that this number increases with time at a rate equivalent to Moore's Law. Today, if you are willing to wait about a week for each key, you can recover them for about the price of a nice car. Let's hope that

continued...

secret. This allows data exchange with untrusted without giving the untrusted user the ability to forge or read other protected content. The down side of public key algorithms is that they typically require more complex computations and are thus slower than symmetric ciphers. Public key ciphers also tend to require longer keys for equivalent security. As a result, if large amount of data is to be exchanged, public key ciphers are often used to encrypt a key for a symmetric cipher that is used to encrypt the bulk of the data. This symmetric cipher key can be unique to each transaction and hence it is often referred to as a "session key".

SHA-1 Hash

SHA-1 is the Secure Hash Algorithm recommended by the Federal government in FIPS publication 180-1 (`http://www.itl.nist.gov/fipspubs/fip180-1.htm`). Devised by the NSA and based on Ronald L. Rivest's MD4 message digest algorithm, SHA-1 works on messages of any length less than 2^{64} bits in length, and it produces a 160 bit output. The SHA-1 hash algorithm starts with a deterministic 160-bit seed state; this state is blended with a block of 512 bits of message data over four rounds. Each round consists of a series of non-linear functions, rotations, shifts

banks do not use DES to encrypt their account data!

The successor to DES, AES, is a cipher that can use 128, 192, or 256-bit keys. These keys are large enough to be considered impervious to brute-force attacks (i.e., a very difficult problem). According to the AES Q&A published by NIST (`http://csrc.nist.gov/encryption/aes/aesfact.html`), a machine powerful enough to recover one DES key per second through brute force (trying on average 2^{55} keys per second) would still require 149 trillion years to recover a 128-bit AES key. My favorite analysis of the strength of 256-bit keys against brute force attacks comes from Bruce Schneier's book, *Applied Cryptography* (Wiley Publishers). In his book, he uses an argument based on the amount of energy required to crack a 256-bit key. It turns out that even with a thermodynamically ideal computer, it would require over 32 times the annual energy output of our sun to just *count* to 2^{192}, much less do anything useful with that count. I must stress that all of this assumes that the most efficient attack is brute force. Who knows, maybe someone will discover a weakness in the algorithm that can be used to mount a much more efficient attack. New analysis techniques are constantly being invented that slowly chips away at the strength of a cipher.

Public-key ciphers are a different story from symmetric-key ciphers. Public key ciphers are based on a wide variety of difficult to reverse mathematical operations, such as prime number multiplication and modular exponentiation. As a result, the key space for many public key ciphers is sparse, so more key bits are required for equivalent symmetric ci-

continued...

and XORs. The result of a round is used to seed the next round's computation. In general, 2^{80} random messages need to be generated, hashed and "simultaneously" compared in order to find two messages that have the same hash value (i.e., a hash collision). Finding two random messages that have the same hash is known as the "birthday attack", named after the probabilistic phenomenon called the "birthday paradox": the probability that two people share the same birthday in a room of 23 people is better than 50%. On the other hand, 2^{160} random messages need to be generated, hashed and compared in order to find a message that hashes to the same value as a specific message. Thus, the strength of a hash function depends heavily upon the manner in which it is used.

Very Difficult Problems, continued...

pher security. As an example, key lengths in the RSA public-key cipher are typically several thousands of bits long. The exact correlation between the security of RSA public key lengths and symmetric cipher key lengths is unknown. The security of RSA is conjectured to be the difficulty of factoring the products of large prime numbers; however, there may be other attacks as of yet to be discovered on the algorithm. Even so, the effective difficulty of factoring the product of large primes is reduced not only by advances in computing technology (Moore's Law), but also by advances in number theory, such as the invention and refinement of the Quadratic Sieve and the General Number Field Sieve. In August 1999, a group of researches used the Number Field Sieve to factor a 512-bit prime number in 7.4 calendar months, including the time required to set up the factorizing run[1]. In addition, new technologies such as quantum computing promise to enable the factorization of prime numbers in polynomial time. I wouldn't hold your breath, however; there is still debate as to whether it is possible to build a quantum computer large enough to factor an interesting prime. As of today, RSA Security, Inc. recommends key lengths of 1024 bits for most corporate uses, and 2048 bits for "extremely valuable keys"[2]. Bruce Schneier estimates in the second edition of his *Applied Cryptography* book that a 2304 bit public key length gives the equivalent security of a 128 bit symmetric key, and that a 1792 bit public key length corresponds to about a 112 bit symmetric key.

As you read through the sections about the Xbox security scheme, keep in mind these basic guidelines about how difficult it can be to crack these security schemes using brute-force methods. Time after time, messages are posted on hacking forums and bulletin boards asking, "why don't we start a distributed key search effort for these keys?" Now you know the answer.

---

[1] http://www.rsasecurity.com/rsalabs/challenges/factoring/rsa155.html

[2] http://www.rsasecurity.com/rsalabs/faq/3-1-5.html

```
void encipher(unsigned long *const v,unsigned long *const w,
            const unsigned long *const k)
{
  register unsigned long
          y=v[0], z=v[1], sum=0, delta=0x9E3779B9,
          a=k[0], b=k[1], c=k[2], d=k[3], n=32;

  while(n->0) {
     sum += delta;
     y += (z << 4)+a ^ z+sum ^ (z >> 5)+b;
     z += (y << 4)+c ^ y+sum ^ (y >> 5)+d;
  }

  w[0]=y; w[1]=z;
}
```

Listing 7-1:
TEA Algorithm in ANSI C[3]

TEA

TEA stands for "Tiny Encryption Algorithm". David Wheeler and Roger Needham at the Computer Laboratory of Cambridge University developed it. The developers have a web page for TEA at `http://vader.brad.ac.uk/tea/tea.shtml`; much of the material presented here is gleaned from that page. As its name implies, TEA is a compact, fast encryption algorithm suitable for encrypting real-time data streams and embedded applications where processor performance and storage space is tight. TEA has a 128-bit key and it operates on 64-bits of data at a time, and each of its 32 rounds uses only shifts, XORs and additions. The algorithm, given in Listing 7-1 and Figure 7-2, is optimized for implementation on 32-bit general-purpose processors.

The bantam TEA algorithm is believed to be quite secure when used to encrypt and decrypt data. However, TEA is not used for encryption in the Xbox. It is actually used as a hash function by operating the cipher in a modified Davies-Meyer mode. The region to be hashed is divided into 64-bit blocks. These source data blocks are used as half of the key input to TEA. The other half of the key input comes from the result of the previous TEA operation, and the first TEA operation uses a magic number as its input. The result is a 64-bit hash function, as depicted in Figure 7-1. This hash is weak against birthday attacks, especially given the computational efficiency of TEA, as only 2^{32} message pairs need to be tested on average to find a collision. Even though a birthday attack does not apply in the Xbox's

[3] Code is from `http://vader.brad.ac.uk/tea/source.shtml#ansi`

TEA in a cipher application

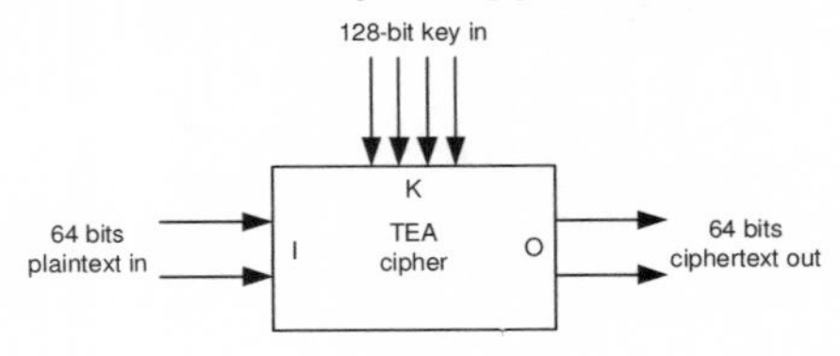

TEA used as a hash function

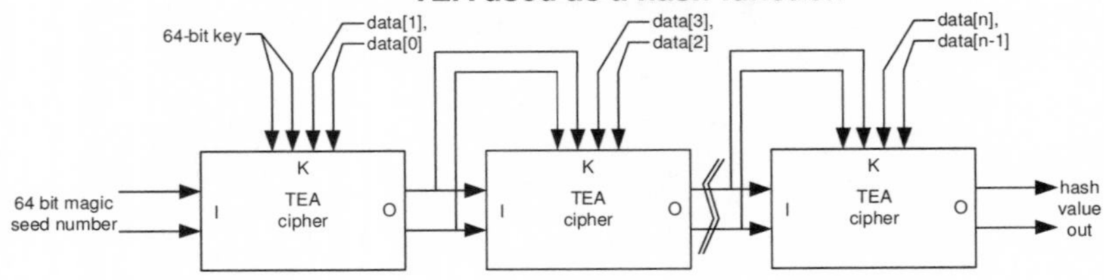

Figure 7-1:
Tea cipher usage scenarios.

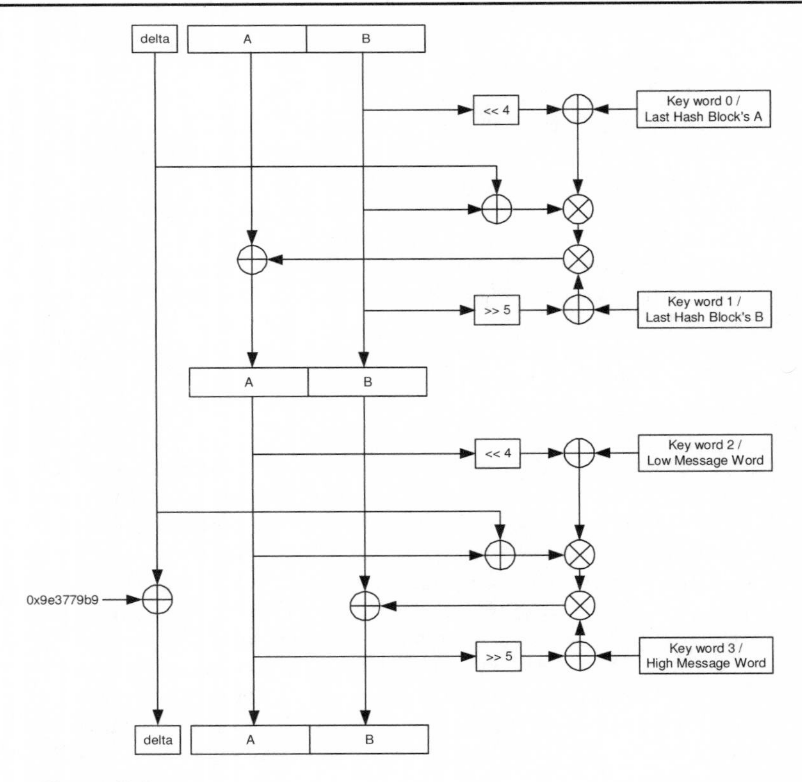

Figure 7-2:
Inner structure of TEA. This diagram depicts a single round of TEA, which is repeated 32 times for the full cipher. The key schedule is described in the boxes on the right for use as both a cipher and as a hashing function.

usage scenario, the Xbox runs the hash twice, each time with a different magic number seed, and concatenates the results to generate a single 128-bit hash value—probably in an attempt to foil brute-force attacks. Unfortunately, TEA has a weakness in its key schedule: every TEA key has four related keys. In other words, for every key, you can generate three other keys that produce the same ciphertext result with the same input data. Related-key generation is as simple as complementing pairs of key bits (bits 31 and 63 is one pair, bits 95 and 127 are the other pair). This makes TEA unsuitable for use as a hash function, and this weakness is well documented in the paper "Key-schedule cryptanalysis of IDEA, G-DES, GOST, SAFER, and triple-DES", written by John Kelsey, Bruce Schneier, and David Wagner, and presented many years ago in CRYPTO 1996. This weakness is leveraged later on by a team headed by Andy Green to break the second version of the Xbox security scheme.

RC-4

RC-4 (Ron's Code or Rivest Cipher 4) is a variable key-length stream cipher by Ron Rivest. The heart of RC-4 is the keystream generator. It can be thought of as a cryptographic pseudo-random number generator (CPRNG). The output of the CPRNG is XOR'd one byte at a time with a plaintext stream to generate the ciphertext. Decryption is accomplished in a similar fashion. Loosely speaking, the generator is "seeded" with a value (the key) of up to 256 bytes (2048 bits) long. If the key is shorter than 256 bytes, it is repeated to fill out the 256 bytes before use as a seed; this enables variable-length keys. In the Xbox, the key is 16 bytes (128 bits) in length, and thus the cipher is dubbed RC-4/128. RC-4 is thought to be a strong cipher, although there is a few known weaknesses in the key scheduling algorithm that can be leveraged in poorly designed cryptosystems, such as WEP. Scott Fluhrer, Itsik Mantin, and Adi Shamir document these weaknesses in a paper titled "Weaknesses in the Key Scheduling Algorithm of RC4" that was presented in the Eighth Annual Workshop on Selected Areas in Cryptography (August 2001). None of these weaknesses can be applied against the Xbox's implementation of RC-4.

There is, however, a potential problem in the way that RC-4 is used in the first version of the Xbox security. RC-4 is used on the Xbox to encipher a stream of x86 code, and no significant check is performed on the deciphered code to ensure the integrity of the plaintext. This means that changes in the ciphertext will lead to changes in the code that the Xbox executes. The trick is to figure out a change in the ciphertext that leads to a meaningful code modification. Since RC-4 encrypts one byte at a time and x86 opcodes can be as short as a single byte, it requires no more than $2^8 = 256$ iterations to "brute force" an instruction into a single known location by mutating the ciphertext. Figuring out which location to brute force can be tricky, but I suspect a lot of information could be derived by mutating ciphertext bits and observing what happens to the pattern of instruction fetches, even with the caches turned on. The goal would be to try and identify the location of a jump opcode's operands and modify the jump destination such that the secured program jumps into an unsecured region of memory. The process would be similar to playing the classic board game "Battleship". Keep in

```
typedef struct rc4_key {
     unsigned char state[256];
     unsigned char x;
     unsigned char y;
} rc4_key;

void prepare_key(unsigned char *key_data_ptr, int key_data_len,
                 rc4_key *key) {
   unsigned char swapByte, index1, index2;
   unsigned char* state;
   short counter;

   state = &key->state[0];
   for(counter = 0; counter < 256; counter++)
     state[counter] = counter;
     key->x = 0;     key->y = 0;
     index1 = 0;     index2 = 0;
   for(counter = 0; counter < 256; counter++) {
     index2 = (key_data_ptr[index1] + state[counter] +
              index2) % 256;
     swap_byte(&state[counter], &state[index2]);
     index1 = (index1 + 1) % key_data_len;
   }
 }

 void rc4(unsigned char *buffer_ptr, int buffer_len, rc4_key
        *key) {
     unsigned char x, y, xorIndex;
     unsigned char* state;
     short counter;

     x = key->x;     y = key->y;

     state = &key->state[0];
     for(counter = 0; counter < buffer_len; counter ++) {
          x = (x + 1) % 256;
          y = (state[x] + y) % 256;
          swap_byte(&state[x], &state[y]);
          xorIndex = state[x] + (state[y]) % 256;
          buffer_ptr[counter] ^= state[xorIndex];
      }
      key->x = x;     key->y = y;
 }
```

Listing 7-2:
RC-4 code in C, From Original Usenet Posting[4]

[4] Code from http://www.cc.jyu.fi/~paasivir/crypt/rciv/rc4article.txt. Minor white-space modifications to make it all fit on one page. The swap byte function definition is also not included, but you can guess what it does by its name.

mind that the attack is so easy that guessing through a kilobyte of code only requires a maximum of 2^{18} iterations. The guessing process could be automated by integrating a logic analyzer with a ROM emulator via a control script running on a host computer.

The history behind RC-4 is actually quite interesting. RC-4 was invented in 1987 by Ron Rivest, and was kept as a trade secret by RSA Security, Inc. until it was released in 1994 by an anonymous post to a cypherpunks mailing list (see Listing 7-2). As a result of RC-4's virtues of simplicity and robustness, it has found its way into numerous applications, including WEP, SSL, SQL, and CDPD. While the source code for RC-4 is widely distributed and well known, the cipher is still the intellectual property of RSA Security. I wouldn't recommend integrating it into a commercial product without first obtaining a license from RSA Security.

RSA

RSA is a public-key algorithm devised by Ron Rivest, Adi Shamir and Leonard Adleman in 1977. In a public-key algorithm, two distinct keys are used, a public key and a private key. As their names imply, the private key must be kept a secret, while the public key can be freely distributed. The math behind RSA is briefly described in the sidebar titled "The RSA Algorithm". You need not understand the details of the math behind RSA to grasp how RSA is used in the context of the Xbox. Note that brute-force attacks are currently thought to be infeasible on RSA with keylengths in excess of about a thousand bits. Also note that one cannot be too cavalier about how RSA is integrated into a cryptosystem. There are some attacks against protocols that use RSA, such as tricking the private key holder into signing carefully crafted messages that can then be used to derive the signer's private key.

Encrypting a message using RSA is as simple as invoking RSA on a message. However, RSA encryption works on message blocks that are too short and the encryption process is too slow to be practical for most messages. Thus, RSA is typically used to encrypt a single-use random key, called a session key, for a fast symmetric cipher such as AES that is then used to encrypt the bulk message. This process is illustrated in Figure 7-3.

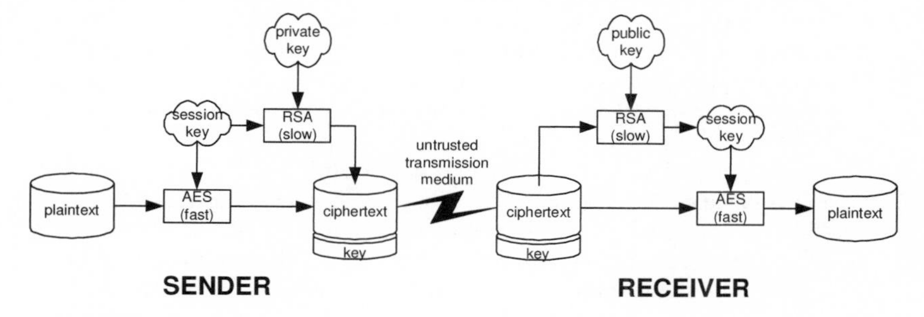

Figure 7-3:
Use of RSA with session keys.

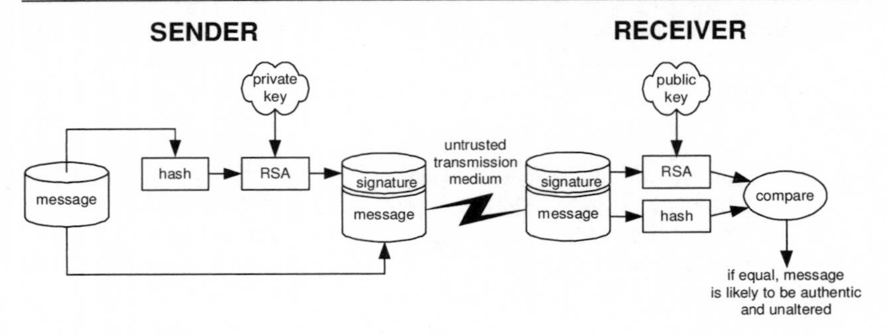

Figure 7-4:
RSA used to implement digital signatures.

In addition to encryption, RSA enables digital signatures. A digital signature allows parties exchanging messages over an insecure medium to guarantee that messages are not forged and are not modified. The message does not have to be encrypted. A typical digital signature protocol works as follows. The sender computes a hash of the message to be sent. This hash is then encrypted with the sender's private key and included with the message plaintext. The receiver decrypts the encrypted message hash using the sender's public key, and compares this hash against a locally computed hash of the received message. If the decrypted hash sent with the message and the locally computed hash agree, then the receiver could conclude that the message is authentic and unaltered. This process is outlined in Figure 7-4. If this protocol sounds complex to you, then you are right. There are a lot of places where things can go wrong. The receiver could have a false copy of the sender's public key. The sender could have had his private key compromised. The hash could have weaknesses. Employing digital signatures in an adversarial environment requires attention to detail at all levels of the system design.

In the Xbox, digital signatures are used to control the distribution and sales of programs for the console. Microsoft is effectively in control of both the sender and the receiver of messages. The receivers—Xbox consoles—are programmed to only run programs that are digitally signed by Microsoft. In an ideal world, this guarantees that Microsoft has the final word on who can or cannot run programs on the console, and hackers cannot modify games to insert viruses, Trojan horses or back doors. Saved games are also sealed using encryption, and as a result, it is nominally impossible to hack a game and cheat by patching the executable or by jacking up your character stats.

Clearly, a pivotal issue in hacking the Xbox console is their implementation of the digital signature system. The Xbox uses a SHA-1 hash with 2048-bit RSA keys, making the chance of a successful brute force attack very, very slim. Of course, the probability is zero if you never try, but the odds are stacked against you (see the section on Very Difficult Problems). You'll have better luck trying to win the lottery. This is by no mistake; the discovery of the private key would make game copying trivial and developers would not have to pay royalties to Microsoft (legally, they may be obligated but there is no

The RSA Algorithm

The RSA algorithm was patented by the Massachusetts Institute of Technology and exclusively licensed to RSA Data Security, Inc in 1983. The patent on the RSA algorithm has since expired in September 2000. Thus, today RSA is free to use in any application. Many excellent tutorials and educational examples using RSA can now be found on the Internet. Perform a Google search using the keywords "RSA algorithm" to find some of these examples.

The RSA algorithm is as follows (adapted from `http://world.std.com/~franl/crypto/rsa-guts.html`):

1. Find two large (thousands of bits long) prime numbers, "P" and "Q".

2. Choose "E" such that E > 1, E < PQ, and E is relatively prime to (P-1)(Q-1). E does not have to be prime, but it must be odd. **The pair of E and PQ are the public key**.

3. Compute "D" such that (DE - 1) is evenly divisible by (P-1)(Q-1). This can be accomplished by finding an integer X which causes D = (X(P-1)(Q-1) + 1)/E to be an integer. **D is the private key**.

4. Plaintext "T" is encrypted using the function $C = (T^E) \bmod PQ$

5. Ciphertext "C" is decrypted using the function $T = (C^D) \bmod PQ$

Note that T < PQ. Messages larger than PQ must be broken down into a sequence of smaller messages, and very short messages must be padded with carefully selected values to foil dictionary attacks, among other things.

technical reason preventing them). Given that this key is probably worth a few billion dollars to Microsoft, it is quite likely that no single human knows the full key, as rubber-hose (beatings) and green-paper (bribery) cryptanalysis techniques tend to be quite effective on humans (do *not* discount real "brute force" as a possibility if you are trying to protect an extremely valuable secret!). Products such as BBN's SignAssure™ certificate authority management system ensure the physical security of high-value keys and implements secret-sharing schemes that require multiple trusted users to activate the machine.

As mentioned previously, there are a few known viable attacks against RSA, but all of them do not apply in the Xbox scenario, as they rely on groups of users or require chosen-ciphertext. In addition, the list of weaknesses is widely known and most implementations of digital signatures implement the proper countermeasures to protect against such attacks.

The Rest of the Picture

An effective security system needs good key management, strong protocols and in the case of the Xbox, physical security in addition to strong ciphers and hashes.

Key management is perhaps one of the most difficult system implementation tasks that face any security architect. Ultimately, the decryption keys need to go into the hands of a user. The user interface must be designed so that the average user with minimum training does not accidentally leak key information. As ciphers become stronger, the easiest path of attack is increasingly through the user. Eavesdropping through surveillance videos, social engineering, or even analyzing the pattern of sounds made by the keyboard as a password is typed will probably yield more information per unit effort about a passphrase than cryptanalysis. Public key cryptography partially helps solve the problem of key distribution, but public key fingerprints should be compared in person to rule out the possibility of man-in-the-middle attacks. Public key cryptography also does not prevent someone with physical access to the client machine from eavesdropping on the decrypted output.

In addition, protocol attacks find weaknesses in the way keys and data are manipulated, or they find weaknesses in the way strong ciphers are used. The WEP attack on RC-4 and Mike Bond and Ross Anderson's attack on the IBM 4758 Cryptoprocessor are both examples of protocol attacks. The red flags for potential protocol attacks are systems that implement backward-compatibility measures, and systems that are implemented by engineers whose primary job is not crypto-security.

Finally, in a system like the Xbox where one of the goals is to establish a trustable client, back doors and buffer-overrun attacks are also viable attacks on the trust state of a machine. No widely used commercial processors embed execution privileges within instruction streams or data tags. Processors blindly execute any piece of code that it is instructed to jump to, whether or not the jump was induced through a transient hardware failure or through maliciously placed code. Periodic hashes on the machine state can be used to counter this deficiency, but even then the state checks can be spoofed.

As discussed in the beginning of this chapter, establishing the trust state of a client also requires a piece of tamper-resistant hardware to carry the seed of trust. The amount of physical security must be enough to make it uneconomical to defeat the security once, and robust enough such that one instance of broken security does not enable trivial attacks on the remainder of the consoles. Some of the trade-offs when designing physical security as well as the decisions made by Microsoft to this end are discussed in the next Chapter.

The moral of this Chapter is that security requires a well-designed *system*. Although ciphers have become strong enough to make brute-force attacks moot, systems have grown in complexity. This complexity increases the likelihood of a viable protocol or back door attack, yet does little to save users from the more traditional eavesdropping, rubber-hose and user-error attacks.

CHAPTER 8

Reverse Engineering Xbox Security

In this chapter, I will describe how I defeated the initial production version of the Xbox security system that was first encountered in Chapter 6. The security system was discovered after analyzing the FLASH ROM and realizing that the true hardware initialization and boot image decryption sequence was somehow hidden outside of the FLASH ROM. The last chapter introduced some basic cryptography concepts that will be useful understanding the contents of this chapter.

Extracting Secrets From Hardware

The hidden boot code in the Xbox, as concluded in Chapter 6, can be recovered by eavesdropping on one of the following buses: (1) the FSB, (2) the main memory bus, or (3) the Northbridge-Southbridge connection.

The format of the Front Side Bus (FSB) of the Pentium processor used in the Xbox is documented in the Pentium III processor datasheets, available at Intel's Developer Website. The FSB is a bidirectional 64-bit data bus with about fifty some address and control signals, all running at 133 MHz. The bus uses a signaling convention known as AGTL+. Eavesdropping this bus is an expensive and difficult proposition because of the high signal count and challenging physical form factor. Viable approaches include: (a) socketing the processor with a special emulator break-out socket that costs many thousands of dollars, or (b) reverse engineering the meaning of each FSB trace on the Xbox motherboard, and tack soldering a short probe wire onto each of the almost hundred signals. In addition, a logic analyzer that supports AGTL+ signaling is required. The combination of all these factors made me look to someplace else as a starting point for eavesdropping.

Our next eavesdropping candidate, the main memory bus, is a 128-bit data bus plus address and control signals running at 200 MHz with double data rate (DDR) clocking. The memory bus uses a signaling convention known as SSTL-2. The details of this bus can be inferred by reading the datasheet for the Samsung K4D263238M memory part, available at the Samsung Electronics website. Despite its higher speeds, eavesdropping the main memory bus is probably easier than eavesdropping the processor FSB, because of the empty (spare) memory footprints designed into the Xbox motherboard. A relatively inexpensive, standard 100-pin TQFP adapter (Thin Quad Flat Pack, a rectangular chip package with 100 gull-wing shaped pins) could be soldered onto the empty memory footprints. These adapters would provide convenient probe points for connecting a logic analyzer. The problem with this approach is that you can only capture data that is written to main memory. Decryption keys are generally read-only data, and read-only

More About High Speed Information Transmission

Eavesdropping and modifying data on computer buses is a powerful technique that is difficult to counter. In order to understand how to eavesdrop, you will need a little bit of background on how digital information is transmitted inside a computer.

There are two major categories of signaling standards, single-ended and differential. The transmission of digital information over a wire requires a translation into physical quantities such as voltage and current. Classically, signals were defined in terms of voltages measured with respect to a common reference potential called the "ground". This kind of signaling is known as single-ended or unbalanced signaling. Unfortunately, the idea of a ground reference point only works when signals change slowly with respect to their propagation time. In reality, every change in potential is accompanied by a flow of current. The laws of nature demand that current be conserved, i.e., for every flow of current in one direction, there must be a flow of current in the reverse direction. In single-ended signaling, the reverse current, also known as a return current, must find its way back through the "ground". At very high speeds, the return paths for current do not necessarily follow the same path as the signal current. This imbalance results in a distorted signal.

Differential signaling combats this problem by using two wires to transmit a signal, with one wire used for the signal current and the other used for an explicit return current path. The differential approach allows the signal and return paths to be laid out so that they track each other, ensuring that the flow of current is balanced. The result is a more robust signal transmission system at the cost of twice the number of wires.

continued...

data will go straight from the hidden boot ROM into the processor cache without ever being stored into main memory. Once the processor is done with the cache line containing the key, it will be overwritten, so the key should never leave the physical perimeter of the processor.

The third potential eavesdropping candidate, the Northbridge to Southbridge connection, is a pair of unidirectional, 8-bit wide differential busses, each with just one control signal and one clock signal. The bus uses the HyperTransport signaling convention and runs at 200 MHz with DDR clocking. The signaling convention of the bus was deduced from the publicly available information at nVidia's website about the nForce, a chipset closely related to the Xbox's chipset. A few measurements with an oscilloscope, cross-checked against the open HyperTransport specifications available at the HyperTransport consortium's website, were used to verify the

A specific standard for interpreting voltages as logic values is called a signaling convention. The venerable TTL and 3.3V CMOS signaling conventions were invented in a era when transistors performed so poorly that large signal excursions were necessary. Lately, a host of new and even old signaling conventions have been gaining popularity, such as SSTL (series stub terminated logic), GTL (gunning transceiver logic), LVDS (low voltage differential signaling), and PECL (pseudo emitter coupled logic). These high-speed signaling conventions account for the fact that electric waves travel slowly with respect to the rate of data transmission. They also account for the fact that electric waves carry energy that must be dissipated upon the termination of its journey, otherwise the energy will reflect and cause interference with incoming waves. In high-speed applications, wires are often called "transmission lines" in order to emphasize the fact that these waves travel slowly in comparison to the signal transition time (the time required for a signal to transition between a "1" and a "0" state). Note that the speed comparison is made relative to transition time of the signal, and not its gross signaling frequency. A common mistake is to think that transmission line effects can be ignored because the clock frequency of the signal is slow. Even if there is only one transition every year, problems can still arise if the duration of that transition takes only a picosecond (one trillionth of a second).

The good news for novices is that the latest FPGAs from vendors such as Xilinx come with built-in support for almost every widely deployed signaling standard. The other piece of good news is that signaling standards are becoming increasingly well documented. The Xilinx FPGA data sheets, for example, illustrate the expected position and value of the termination resistors for every supported signaling standard. By following the recommended practices in the datasheet and application notes, you can use the FPGA to eavesdrop on a wide range of signals. Just remember to keep your eavesdropping taps as short as possible and you shouldn't go wrong.

assumption that the HyperTransport signalling convention is indeed being used.

The HyperTransport bus is implemented on the Xbox motherboard with all the signals parallel and evenly spaced, a decision likely driven by the high operating speed of the bus. This makes the bus an ideal target for eavesdropping, except for the fact that it runs at such a high data rate. Eavesdropping a bus that runs at this speed requires special attention to the stub length of the eavesdropping traces (in order to preserve the integrity of the signals) and it also requires a rather expensive logic analyzer or a custom analyzer circuit.

Ultimately, the Northbridge-Southbridge connection was chosen as the first bus to eavesdrop because it has by far the fewest wires, and therefore requires the least amount of soldering. The Northbrige-Southbridge connection has only ten unique signals, whereas both the FSB and the main memory have about a hundred signals each. Soldering a large number of connections not only consumes a large amount of time, but also greatly increases the risk of hard failures due to solder bridges or damaged traces. Thus, minimizing the number of solder connections minimizes the risk of collateral damage to the motherboard.

Eavesdropping a High Speed Bus

I had committed to the HyperTransport eavesdropping approach in late January 2002. The significant technical issues with this approach were

- Tapping the high-speed differential bus without disrupting signal integrity
- Finding or building a logging tool that could keep up with the 400 MB/s data rates on the HyperTransport bus
- Determining the polarity and bit ordering of the differential HyperTransport bus traces on the motherboard

Tapping the Bus on a Budget

The first two issues are intimately linked. High-speed bus analysis and logging tools typically have proprietary interfaces that would require a custom adapter to the Xbox motherboard. The last issue, determining bit polarity and ordering, just requires a lot of post-processing and data massaging after the data logger is attached and functioning.

HyperTransport is an open standard that has gained industry acceptance, meaning that off-the-shelf protocol analyzers and logging tools are available for the bus. One such example is the HyperTransport protocol analyzer by FuturePlus. Unfortunately, this protocol analyzer was priced in excess of $25,000 at the time the work was being done. In addition, the protocol analyzer requires the target board to be specially designed to accommodate the protocol analyzer's bus interface pod.

Instead of buying a protocol analyzer and investing the time and effort to adapt it for use with the Xbox, I just built my own simplified protocol analyzer. This task is feasible because the HyperTransport protocol is quite simple. The Xbox implementation of HyperTransport uses two 8-bit unidirectional buses, one for transmit and one for receive. Each bus has a clock and a strobe line associated with it. The signaling standard requires valid data to be presented on each edge of the clock. The beginning of a new packet is indicated by the data lines leaving their idle state. The strobe line differentiates between command and data packets. All of the sideband signals typical of other busses, such as the address, read/write control, chip select, and interrupt lines, are handled in HyperTransport using in-band command packets. Hence, just ten differential signals (twenty wires) are all you need for eavesdropping the bus—great news for hackers.

The HyperTransport protocol is simple enough, but what about finding something that can both physically interface to the Xbox bus and keep up with the 400 MB/s speeds? The ideal tool for building this HyperTransport bus tap would be an FPGA. However, at the time, no FPGA was available that could keep up with the high data rates and more importantly, no FPGA was available that was certified by the vendor for use with HyperTransport. Theoretically, a Xilinx Virtex-II FPGA would work for this application, but the product had just been launched and the devices were extremely pricey and hard to get (today, you can purchase a low-end Virtex-II FPGA for well under a hundred dollars). The best FPGA that I had on hand at the time was a Xilinx Virtex-E FPGA that I had previously designed into a prototype supercomputer network router as part of my thesis. The network router board used CTT (Center Tap Terminated) signaling for its network interfaces, and also had an Intel StrongArm processor on board for configuration, control and debugging purposes.

The challenge therefore boiled down to figuring out how to interface HyperTransport signals to CTT signals, and how to coax 400 MB/s performance out of an FPGA that wasn't intended to run at those speeds.

The HyperTransport signaling convention, it turns out, is a close relative of the more common LVDS (low voltage differential signaling) signaling convention, specified in the TIA/EIA-644 standard. HyperTransport drivers create a signal with a differential swing of 600 mV typically, centered around a common mode voltage of 600 mV. LVDS receivers, on the other hand, can make sense out of data that has a differential swing of greater than 100 mV and a common mode voltage anywhere between 50 mV and 2.35 V. So LVDS receivers are directly compatible with HyperTransport drivers! Although the Virtex-E supports a direct interface to LVDS signals, I could not take advantage of this because the Virtex-E parts I had were already designed into a system that is hard-wired for CTT signals. If you are designing your own tap board, the best approach would be to use the native LVDS capabilities of the FPGA instead of the hack described here. In addition, the LVDS receiver must be located very close to the Xbox motherboard in order to not corrupt the target signals. A long cable would dissipate energy out of the wires and introduce noise and reflections that might cause the system to cease functioning.

What about Driving Signals onto HyperTransport?

The eavesdropping application described in this chapter only requires a HyperTransport receiver. Applications such as "man-in-the-middle" attacks require a device that can override HyperTransport signals and insert a false bit or two. Such a device is feasible because HyperTransport, like LVDS, uses *current-mode drivers*. In other words, the drivers are designed to drive only a measured amount of current into the wire, regardless of the voltage it creates. In a normal situation, this works perfectly well because the impedance of the wire transforms the current into a voltage in accordance with Ohm's Law. However, currents can sum and cancel each other out. An antagonistic differential driver that applies an overdrive current that cancels out the intended signal can be attached to a HyperTransport line. This kind of overdrive can be accomplished using the flexible, programmable I/O provided in FPGAs such as the Xilinx Virtex-E and Virtex II.

The simplest application of such a bus override device would be one that modifies the destination of the reset vector as it is transmitted to the CPU, enabling you to gain control of the Xbox. The reset vector destination is coded into a single byte that follows the "jump" opcode located at 0xFFFF.FFF0. The reset vector is likely transmitted a deterministic number of clocks from the de-activation of reset, so the timing element for this attack can consist of just a timer that is clocked by the HyperTransport bus clock and synchronized to a reset signal. A "man-in-the-middle" attack like this will defeat even a cryptographically secure public-key boot block implementation.

The solution to the problem of getting the HyperTransport signals to the FPGA is to use a signal conversion chip. LVDS is a popular standard for LCD panel interfaces and backplanes used in telecomm systems, so numerous inexpensive LVDS-to-CMOS converters are available. Of course, the desired signaling convention is CTT, but a closer look reveals that interfacing CMOS drivers to CTT receivers is actually not a problem. CTT is a current-mode signaling convention that drives +8 mA or -8 mA into a 50 ohm transmission line terminated at 1.5 volts. The receiver is a differential amplifier that compares the reference termination voltage with the transmission line voltage. In the Virtex-E, a CTT receiver amplifier is specified to work as long as the received voltage swings more than 200 mV up or down from the reference voltage. Most CMOS transmitters driving a CTT terminated line will have no problem sourcing or sinking 8 mA of current into a 50 ohm load. Also, CMOS transmitters should have no problems driving a wire terminated into a fixed voltage. Thus, a standard LVDS to CMOS converter chip can be used to take the Xbox motherboard's HyperTransport signals and feed them into the board I had previously built for my thesis. The chip I chose was the Texas Instruments SN65LVDS386, and you can find data sheets for this chip at Texas Instruments' website.

Attaching the LVDS-to-CMOS converter chip to the board is made delightfully simple by the clean layout used for the HyperTransport bus on the Xbox motherboard. Figure 8-1 is a picture of what the HyperTransport bus traces look like. Notice how all the wires run in parallel and how the wires are evenly spaced. Some of the wires, such as the clock (`TX CK/TX CX*` and `RX CK/RX CX*`) and the strobe line (`TXD8/TXD8*` and `RXD8/RXD8*`), are even labeled for us with polarity markings! This simple layout enables the use of an easy-to-engineer tap board.

The tap board contains just the LVDS-to-CMOS converter chip, some power conditioning circuitry, and a set of traces laid out right up to the edge of the board that are identically spaced to the HyperTransport bus on the Xbox motherboard. For identical spacing and easy alignment and mounting, I measured the dimensions of these traces using a digital caliper tool. Figure 8-2 illustrates the dimensions of the HyperTransport bus traces. The measurements were a little tricky to make. My approach was to measure the overall width of the bus and divide the width by the number of traces and spaces to get the average expected spacing and trace width. I then laid out

Figure 8-1:

HyperTransport bus traces as laid out on an Xbox motherboard.

these traces with a PCB CAD program and printed the layout on paper at a 1:1 scale. I compared the printed traces with the board traces and made a few adjustments by hand. Note that many printers have some small amount of scaling error, so if you are trying this, calibrate yourself by printing out a few long lines of known length and measuring them. Printers can have different scaling errors along the horizontal and vertical axes, so be sure to print lines in both directions.

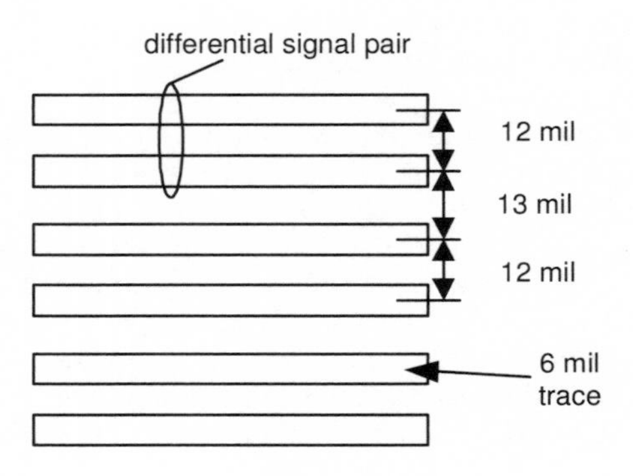

Figure 8-2:
Dimensions of the HyperTransport bus traces on the Xbox motherboard. A "mil" is 1/1000th of an inch or 25.4 microns.

Designing your own boards is fairly easy with the right software. You can find out more about how to make your own boards by reading the Appendix on Getting Into Board Layout.

Once the component selection process was finished, the design and layout of the HyperTransport tap and signal conversion board took just a few more hours. A schematic of the board's design can be seen in Figure 8-6. The board was then fabricated by an order placed via the Internet. Many board houses offer affordable, quick-turn board fabrication services that take board designs in Gerber file format via an email or ftp upload. In this case, I had two copies of the board built in five days for a price of $33 per board (see Appendix C, "Getting Into Board Layout", for more information on how to build your own boards). This price only includes the price of cutting the board into a square piece. However, I needed the side of the board with the HyperTransport tap to have a special shape that facilitates board mounting without interfering with the existing components on the Xbox motherboard. I also needed the mating edge of the board to be beveled such that the board mounts at a slight angle, to simplify the task of soldering the tap board to the motherboard. I used a belt sander to manually sculpt the edge into a shape described in Figure 8-3. When sculpting, the board had to be oriented such that the belt sander's abrasive belt made contact with the trace side of the board first. This prevents the belt sander from tearing the copper traces off of the board. Be careful when using a belt sander to sculpt small boards like the tap board — a belt sander could just as easily sculpt your fingers by accident.

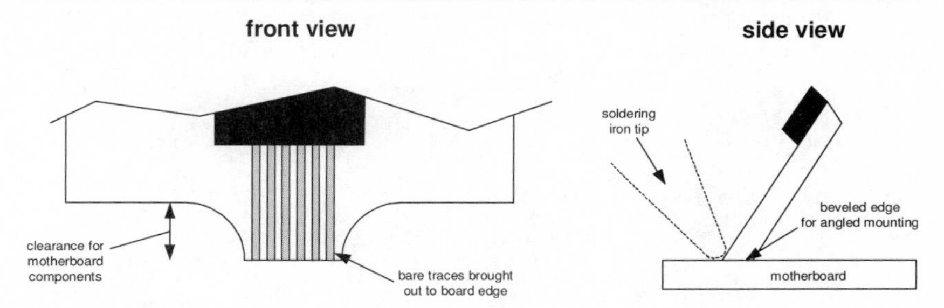

Figure 8-3:
Shaping of the HyperTransport tap board edge.

After sculpting the beveled edge, all the parts were soldered onto the board. Appendix B, "Soldering Techniques", covers the techniques used to attach all the components to this board.

The finished tap board now had to be attached to the Xbox motherboard. This critical step was perhaps the most difficult step. First, the Xbox motherboard was prepared by using a fine grit sand paper to strip away the green soldermask, revealing the bright bare copper of the target traces. These traces were fluxed and a thin coat of solder was applied using a hot soldering iron tip.

The procedure I used for the attaching the tap board to the motherboard is shown in Figure 8-4. The prepared tap board was tacked onto the motherboard at the approximate location and angle using a thin (30 AWG) wire soldered between a trace on the tap board an the motherboard. The

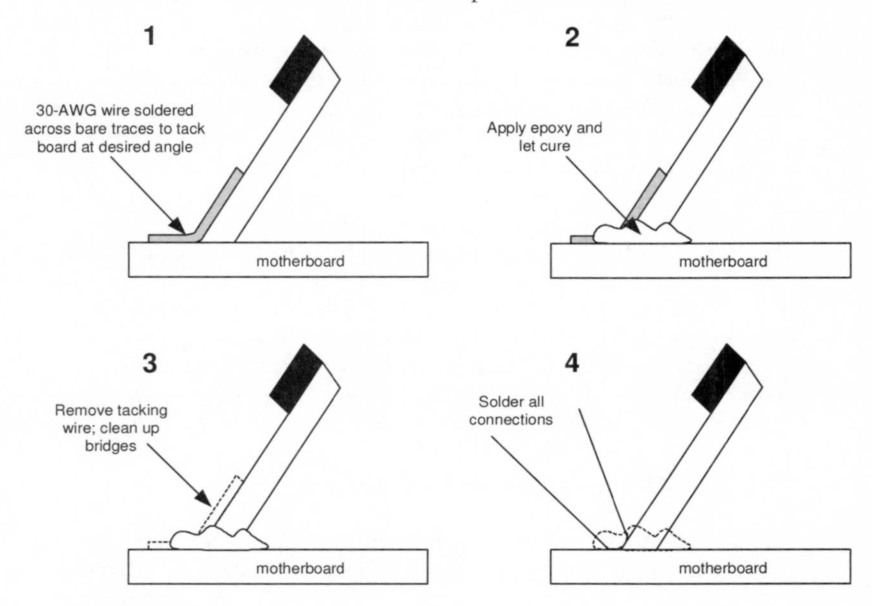

Figure 8-4:
Tap board soldering procedure.

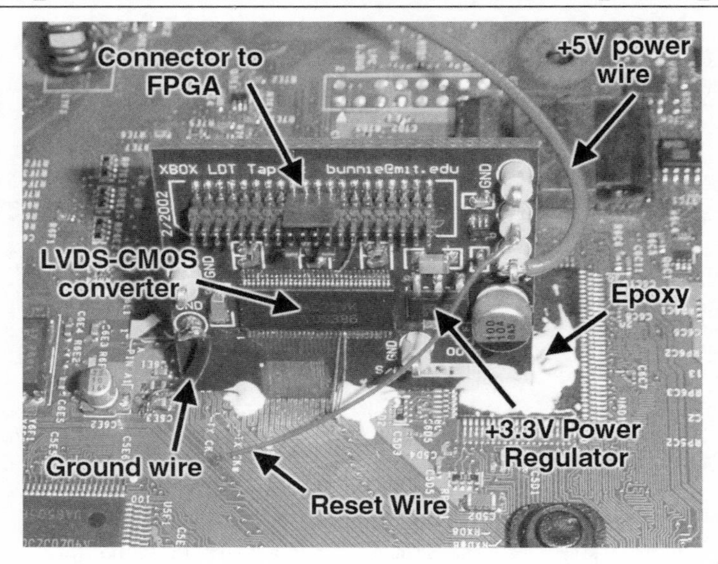

Figure 8-5:
HyperTransport tap board mounted on the Xbox motherboard.

tack wire serves only as a temporary aid for holding the board in place and will be removed, so it does not matter if the wire bridges across multiple traces. Once the wire was attached, I carefully adjusted the position of the tap board on the motherboard, heating the wire to release its bond to avoid lifting any of the copper traces. I used a microscope to aid in determining the optimal alignment. Once I was satisfied with the position of the board, I applied a strong epoxy to the board joint to hold it all in place. The epoxy should cure and form a rigid, stiff joint. Note that some epoxies when applied incorrectly cure into a gel; this is not acceptable, as the entire mechanical integrity of the joint must come from the epoxy and not the solder joints. I used Miller-Stephenson Epoxy formula 907, and it sets with enough strength for me to lift the Xbox by the tap board and not disturb the tap connection.

Once the epoxy had cured, I removed the temporary tack wire that was used to hold the tap board in place, and cleaned the bare mated traces with a bit of solderwick and flux. The last step of soldering the tap board traces to the bare motherboard traces was now no different from soldering any surface mount component onto a board; most of the standard techniques described in Appendix B, "Soldering Techniques", applied directly to this situation. Figure 8-5 illustrates what the finished assembly looks like.

Building the Data Logger

The second challenge of eavesdropping the HyperTransport bus is acquiring or building a logging device that can keep up with the 400 MB/s data rate of the bus. Considering my budget, I decided that my only option was to build a logger, as buying any tools with sufficient performance for this job was well outside of my budget.

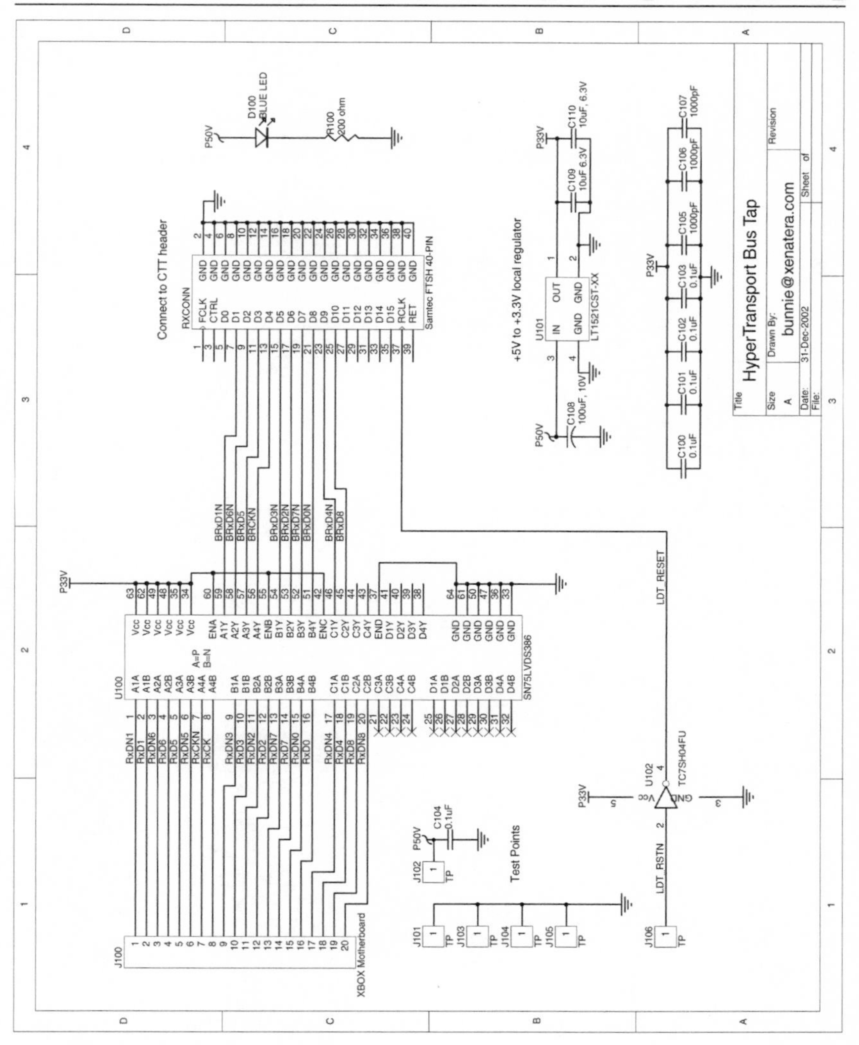

Figure 8-6:
Schematic of the HyperTransport tap board.

In building the logging device, I had settled on using a Virtex-E FPGA that was integrated into a board that I had previously built. However, the one problem with using the Virtex-E FPGA is that the performance of the FPGA (as specified in the databook) is insufficient to keep up with the HyperTransport bus. Fortunately, FPGAs overclock well because their manufacturing margin is very conservative, and because FPGA performance is largely limited by signal propagation delays in the configurable wiring fabric. As a result, some key performance-limiting paths can be manually identified and compensated using soft delay lines and selectively inverted clocks. The most performance sensitive blocks can be hand-placed to optimize the delays, while the compiler and automated place-and-route tool

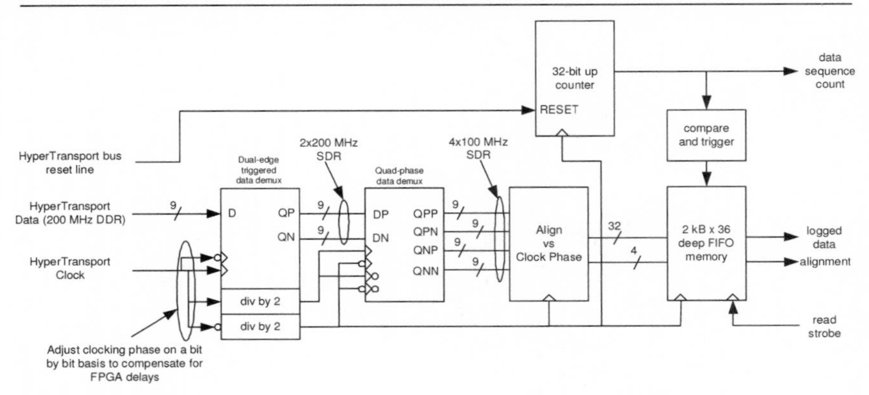

Figure 8-7:
Block diagram of the data logger built in the Xilinx Virtex-E FPGA.

handle the non-critical parts of the circuit. The overall design that was used to capture the data on the HyperTransport bus is illustrated in Figure 8-7.

The design is fairly simple in concept: take the high speed data off of the HyperTransport bus and clock it into four phases of a quarter speed clock, creating a data stream that is four times slower but four times wider. This confines all hand-placing and tweaking to just the first few input flip flops. Next, re-align the data using a set of delays and rotators, and store the data one piece at a time inside a first in, first out (FIFO) memory. The signal that triggers the start of FIFO capture is generated by a timer-comparator that starts counting up from first reset. Long windows of data can be captured by concatenating the results of multiple runs, each with the capture trigger point delayed from the previous. A later optimization applied to the trigger circuit is a "do not store zeros" (DNSZ) function. In the DNSZ mode, data consisting of all 0's is not stored in the FIFO. This is helpful in culling out all of the idle data on the HyperTransport bus. The resulting data traces are time-stamped series of 32-bit words.

The most difficult part of the FPGA data logger design was calibrating the delays on the input paths. Delay calibration was accomplished by using an oscilloscope to probe a small window of data on the HyperTransport bus. Wire delays and byte-wide rotations were tweaked until the probed data matched the log data. This process was aided by the fact that during idle times, a common sequence of commands was repeated on the bus every few hundred microseconds that served as the calibration reference.

Determining the Bus Order and Polarity

The final challenge after logging the data is figuring out the order of the signals on the HyperTransport bus and their polarities. Note that while the two most important signals of the HyperTransport bus on the Xbox motherboard are labeled for us, the remaining eight data lines have ambiguous polarity and bit ordering.

The correct polarity of the eight data signals was determined by observing the idle bus data bit pattern. The HyperTransport bus spends most of its time in an idle state, so this is not difficult. If the idle pattern is supposed to be all "0"s, then any bit position that shows up as a "1" has its polarity inverted. This was corrected in hardware by inserting an inversion term in the FPGA on the appropriate wire.

Determining the correct bit ordering is much more difficult, however. Operating under the presumption that data coming across the HyperTransport bus must in large part come from the FLASH ROM, a 1's count was performed on a byte by byte basis. The theory is that the bus ordering is a pure permutation, meaning that the number of binary 1's in a byte is preserved between the FLASH ROM data and the data captured by the logger. Patterns of 1's counts were lined up against each other to identify candidate regions of correspondence between FLASH ROM and logged data. Fortunately, the first few words to come across the HyperTransport bus are some chipset-specific initializations that are located near the bottom of FLASH memory, so finding a set of patterns that lined up correctly did not take too long. A set of bytes from each of the ROM and the logger were tabulated and with the aid of a short C program, columns of bits were transposed until an ordering was found that made all of the row values match up.

Making Sense of the Captured Data

Now that valid data traces have been extracted, the problem remains of deciphering the meaning of it all. Before doing so, let us recap what we know about the data we have collected thus far.

- **Temporal correlation.** The logged data, on a macroscopic scale, should have a strong time correlation to the expected sequence of initialization events: jam table initialization, followed by a decryption step, followed by execution from RAM. The regions of the log traces that correspond to each of these events can be determined by just observing when large bursts of activity happen, followed by regions of silence.
- **Transaction lengths.** Since the Pentium processor has both a data and an instruction cache, all fetches on the HyperTransport bus to FLASH ROM or the hidden boot ROM should come in even-length bursts of traffic.
- **Guaranteed ordering.** The collected data is time stamped and chronologically correct, so if the first instruction fetched in the reset vector can be identified in the data logs, the position and structure of the remainder of the instructions can be deduced.

Initially, I neglected to check the macroscopic organization of data coming across the HyperTransport bus, and this caused me some problems. The simplified block diagram of the logging machine in Figure 8-7 would have the log FIFO resetting each time the HyperTransport bus is reset. This seems like a fine idea, however I originally incorrectly assumed that the HyperTransport bus is reset only once upon the application of power. In reality, the HyperTransport bus is reset a second time following the jam table initialization step. Thus, when I first started looking at traces, all I saw was the encrypted data plus a smattering of code, none of which could really be lined up in any logical fashion with a boot vector.

Imagine how disappointing that was! I took a step back and observed the HyperTransport bus events on an oscilloscope with the time scale set at the milliseconds per division. I observed that there was an earlier reset pulse, and after adjusting the trigger mechanism to catch only the first pulse, the boot instruction was easy to identify. The sixteen bytes at `0xFFFF.FFF0` in the secret ROM happened to be identical to the same sixteen bytes in the FLASH ROM. From that point, I tracked the current value of the program counter by performing a lot of grungy tracing and disassembling with bookkeeping, so that I could place each instruction block at the correct location in memory. Every cache line fetch consisted of 16 or 32 consecutive bytes of memory, resulting in a distinctive data logger time stamp pattern which aided the reverse engineering process. After a few hours of sifting through traces looking for cache lines, I had collected enough code to feed

More Tools of the Trade: Software Analysis Tools

Inevitably at some point in your hacking experiences, you will come across a need to disassemble some assembly language code. I was introduced to an excellent tool for this job by some fellow software hackers in January 2002 while I was reverse engineering the Xbox security. The tool is called "IDA Pro" by Ilfak Guilfanov, sold by DataRescue Corporation (`http://www.datarescue.com/idabase/`). IDA Pro is capable of disassembling not only x86 code, but a huge variety of embedded processors' code as well. The quality of IDA Pro's output is also very high; code segments are automatically annotated and organized for readability. IDA Pro also features a vast array of useful and fun tools. Some of my favorites include the ability to automatically pattern match code library signatures to function calls, and the ability to follow jumps at the press of a key.

Another tool that is quite handy during the code analysis was HackMan. HackMan is freeware made by TechnoLogismiki Corporation (`http://www.technologismiki.com/hackman/`). HackMan is nominally a "hex editor", i.e., a file editor that allows you to manipulate binary data directly, but it has a lot of unique capabilities that go far beyond simple editing. For example, HackMan has a built in disassembler. The disassembler is not as powerful as IDA Pro, but it is interactive with the hex editor. This allowed me to rapidly test candidate cache lines for valid code while tracing through the data logs, while assembling the final binary image of the secret ROM.

into a disassembler. See the sidebar on "Software Analysis Tools" for more information about the disassembler that I used.

After a bit of data massaging and a good bit of help from some on-line hacker friends, we had determined that the cipher being used was RC-4/128. RC-4 is a symmetric cipher, and the key had to be stored somewhere in the Xbox, but I was having difficulty trying to identify the key in the data stream. The key seemed to span cache line fetches that were shared with pieces of code which at the time I could not map to a definitive location.

As the night was drawing long and I was growing weary of staring at hex digits, I decided to try something that should never have worked. I adapted an RC-4 decryption program to decrypt the target image in FLASH ROM using a key that was derived from a sliding window within the data log. This is a fairly brute-force approach, as it requires tens of thousands of decryptions (one for every byte in the log) to search the whole data stream. I automated the process by feeding the output of the RC-4 decryption into a histogram routine. If the key did not match, the output should be statistically "white". In other words, a histogram of the output should show that all values are roughly equally probable for a non-matching key. However, if the key was the correct key, the histogram should be biased, with some values being significantly more popular than all the other values.

Eventually I finished the program, `trykeys`, to perform this brute-force search around 5 AM. Bleary-eyed and tired, I decided to give the program a test run before calling it quits for the night. Imagine the dumbfounded look on my face as I watched the output of the program as it crunched away at the candidate data stream:

```
$ ./trykeys.exe ms4.bin binout.full
.........................................................
....................found possible key combo: avg 96, min 5,
offset 8745..............................................
.........................................................
```

FLASH ROM image is named `ms4.bin`, and the binary data logger trace is named `binout.full`. The `trykeys` program had identified a statistically different histogram (with an average value of 96 and a minimum bucket height of 5) for a decryption of the ROM image using, as a test key, data starting at offset 8745. I then isolated the candidate key from the data stream and analyzed the decrypted output using the candidate key. The output looked like real, valid code. I had found the key in a hidden boot sector, stored in the Southbridge chip! A few days later after getting some sleep and catching up on my schoolwork, I finished doing a proper analysis of the data stream and I had patched together an image of the entire secret boot sector.

With the secret boot code's RC-4 key in hand, I had the ability to generate FLASH ROM images that could be accepted by any Xbox at the time. The implication is that the entire trust mechanism of the Xbox could be violated by just overriding or replacing the ROM on the Xbox motherboard. This is accomplished by using the test structures provided by Microsoft to override the FLASH ROM during manufacturing for test and diagnostic purposes. Xboxes must roll off the production line at a rate of one every couple seconds, therefore Microsoft had designed a set of quick-connect test points that enable FLASH ROM override. The ability to boot to an alternate ROM image is valuable for running production test programs using the native Xbox CPU. The physical structure of the Xbox LPC interface implementation allows users, as well as Microsoft's contract manufacturer, to install a

The Legal Challenges of Hacking

In retrospect, hacking the Xbox was less challenging technically than it was socially and legally. After retrieving the secret key from the Southbridge chip, I met with my research advisor, Prof. Tom Knight, at the MIT Artificial Intelligence Laboratory to discuss my results. My advisor pointed out that my work could possibly be in violation of the DMCA, so prior to publishing we contacted MIT's legal department for counsel. MIT Legal eventually responded that the DMCA made the case too risky and that I had to publish as an individual, despite the fact that my work was conducted at MIT as a part of my research in computer architecture. I despaired, thinking I would never be able to afford a lawyer and that I would never be able to publish my results, but then Prof. Hal Abelson connected me with the Electronic Frontier Foundation (EFF). As a result, Lee Tien and Joe Liu from the EFF and Boston College were assigned to help me publish my work. Months of deliberation and positioning ensued. It was a battle fought on two fronts: we had to convince MIT to accept the work, while trying to appease Microsoft at the same time. After four months, MIT capitulated after an encouraging review of my work by Microsoft, and the overwhelming support of my laboratory colleagues and professors. MIT decided that I could publish my work as a student of MIT, instead of as an independent entity. The result of five months of legal stalemate was an AI Laboratory technical memorandum, followed by an academic presentation of the work at the conference on Cryptographic Hardware in Embedded Systems (CHES) in August 2002.

While the ending of this story may be happy, things could have been very different if not for the support of my advisor, my laboratory and the talented lawyers at the EFF. The DMCA draws a fuzzy line between a rogue hacker and a legitimate researcher; perhaps without MIT's endorsement, I would not be able to satisfy the DMCA's research exemption and my research would never have been published, or published and be contested by Microsoft. Free speech applies to all, not just to those who are lucky enough to sit in the ivory towers of esteemed academic institutions. There are countless others who were also working on the Xbox with excellent results, but their voices shall remain forever silent behind the curtain of the DMCA.

properly designed FLASH ROM override device without any soldering.

Clearly, the ability to override the trust mechanism used in the Xbox has sticky legal implications. While *my* intent was mostly to satisfy my curiosity and secondly to run my own code on the Xbox under my fair-use rights, other people have a desire to copy games and to modify and redistribute Microsoft's copyrighted kernel code. Because a cipher is blind to its application, the extraction of the RC-4 key enables all applications equally. As a result, I contacted the Electronic Frontier Foundation (EFF) to help me sort through the legal issues. The legal process is a slow and ponderous one. I had extracted the key in February, 2002, and it took until almost June before I was allowed to publish the results of my study in the appropriate academic forum.

Never had I experienced so much ado over 128 bits. The Digital Millennium Copyright Act (DMCA) of 1998 has eternally changed the landscape of hardware hacking. Reverse engineering used to be a protected act, deemed part of what makes a marketplace healthy and competitive. Now, tinkering with and bypassing a cryptographic security system to exercise your fair-use rights in the privacy of your own home could serve you thousands of dollars of fines and lawsuits. I strongly recommend that you read Chapter 12, "Caveat Hacker", so that you understand your legal rights and responsibilities.

There is an upside, however. The next chapter introduces the findings of my colleagues, many of which include the discovery of back doors in the

Security Through Obscurity

The technique used by Microsoft in the first version of the Xbox security is an excellent example of security through obscurity. A strong cipher, RC-4/128, was used to encrypt the ROM image in order to prevent people from analyzing the ROM contents or from creating their own ROMs. However, RC-4/128 is a symmetric cipher, which means that the Xbox must contain a decryption key also usable as an encryption key. This decryption/encryption key is the important piece of information buried inside the secret boot ROM. Hiding this key is security through obscurity: once the key is found, the cipher is moot and all security is lost.

True security would require that the user have access to every single piece of the Xbox and still be unable to encrypt their own valid FLASH ROM image. This implies that some secret must be kept outside of the Xbox. Public-key cryptography was invented for precisely this scenario. If Microsoft had used a public-key cipher to encrypt or sign the Xbox boot code, then knowing the entire contents of the secure boot ROM would be useless, since the main secret, Microsoft's private key, remains safely out of our reach in a vault somewhere in Redmond, Washington.

Xbox initialization sequence. These backdoors enable you to run your own code on the Xbox without enabling access to Microsoft's copyrighted works, and without enabling the copying of games. The next chapter will also introduce Xbox security version 1.1, which was cracked in just a few days by Andy Green in the UK.

CHAPTER 9

Sneaking In the Back Door

The full range of viable attacks on the Xbox are too numerous to describe in this book. The Xbox is based on the PC architecture, a complex, evolved architecture originally designed with no thought for security. Many of the classic hardware security holes exploited by smart card hackers, such as power supply modulation, sideband attacks and clock glitching have not even been touched on the Xbox, to the best of my knowledge. More information on these security weaknesses can be found in the proceedings of the Cryptographic Hardware in Embedded Systems (CHES) conference, available through the Lecture Notes in Computer Science series published by Springer-Verlag.

Unfortunately, console and secure PC manufacturers are not concerned about hardware security weaknesses, because hardware attacks are "too difficult for the average consumer to execute" and therefore of little threat. While it is true that researching an attack requires a skilled hacker with the correct tools, implementing an attack can be very cheap and easy. This situation reminds me of the parable where a mechanic, called in to fix an important piece of broken machinery, spends an hour looking at the situation and repairs the machine by tapping on it at just the right spot. Upon receiving a bill for $1,000 for services, the machine's owners demanded to know why a tap costs so much. The mechanic responded with, "the tap costs a dime. Knowing where to tap costs $999.90". The corollary to this parable is anyone could have executed the tap to repair the machine, given specific instructions. Security attacks are often the same: difficult to figure out, easy to share and implement. Secure hardware manufacturers should also be concerned about adopting mainly reactive policies to hacker intrusions. Many hackers work in secret, and they keep their methods and results quiet so that vendors are unable to develop proper countermeasures. These hackers also maintain a library of known attacks and back doors, disclosing only one at a time, so that vendors with reactive hardware security policies are always playing catchup.

A Commentary on Naming Conventions

Hacking communities often invent their own terminology for important concepts; these terms can vary from community to community and from industry standard terminology. The following is the list of terminologies accepted by the Xbox-Linux community. Any deviations from the terminology I use in this book are noted.

- **X-code**: Jam table opcodes; the opcodes used by the secret Southbridge (MCPX) boot ROM to initialize the Xbox hardware
- **2BL**: Second boot loader. This is the code that is decrypted by the secret boot ROM. It is called the second boot loader because this code's primary responsibility is to decrypt and decompress a kernel image.
- **Flash Boot Loader:** In version 1.1 security, this is an intermediate boot loader in between the secret boot ROM and the 2BL. The FBL is verified by a lightweight hash against a hard-coded value within the secret boot ROM. As a result, the FBL cannot be changed without changing the MCPX silicon. The FBL is responsible for verifying the digital signature on all critical portions of the FLASH ROM.
- **Kernel**: The Xbox kernel code. It is stored compressed and encrypted in the FLASH ROM.
- **Version 1.0 security**: The original Xbox security system using RC-4 encryption on the 2BL.
- **Version 1.1 security**: The second Xbox security system using the TEA hash to verify regions of the FLASH ROM. The earliest manufacturing date seen on boxes with version 1.1 security is around August 2002.

The previous chapter described my eavesdropping attack on the Xbox security mechanism that eventually yielded the RC-4 key hidden in a block of secret code. This chapter describes a few of the other attacks available on the Xbox that were devised by my colleagues, as well as the attack that was mounted on the revised Xbox security scheme, herein referred to as security version 1.1.

Back Doors and Security Holes

A class of back-door attacks on the Xbox leverage a fundamental weakness in the way the hardware is initialized by the secret boot code. This weakness stems from the fact that hardware initialization is accomplished by way of a powerful jam table opcode interpreter that stores its commands in unverified cleartext.

Visor Jam Table Attacks

One class of attacks on the Xbox involve modifying the hardware initialization sequence. Recall that hardware initialization of the Xbox is accomplished by means of an opcode interpreter that retrieves its commands from an unencrypted portion of the FLASH ROM called the "jam table". The relationship of the jam table entries to the rest of FLASH ROM is illustrated in Figure 9-1. Jam table entries are stored as `<opcode, arg1, arg2>` tuples near the lowest FLASH ROM addresses. The available opcodes include memory read and write functions to all the address spaces in the x86 architecture. Since the jam tables are stored unencrypted and never checked for modification, opcodes can be inserted into the jam table that can "seed" the Xbox memory with rogue instructions or modified hardware state *before* the RC-4 decryption of the FLASH ROM 2BL.

One application of jam table modification is to recover the plaintext of the kernel without knowledge of the RC-4 key. A hacker, known only as Visor, first described this approach to me. Here is a summary of Visor's approach:

1. Boot the Xbox normally. Part of the normal boot process will place a decrypted kernel image into main memory.
2. While maintaining power to the Xbox, switch the contents of the FLASH ROM's jam table to an alternate table that copies regions of main memory to an easily monitored location, such as the FLASH ROM's bus.

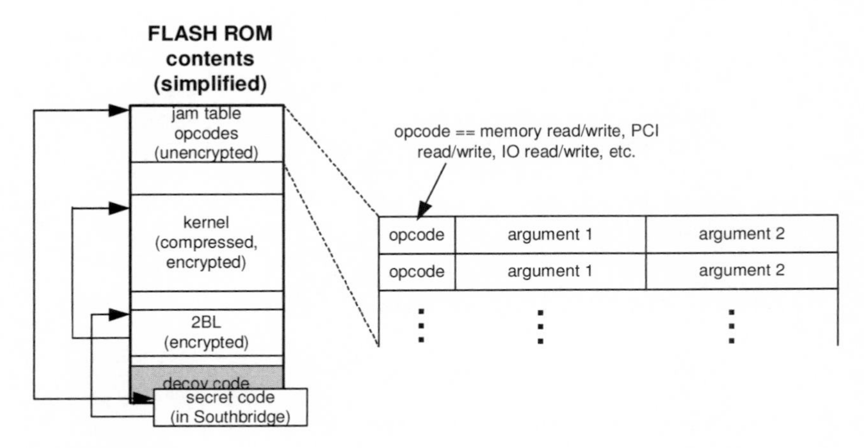

Figure 9-1:
Jam table opcodes in relation to the rest of FLASH ROM.

3. Perform a soft-reset of the Xbox CPU. This forces a hardware re-initialization without erasing the main memory.
4. Record the contents of main memory as the modified jam table program is executed.

Dynamic switchover of the FLASH ROM contents, required in step 2, can be accomplished by means of a ROM emulator, or by using an oversized ROM with the excess address bits wired to a bank of switches.

Visor also described how the jam table can be used as part of an elaborate hack to gain control over the Xbox's instruction pointer (IP). To better understand this hack, we will further investigate how the secret boot code handles the case of an invalid FLASH ROM image.

After decrypting the 2BL in the FLASH ROM image, the secret boot code checks for a magic number at a location near the end of the 2BL. For an invalid FLASH ROM image, this number does not match, and causes the CPU to jump to a short sequence of instructions located at `0xFFFF.FFFA`. This set of instructions continues all the way to the very last addressable location in physical memory, location `0xFFFF.FFFF`. Once the CPU executes this last instruction of the invalid ROM image, it should crash and halt execution due to a code segment boundary error when the IP rolls over from `0xFFFF.FFFF` to `0x0000.0000`. However, this does not happen; rather, the CPU happily attempts to execute whatever instruction, valid or invalid, is located at location `0x0000.0000`. Nominally, this instruction is invalid and the CPU halts anyway due to an instruction fault. However, a valid instruction can be placed there during the Xbox jam table initialization sequence using a jam table memory write opcode. Thus, by corrupting or erasing the encrypted FLASH ROM image and by modifying the jam tables to insert a jump instruction to your own unencrypted code in FLASH ROM, you can gain control of the Xbox CPU IP without ever touching a cipher or any similar technological measure that effectively controls access to a copyrighted work. Hence, this hack might be legal under the DMCA. I say *might* because the DMCA is an often times vague piece of legislation, and there is little court precedent to clarify the ambiguities. The argument for the legality of this approach lies in the fact that no significant Microsoft copyrighted code is ever decrypted or executed. The only exception is the portion of the secret boot ROM that must execute because they are hard-wired into the Southbridge's silicon. See Chapter 12, Caveat Hacker, for a more in-depth discussion of the legal issues that are facing the hacking community today.

MIST Premature Unmap Attack[1]

In order to protect the secret boot code in the event that a hacker gains control of the Xbox, the secret boot code in the Southbridge chip unmaps itself shortly before it exits. In other words, the secret boot code hides itself permanently from the system when it is finished executing. A user program

[1] From Andy Green's 19th Annual Chaos Communication Congress presentation on Xbox security hacking.

attempting to access any of the top 512 bytes in memory will see the decoy block in FLASH memory instead of the secret boot code. Michael Steil, the lead of the Xbox-Linux project, discovered a way to leverage this feature.

The unmapping process is accomplished by writing to `0x8000.8008`, a hardware register in the PCI configuration space. The basic strategy is to include a jam table opcode that writes to `0x8000.8008` and unmaps the secret boot code before the initialization sequence is finished. Since the caches are off at this time, the processor will start fetching and executing instructions from the decoy block, and fortunately the decoy block can be freely modified since it is part of the FLASH ROM. The catch, however, is that the jam table interpreter blocks writes to location `0x8000.8008`, so this shouldn't work. However, a bug in the decoding of the PCI configuration space in the Southbridge chipset makes the unmap instruction respond to multiple aliased addresses. In particular, the "function" bitfield is ignored. Thus, a write to `0x8000.8X08` where `X` is not equal to `0` also does the trick, and these writes are *not* blocked by the jam table interpreter. Therefore, in order to gain control of the CPU IP using the MIST hack, you must modify the decoy block in FLASH to contain your code, and you must add the appropriate jam table opcode to unmap the secret boot ROM during hardware initialization.

Microsoft Retaliates

The discovery of security holes prompted many to speculate that Microsoft will be swift to rotate its security scheme. In August 2002, Xboxes with a new motherboard quietly started to appear in Australia. The first official word of the new security system came from an unlikely source: nVidia, the producer of the chipsets used in the Xbox. Following an unspectacular second quarter in 2002, an nVidia spokesperson cited this as the last of a few reasons for why the quarter went poorly:

> "What we said about Xbox was that we reached a volume discount milestone, further reducing the margins. And that we will be taking an inventory write off in Q2 related to the amount of Xbox MCPs that were made obsolete when MSFT transitioned to a new security code (by way of the MIT hacker) and excess in nForce chipsets that we built in anticipation of higher demand of Athlon-based PCs." — Derek Perez, PR Director nVidia [2]

[2] From an article by the Inquirer, `http://www.theinquirer.net/?article=4735`

Reverse Engineering v1.1 Security[1]

The specifics of the security code changes where not revealed until October 2002, when a hacker named Andy Green began investigating the first version 1.1 Xboxes available in the United Kingdom. The outward physical differences between Xbox version 1.1 and 1.0 on the motherboard were subtle: the GPU traded its fan for a larger heat sink, the USB daughtercard was merged into the motherboard, and a PLL clock synthesizer chip was missing . Also missing were filter capacitors here and there, but nothing significant seemed to have changed. Further probing revealed that the hole leveraged by the MIST attack was patched, but the jam table opcodes were unchanged. The LPC bus, a key vector for gaining access to the Xbox, was also present and unchanged.

Andy was able to extract the MCPX ROM in one day using a procedure thought up by a fellow hacker named Asterisk. The procedure leveraged an undisclosed combination of previously identified security holes and back doors. The initial analysis of the ROM contents revealed that the security was implemented in a radically different fashion. A cursory overview of the version 1.1 Xbox revealed that the old security through obscurity scheme was tossed out, and replaced with a scheme that nominally gets its security from the strength of public-key ciphers.

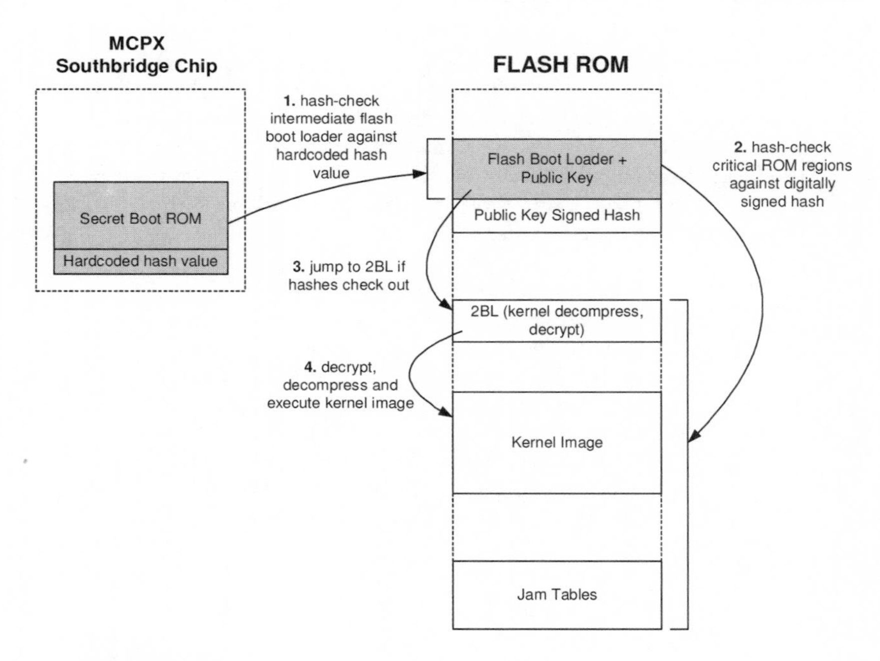

Figure 9-2:
Xbox Security Version 1.1. Regions that cannot be changed without replacing the MCPX silicon are shaded gray.

Microsoft's implementation of the new security scheme was a little bit counter-intuitive, however. The secret boot ROM within the MCPX remained the same size, 512 bytes. As a result, they could not fit the full public-key digital signature algorithm within the secret boot ROM. Their solution was to instead use a lightweight hash in the secret boot ROM to verify a region of FLASH ROM dubbed the Flash Boot Loader (FBL). The FBL contains the code (RSA cipher, SHA-1 hash, Microsoft's public key and the driver program) for digital signature verification of the FLASH ROM. The FBL is executed only if the FBL's hash can be verified against a constant stored within the secret boot ROM. Thus, the FBL is in theory as immutable as the secret boot ROM, even though the FBL is stored in the mutable FLASH ROM.

Although this scheme sounded fairly bulletproof, the hacking community did not give up so easily. They examined the secret boot ROM's hash in detail and discovered that it is based on TEA, a Tiny Encryption Algorithm by David Wheeler and Roger Needham at the Computer Laboratory of Cambridge University. Franz Lehner, a collaborator in the effort, sent a query to the newsgroup sci.crypt regarding weaknesses in the TEA hash.

On Friday afternoon, October 11th, their query was answered. A paper written by John Kelsey, Bruce Schneier, and David Wagner, presented in CRYPTO 1996 pointed out that the TEA cipher has a weakness in its key scheduler where every key has three related keys that can be generated by inverting certain pairs of bits (this weakness, along with the TEA cipher, is discussed in more detail in Chapter 7). On Saturday, Andy Green posted this to XboxHacker.net:

```
Aw, I'm a mere mortal, my feet are definitely made of
clay.

OK, I don't think its giving too much away to say the
first 5 bytes of the region.

ffffd400: E9 83 01 00 00

This is a relative longbranch to 0xffffd588

If I flip b31 of that as a DWORD (and flip its friend at
DWORD address +1 the same way) I branch instead to
0x7fd588.... Hmmmm that's, what, 8M up, where...

where
there's
RAM

Xcodes.. visor ram push method... (looks at MCPX for RAM
Write X-Code)

X-Code opcode 3 ... unrestricted
```

```
Hold on to your hat, boys!  Its testing time!

(mviz, a marvelous and well-timed revelation, I feel
mysterious and invisble forces helping me along, for which
I am grateful![3]
```

In other words, the related-key weakness of the TEA cipher means that every adjacent pair of double words in the FBL can be modified by one bit, the most significant bit, without any change to the resulting hash. This weakness gave Andy and his team enough breathing room to modify the target of a single jump instruction to point to a location in main memory.

Profile: Andy Green

Can you tell us a little bit more about yourself, and how you got into hacking?

I am 37, living in England, near Kettering in the East Midlands, with my wife, our four children and two cats.

I have been interested in computers from the age of 12 or so, when my brother bought a Commodore Pet. This 1MHz 6502 kept me occupied for months and months trying to write first BASIC code typed in from magazines, then games for it; eventually I wrote a fantastic character-cell Space Invaders thing in machine code. Machine code is where you are actually programming the CPU directly in hex; I still remember the common 6502 opcodes in hex now. This was such a dificult effort that I decided my next project would be an assembler written in machine code. 1978 was before the days of the Internet: I couldn't afford the commercial assemblers because I was just a kid and there weren't any people around us that I knew to warez a copy from.

This was fairly pathetic as assemblers go, but it worked fine. I learned from this the value of having the right tools, I could write far faster in Assembler, and whole kinds of errors miscomputing relative branches by hand, for example) went completely away. Next I had a BBC Model B computer, and again I was interested to make tools and games. I was offered a scholarship at a public school, but turned it down and instead left school at 16 with no further education. I was quite content to teach myself anything that interested me.

I sold a few games for this and another 6502 platform called the Oric, and with that money started up a company making Assemblers and other development tools. On the way I learned C and C++, and each time I stepped up

continued...

[3] Posting from `www.xboxhacker.net` under the Xbox Hacker BBS- > Xbox Hacking (TECHNICAL) -> BIOS/Flash ROM/Firmware -> News from the Xbox Linux Team, MS 'made a hash of it', guts exposed

That single location can be pre-loaded with a follow-up jump instruction back into any piece of user code using the previously discussed jam table codes. The Xbox hacking community had come together in a heroic effort and cracked Xbox security version 1.1 in three days. A separate effort, no less valiant, by Xecuter had also cracked the security in the same time frame.

The first moral of this story is that security is only as strong as its weakest link. While there is little doubt about the robustness of the RSA cipher and the SHA-1 hash for digital signature purposes, these were not the only elements of the security system. The TEA cipher used to extend the secure boot ROM's trust sphere into the FLASH ROM had flaws that allowed hackers to walk around the strong digital signature algorithms. This leads us to our second moral: complexity breeds weaknesses. Complex systems are difficult to design, test, and analyze. The version 1.1 security for the Xbox was probably implemented on a short fuse, so there was insufficient time to analyze the system for weaknesses. Either that, or Microsoft knew about the

whole rafts of bugs and timewasting miseries disappeared. Its like that picture on the Ascent of Man, from Nethanderal relative branch computation through to Homo Erectus with his virtual functions.

Alongside this I began to explore digital hardware design, again teaching myself from experience. I discovered that hardware and software are two sides of the same coin, although they are treated completely separately in education. Its really an implementation detail whether you choose to make your logical function in software or in hardware, or some mixture of the two. Having a foot in both camps gives greater insight into the nature of design: for example, C++ can be said to borrow many concepts from electronics in terms of the importance of interfaces.

Recently before becoming interested in the Xbox I had been working for a US-owned company with an office in Oxford, doing many jobs but the last one was designing smartcard silicon. Although the design was interesting and there were some great people working in the trenches there, I became increasingly despondent about the politics and problems with the management. Nor did it help that despite being spread across several projects, I was paid 2/3rds the salary of staff in San Jose simply because I was based in the UK. And don't get me started about the patents they had from me with no reward. In December 2001 I discovered that integrity was more important than money, resigned, and decided to go back to working for myself.

I had been rather tenderized by some unpleasant experiences on leaving this company, while digesting these I found myself snagged by the vast difference in outlook between the ugly, grabbing, controlling instincts of your average company involved in Intellectual Property, and the nature of GPL projects and the people involved in encouraging a reduction in the severity of patent and copyright laws. As

continued...

TEA weakness and designed this back door into the system to mitigate the risk of locking their FBL into silicon. It seems rather doubtful that Microsoft intentionally included this back door, since modifying the MCPX silicon is a very expensive proposition (although the expense ended up on nVidia's books). On the other hand, complexity is hard to avoid. My advisor at MIT, Tom Knight, once told me, "There are two kinds of designs in this world: those that are useful, and those that you can formally prove to be correct." To some extent, the only way to ensure the security of a real-world system is to make its details open (no security through obscurity!) and subject the system to analysis from all angles. In a way, a thorough analysis of Xbox security is being conducted at no expense to Microsoft, thanks to the hacker community.

Even if Microsoft had used a stronger hash function in the secret boot ROM, there are still a number of viable attacks on the Xbox that have yet to

Profile: Andy Green, continued...

time went on I increasingly came to see Microsoft, and the previous company I was working for in the same light.

It was after this that I read about Bunnie's hack on Slashdot. I read about Bunnie's methods with some tart emotions. My main thoughts were that this was something that I could have done, since I have been using the FPGAs that Bunnie used since 1989, admiration for the conciseness of the attack, and dismay with myself that I had not been doing something equally cool and interesting - and that matched with my philosophical predilictions - with my time. Instead I was sitting there reading Slashdot, drinking coffee, contributing nothing. (An aside, I think this is a fairly common experience for many Slashdot readers, to be a little jealous and challenged when they read about someone else's cool hacks. I think it explains the constant background noise there of jeering and questioning why someone would want to do such a thing.)

Over the next few weeks I gathered as much information as I could on the internals of the Xbox, Xboxhacker.net was crucial for this. Its also where I met Michael Steil as the Xbox Linux project was starting. Pretty soon I was able to identify interesting projects that I could contribute to, for example the Milksop project. Again from this, with Surferdude's help, it became possible for me to put together the very first clean ROM which was able to boot and keep up the Xbox without being reset. This later became the basis of the crom 1MB Linux and cromwell, the Xbox Linux clean ROM. After the initial hacks and designs, I decided to work almost entirely towards the Xbox Linux goal.

Can you tell us why you hack the Xbox?

Why? Everyone has different reasons, but for me it was my comprehension of Microsoft's outrageous antitrust behaviour - deny everything, appeal everything, delay everything, and in the meanwhile, create and dump (for they are sold at below cost) on the market millions of Microsoft-only PCs -

continued...

be tried. One can mount a man-in-the-middle attack on the HyperTransport bus (see Chapter 8) by overdriving the signals with carefully timed pulses. This attack is fairly simple to implement, since each HyperTransport bus trace has a test point visible from the component side of the motherboard. A complete hardware solution would involve an FPGA on a board with "pogo-pin" bed-of-nails style test connectors. This board can be impressed upon these test points without any solder. Another attack, suggested by Adi Shamir to me at the CHES conference, is to employ a timed glitch in the CPU clock or power supply to upset the calculation of a jump target address. This kind of attack has been applied with success to the processors in cryptographic smart cards. Again, this kind of attack can be implemented fairly easily and cheaply as a user-installable module. Keep in mind that a much broader range of attacks is available to hackers if the goal is a onetime defeat of the security to recover, for example, a secret key or a block of critical code.

The Threat of Back Doors

As this chapter demonstrates, searching for back doors is a practical method for attacking cryptographically secured hardware. The relatively high success rate of finding back doors in the Xbox is partially because the Xbox

the Xbox. Since our representatives here in Europe and US don't seem to care (perhaps, as was the case recently in the EU, because they plan to go work for Microsoft and take their silver pieces), it would be an honour to be part of pricking this evil plan of a bloated monopoly using the weapons of the GPL and Linux. I know that people shut their eyes and think of their share options, but it must be hard for decent people - and surely most of the people working there are this - to work for such a monster.

I was lucky enough to get a couple of contracts through 2002 that allowed me to spend the latter part of the year working exclusively on getting the first Linux kernel up in crom and bringing Cromwell up so it was able to control the main peripherals of the box and boot Linux from HDD or CD. Since then my share of the Project A prize money thanks to donor Michael Robertson will allow be to continue working full time for the next few months at least.

Do you have any advice you'd like to share?

My final thought is to encourage people, especially young people, to listen to their brain when it comes to things that interest them. Don't be afraid to dig around and try to learn about things that snag your attention. That feeling you get when you wish you understood something, a kind of yearning, is your brain's way of telling you that it thinks the knowledge might be useful later. If you listen to it enough, you stand a good chance of knowing the right thing at the right time to make some small difference.

Profile: Franz Lehner

Franz Lehner, 29, lives in Austria with his girlfriend. He studied Electrical Engineering for 5 years. Now, he programs "automated solutions" while running an ISP. In his spare time, he searches for projects that are fun and educational.

After finding bunnie's Xbox hacking document, he met the Xbox-Linux team on sourceforge.net. He joined the Xbox-Linux project to learn about team programming, Linux kernel hacking and debugging, and cryptographic systems. He also joined the Xbox-Linux project to develop a better understanding of related systems, such as Palladium.

represents the first significant attempt made by a vendor to cryptographically secure a PC. Despite the lessons learned from the Xbox experience, future secure PC implementations are still at risk of having hardware security weaknesses, since the legacy of the PC is an open and unsecured hardware architecture.

PC hardware is complex yet fragile, and building a chain of trust out of PC hardware is difficult because of this brittleness. Fundamentally, each component in a PC is designed to be "trusting" of its physical environment. The specifications for any commercial integrated circuit component clearly state that the IC is guaranteed to operate over a bounded range of temperatures, voltages, frequencies and other conditions. If these maximum ratings are violated, then the behavior of the device is "undefined", and all bets are off. Most chip engineers do not even consider trying to make their circuits recover gracefully from an out-of-range condition, as it is already hard enough to get a chip to work under the specified operating conditions. Furthermore, most consumer applications are very cost-sensitive, and the overhead of building in robust fault tolerance measures results in a product that is not price-competitive. Thus, chips are typically implemented with no internal error-checking. If, for some reason, the Arithmetic Logic Unit (ALU, the computational "brains" of a CPU) adds two numbers incorrectly, the problem will only manifest itself symptomatically; you can observe only the effects of such an error, sometimes long after the error-causing event. One can think of attacks that take advantage of faults induced by out-of-range conditions as the analogy of buffer overruns in the software world.

Another problem with the PC architecture is that the processor is too trusting of its code environment. The Pentium processor architecture has no provision in hardware for discriminating between code that is insecure or secure. If the instruction pointer happens to find its way into an insecure code segment through a bug or an induced failure, the processor will happily execute this code. Note that code compartmentalization based on hardware security levels is a different technique from sand-boxing. Sand-boxing does not provide an adequate solution for situations where a user program requires direction from or interaction with secret or protected code or data. Lately, new processor architectures have been proposed that can solve this problem through the use of data tags that embed a sort of security audit log.[4]

Another source of back doors are the design bugs that exist in every complex chip. It is common practice to ship chips with plenty of known bugs, also known as errata. For example, the Intel i860 XP processor (first released in 1991, not to be confused with the recently released i860 chipset for the Pentium4 processor) shipped with a book of errata that was comparable in size to the processor's data sheet. Another example closer to home is the bug in the nVidia MCPX's address space decoder that made the MIST Premature Unmap attack possible. Most of these errata have simple work-arounds or have minor implications to the functionality of the chip under nominal conditions. However, some errata, such as those dealing with cache coherence, address decoding, and memory management can result in major *software* security holes.

In the case of the Xbox, the business impact of a hardware back door is probably small. Perhaps Microsoft loses some small fraction of game sales revenue, but the losses due to piracy are dwarfed by the losses Microsoft takes on hardware sales. Also, the Xbox is just a game console—grandma's bank account is not being tapped dry or credit card numbers stolen as a result of security weaknesses in the Xbox. However, more than game revenues will be at risk with the trusted PC. Unless the trusted PC architecture is a fundamental change from legacy PCs, people will be blindly trusting financial secrets and personal data security to untrustworthy hardware. Like most things in life, the first step is education. The more we learn about hardware security, even if it involves poking around a game console, the better our security systems will be tomorrow. Now, on with the lesson...

---

[4] `http://www.ai.mit.edu/projects/aries/Documents/Memos/ARIES-15.pdf`. "A Minimal Trusted Computing Base for Dynamically Ensuring Secure Information Flow" by Tom Knight and Jeremy Brown.

Chapter 10

More Hardware Projects

The similarity of the Xbox to the PC architecture allows hackers to borrow technology and expertise from the PC world when building hardware projects. As a result, PC hardware, monitors, cables, and peripherals have all been adapted to work with the Xbox. This chapter introduces some of these hardware projects, discovered, documented and implemented by hackers around the world.

The LPC Interface

Version 1.0 of the LPC (Low Pin Count) interface was defined by Intel in 1997. The LPC interface is a royalty-free bus that is designed to enable systems without explicit ISA or X-bus (ISA-like expansion bus for memory or generic I/O devices) capabilities. This need for the LPC interface stems from the large number of low bit-rate, high pin count devices and busses with incompatible interfaces found in a standard PC, such as the floppy disk, keyboard, mouse, serial, IrDA, parallel, ISA and boot ROM interfaces. The aggregate bandwidth consumed by all these devices is small, but the number of signals required to support all of them easily exceeds the signal count required by higher-bandwidth buses such as the PCI or AGP bus. Making matters worse, not all configurations of computers requires all of these legacy I/O devices, and wasted pins and functions just eat away at profits. The cost of a pin on a chip package is high relative to the cost of the silicon required to support these simple interfaces (a rule of thumb is that one package pin costs a penny, while in 0.13μ silicon, about ten thousand gates—enough logic to implement a small processor—costs a penny in silicon area, assuming the design is not bond-pad limited[1]).

The LPC interface counters this problem with a single, low-pin count (seven required pins, versus the 36 pins required for an ISA bus) bus that operates at a high speed. All of the legacy I/O and expansion functions are mapped into this high-bandwidth bus, enabling system designers to create so-called "Super I/O" chips that in turn enable Southbridge chips with a much lower pin count. In addition, segregating functions between Super I/O chips and Southbridge chips allows designers to choose Super I/O and Southbridge chip combinations that provide the optimal set of features for a given application.

The LPC physical interface is quite simple. The interface is a 4-bit bi-directional bus that runs at a 33 MHz clock rate. The interface also has two "sideband" signals, one framing signal that indicates the start and end of LPC bus cycles, and one reset signal that forces all LPC peripheral devices into a known state for initialization purposes. In addition, there are a couple of optional signals for the LPC interface that provide DMA and interrupt capabilities as well as power management for more sophisticated I/O devices. More information on the LPC bus and its protocol can be found in the Intel Low Pin Count (LPC) Interface Specification, version 1.1. The specification can be found on the Intel corporate website at `http://www.intel.com/design/chipsets/industry/lpc.htm`.

LPC Interface on the Xbox

The Xbox incorporates an LPC interface on the motherboard. The LPC interface in this case is used to implement a debug and test bus. One can connect a keyboard and mouse through this LPC interface, as well as an alternate boot ROM for diagnostic purposes. The LPC interface is activated to load alternate boot code when the FLASH ROM on the Xbox is not available. The lack of a FLASH ROM device can be simulated by forcing the lowest data bit (D0) of the FLASH ROM data bus to a level of zero volts.

Many speculate that the LPC interface is an essential part of the Xbox production line because of the alternate boot ROM ability provided by the LPC interface. Fully assembled Xboxes can be configured with a comprehensive self-test program via the LPC interface. Applying the CPU as a fast test controller allows defective units to be quickly and efficiently isolated on the factory floor without the cost of expensive testing machines.

For hackers, the alternate boot ROM facility provided by the LPC interface is an ideal mechanism for getting code into the Xbox. Valid LPC-loadable boot ROM images for the Xbox can be created by anyone since the cryptographically secured boot procedure of the Xbox is now fully understood. In fact, some vendors of alternate boot ROM devices for the Xbox have leveraged the regularity of the LPC interface's pinout geometry on the Xbox

---

[1] The circuits on a chip are typically surrounded by squares of metal ("bond pads") that are wired to the pins on the chip's packaging. A chip is said to be bond-pad limited when the area required for the ring of bond pads exceeds the area required by the circuitry inside the chip. The cost of excess pins becomes even higher in the case that a chip is bond-pad limited.

motherboard to create ROM devices that install without any soldering. These devices use a set of spring-loaded "pogo-pins", similar to those used during production for Xbox testing, to contact the LPC interface with just a pressure-fit. The pinout of the LPC bus as implemented on the Xbox can be found in Appendix F, "Xbox Hardware Reference".

Using the LPC Interface

The fact that the LPC interface is an industry standard is quite convenient for Xbox hardware hackers. First, there is a plethora of LPC-compatible interface devices, ranging from Super-I/O chips to firmware ROMs with built-in LPC interfaces. Second, the wide acceptance of the LPC interface as a diagnostic and convenience bus for generic PCs helps mitigate the legal risk of using the LPC interface and selling LPC interface devices. A firmware ROM for the LPC interface can be sold without any Xbox-specific contents since end-users can easily reprogram their LPC bus devices using a simple, cheap adapter for their PC. A further help to the legality of LPC firmware devices is that the Xbox's LPC connector pinout is near identical to the one recommended by Intel for generic PCs. As a result, an LPC firmware device sold for the Xbox is very similar to an LPC firmware device sold for the standard PC.

One of the first LPC boot ROM devices was developed by Andy Green. The project is called "Cheapmod" and it is an SST 49LF020 device (256 kByte FLASH ROM with an integrated LPC interface) in a socket wired to an LPC-compatible header. According to Andy's Cheapmod webpage, "`http://warmcat.com/milksop/cheapmod.html`", "If you can get ahold of the $2.50 SST 49LF020, you can build an alternative BIOS for $4". This device can be programmed using his "CheapLPC" programmer (`http://warmcat.com/milksop/cheapLPC.html`), a delightfully simple PC parallel-port based device that can (slowly) talk to and reprogram an LPC device. Many commercially available alternate firmware devices have been based off of or inspired by his design, including the Xodus/Matrix design The Xodus/Matrix is a particularly interesting variant of Andy's original design, as it is the first Xbox alternate firmware device that implemented an entirely solderless installation procedure. This opened up the world of Xbox hacking to software-oriented hackers who were not inclined to solder wires into their Xboxes. A photograph of the Xodus/Matrix can be seen in Figure 10-1. Note that the Xodus/Matrix device comes without any code programmed in it; the user must provide the alternate firmware image.

There are some important functional considerations when selecting a FLASH ROM chip with an LPC interface for use with the Xbox. The most significant is that the native Xbox architecture allocates a 16 MByte area for the boot ROM. If the physical boot ROM is smaller than 16 MBytes in size, the boot ROM contents are aliased to fill up the entire 16 MByte space. This gives Xbox designers more flexibility in choosing the size of the ROM chip without causing problems with routines that uses both bottom- and top-relative addressing. Let's make the concept of bottom- and top-relative

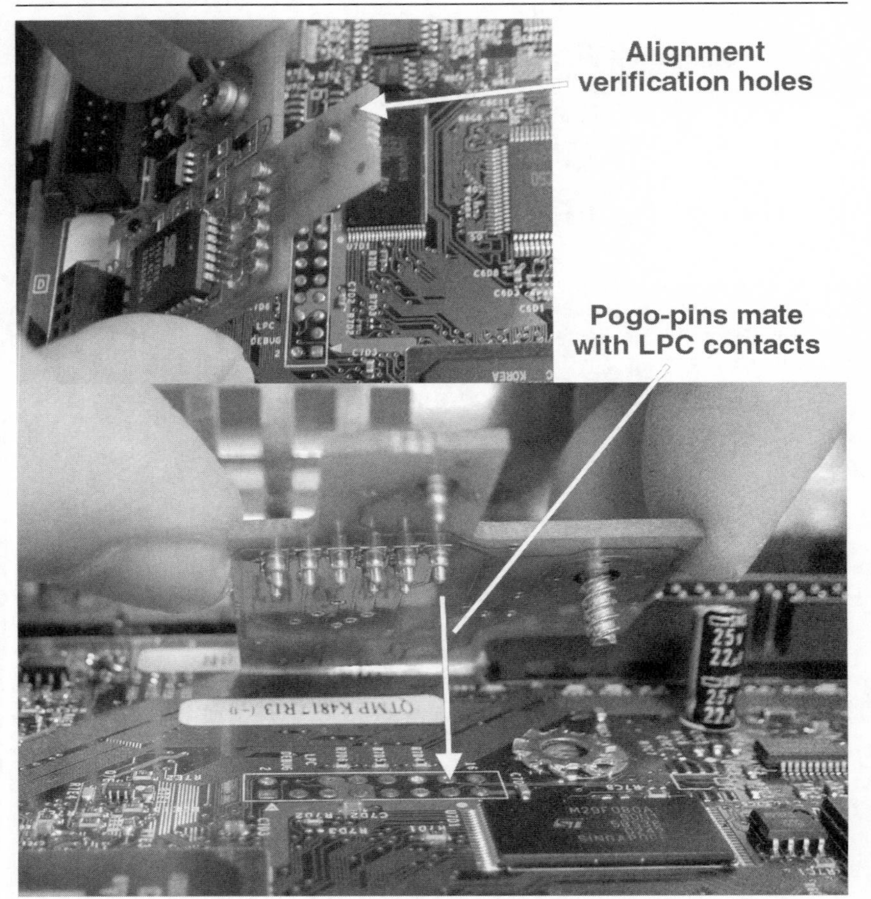

Figure 10-1: The solderless Xodus/Matrix alternate firmware device, showing off the spring-loaded "pogo-pin" contacts that enable a solderless connection to the LPC connector on the Xbox motherboard.

addressing more concrete with an example. The addresses for the 16 MByte boot ROM area in the Xbox spans from `0xFF00.0000` to `0xFFFF.FFFF`. Programs on the Xbox that use bottom-relative addressing will compute addresses using `0xFF00.0000 + offset` (bottom address plus offset), while programs that use top-relative addressing will use `0xFFFF.FFFF - offset` (top address minus offset). Suppose a 1 MByte boot ROM is installed in the Xbox. This means that the processor will see 16 identical copies of this 1 MByte ROM spread evenly over the 16 MByte ROM address space. In other words, the contents of the boot memory appear identical for every address `A + 0xFF00.0000 + n * 0x0010.0000`, `n = 0` through `15`, `A = 0` through `0x000F.FFFF`. As a result, programmers can pack data into the smaller 1 MByte boot ROM using both top- and bottom-relative addressing without having to change any of their code: a valid copy of the ROM image appears near both the top- and the bottom-

Alternate Firmware Devices vs. Modchips

An alternate firmware device is a hardware module that provides a method for running user-specified firmware on the Xbox hardware. Alternate firmware devices are distinguished from the so-called "modchip" in that an alternate firmware device is furnished as a blank device and has no inherent ability to circumvent copyright control mechanisms. A blank LPC-interface ROM device, for example, is an alternate firmware device: you could burn a copy of the U.S. Bill of Rights on it if you wanted. Any user-installed FLASH ROM that comes blank is also an alternate firmware device. A modchip, on the other hand, colloquially implies a device that is crafted for playing game backups and otherwise modifying or removing DRM (digital rights management) policy restrictions. Hence, the term modchip encompasses certain boot ROM devices that *have been programmed with code* that enables DRM policy modifications, as well as devices such as "patchers" that contain no ROM and operate by dynamically patching a few key Xbox firmware locations as the firmware is loaded for execution.

relative base addresses. Now, suppose that Microsoft decided to save on cost and shrink their 1 Mbyte boot ROM down to a 256 kByte boot ROM. The processor now sees 64 identical copies of this 256 kByte boot ROM distributed over the 16 MByte ROM address space, and all of the old code that uses bottom- and top-relative addressing still works. Significantly, the CPU in the Xbox is hard-wired to start executing code on power-up from an address located 16 bytes from the top of memory (its "reset vector"), while the hardware initialization routines wired into the Xbox chipsets use ROM locations located near the bottom of the 16 MByte FLASH ROM space. As a result, the Xbox hardware *requires* an LPC ROM implementation that is either 16 MBytes in size, or else aliases a smaller ROM's contents throughout the FLASH ROM address space. The SST 49LF020 is one of the few LPC FLASH ROMs that aliases the ROM's contents over the whole address space. Arguably, this feature is actually a bug: by ignoring the upper address bits and aliasing the ROM's contents over the whole address space, this chip occupies space that could be allocated to other functions. As a result, SST has released an updated "A-step" of the part, called the 49LF020A, that does not alias the ROM's contents over memory. Likewise, the A-step silicon will not work as an alternate firmware device for the Xbox.

The Other 64 MB of SDRAM

An astute observer will note that there are two missing chips on the top side of the Xbox motherboard, and that these missing chip spots look suspiciously similar to the spots currently occupied by memory chips. Flip

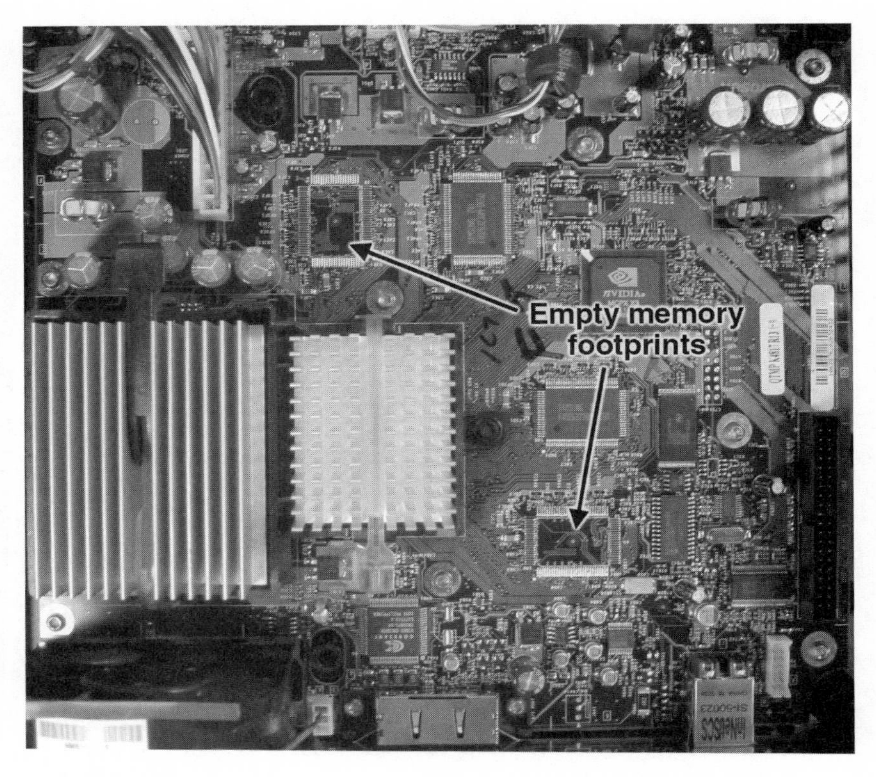

Figure 10-2:
The unpopulated memory footprints on the Xbox motherboard.

Fiduciaries

Look at an unpopulated memory spot on the Xbox motherboard. The silver dot surrounded by a dark annulus inside these unpopulated chip footprints is called a "fiduciary". Fiduciary patterns are used by circuit board assembly machines as reference points for aligning large chips with many pins. Fiduciary patterns are designed to be easily recognized by the machine vision systems employed in board assembly machines. Specially shaped fiduciaries can also be used to enable automatic identification of the orientation and type of a circuit board.

the board over, and there are yet another two unoccupied chip footprints. These empty footprints are in fact for memory chips. The location of these blank spots is illustrated in Figure 10-2.

The next logical question is, of course, "Can you double the Xbox's memory size to 128 MB by soldering suitable memory chips into the open slots on the Xbox motherboard?" The answer is in fact yes, but the initialization code for the Xbox need to be modified in order for the chipset to recognize and use the extra memory. In addition, the extra memory does not help graphics or gaming performance. Xbox games are not designed to take advantage of the extra memory, so the extra memory will typically sit around unused. The extra memory spots are provided primarily for the manufacture of special consoles for game developers. Game developers can use the extra memory to ease the transition of games into the Xbox's relatively tight memory footprint, as well as for keeping debug, performance monitoring and test utilities resident in memory that are not part of the game image. Note that the extra memory could be leveraged by home-brew software, but the difficulty of obtaining and installing the memory chips makes Xbox memory expansions more of an interesting soldering practice exercise than a practical modification.

Xbox-VGA

There is a little bit of confusion about what an Xbox VGA adapter does. Many Xbox VGA adapters are actually "TV-to-VGA converters". In other words, they take the low resolution TV output from the Xbox and they run it through a line doubler to yield a low-quality VGA display. A true Xbox VGA adapter actually configures the Xbox to output a much higher resolution video output, yielding a better-than-TV quality display on a VGA monitor. The VGA adapter configures the Xbox graphics mode using designated pins in the AVIP (Audio Video I/O Port) connector. The main problem with this approach is that a game has to be specially written to support this higher resolution mode. As a result, some games will not work with a true Xbox VGA adapter, but fortunately going back to TV resolution is as easy as plugging in the standard TV adapter cable.

The original Xbox-VGA adapter was developed by Ken Gasper. He sells a version of it on his website at `http://xboxvga.xemulation.com`. Currently, he offers the Xbox-VGA adapter in a "bare board" form as well as in a fully assembled form. If you are looking for an interesting hardware hacking project for the Xbox that is both useful and will hone your circuit assembly skills, it may be worth it to purchase one of his bare boards and attempt to assemble the adapter yourself.

The "Xbox Hardware Reference" in Appendix F at the end of this book contains a pin diagram of the Xbox AVIP.

Mass Storage Replacement

The Xbox contains a DVD-ROM drive and a hard drive; both of these use the PC standard IDE interface for talking to the Xbox motherboard. The DVD-ROM drive also has a proprietary power and DVD tray state connector. A popular and sometimes necessary hacking activity for the Xbox is replacing these drives.

Users replace or tweak the DVD-ROM because the native Xbox DVD-ROM drive is unable to read CD-Rs and many types of CD-RW media. This can be particularly annoying for those who are trying to install Xbox-Linux for the first time, or for users who are trying to rip music from their CD-R collection to the Xbox hard drive.

There are many methods for replacing and tweaking the Xbox DVD-ROM drive. Some Xbox DVD-ROM drive models can have their laser intensity adjusted to improve their ability to read CD-R and CD-RW media. This is a potentially risky operation, since you can permanently damage your DVD-ROM drive by improperly adjusting the power output of the laser, but many hackers have reported that a properly executed procedure results in better media compatibility. I suggest a web-search for the latest news and techniques, since the style and model of DVD-ROM drive used in the Xbox varies frequently. In addition, the Xbox DVD-ROM drive can be outright replaced with a standard PC DVD-ROM. The problem with this method is twofold. First, a regular PC DVD-ROM drive cannot read original Xbox game disks due to physical security measures built into an Xbox game disk. Second, a PC DVD-ROM drive needs to be adapted to the custom DVD power and traystate connector on the Xbox motherboard.

The easiest, but ugliest, method is to install a standard PC DVD-ROM drive but leave the Xbox DVD-ROM drive connected through its proprietary cable. In this method, the gray IDE cable is connected to the standard PC DVD-ROM drive (set to slave mode through jumper configurations on the drive), and power is stolen from the hard drive's power connector using a standard power splitter cable. The Xbox DVD-ROM drive remains in place, but with its IDE connector empty and with the proprietary yellow power-and-tray-state cable installed. The purpose of the Xbox DVD-ROM drive is to serve as a dummy drive that is used to manually relay the state of the DVD drive tray to the Xbox. In other words, the user needs to manually replicate the state of the standard PC DVD-ROM's tray using the Xbox DVD-ROM's tray during a media change event. The exact procedure for operating an Xbox in this configuration varies depending upon the particular PC DVD-ROM drive model and the nuances of the Xbox hardware configuration, so again, I suggest a web-search for the latest information. There are also some websites that describe how to adapt select PC DVD-ROM drive models to work with the Xbox's proprietary tray state and power connector. A project like this is a good intermediate-level project for hackers who are basically comfortable with soldering and screwdrivers. The modifications performed on the standard DVD-ROM drive allows the state of the standard drive's DVD tray to be accurately transmitted to the

Xbox. It does not allow you to play original games, however, unless the Xbox has been modified with additional hardware that circumvents the security checks on the DVD ROM drive. Even without the ability to play games, this is still a useful technique for fettering out Xbox-Linux installation problems and for enhancing the ability of the Xbox to rip your CD collection or to watch DVDs. Note that returning the IDE connector back to the Xbox DVD-ROM drive will restore the original gaming functionality of the Xbox.

Xbox hard drives also need replacing from time to time. Serious software developers for the Xbox find it advantageous to install a higher capacity hard drive into the Xbox, and users with broken hard drives also desire to replace their hard drives. Unfortunately, the OEM Xbox hard drive contains copyrighted Microsoft programs. Xbox hard drives are also protected with a firmware lockout. The firmware lockout makes installing a new hard drive with original gaming functionality rather challenging, especially in terms of legal issues. The firmware lockout is also unique to each hard drive, preventing you from replacing your hard drive with a used Xbox hard drive. However, if you only wish to run Xbox-Linux or other homebrew programs and do not care about playing games, installing a new hard drive in the Xbox is as easy and as legal as installing a hard drive into any PC.

CHAPTER 11

Developing Software for the Xbox

While the focus of this book is educating readers in the ways of hardware hacking and security, one ultimate goal of Xbox hacking is running home-brew software. This chapter is devoted to describing some of the home-brew software projects that are in progress for the Xbox at the time of writing.

Xbox-Linux

The goal of the Xbox-Linux project is to create a user-friendly and legal port of GNU/Linux and of GNU/Linux applications to the Xbox hardware platform. Thanks to the dedication and contributions of hackers around the globe, the Xbox-Linux project has had a great deal of success toward meeting its goals. A picture of the core Xbox-Linux project team can be seen in Figure 11-1, and the sidebars in this chapter and in chapter 9 contain interviews with Xbox-Linux project team members. The homepage for the Xbox-Linux project is `http://xbox-linux.sourceforge.net`. Significantly, the Xbox-Linux project and its principle hackers are not anti-Microsoft. They are pro-"freedom to tinker", and not puerile Microsoft-haters; they have an agenda that touches upon preserving the very freedoms of thought and speech that brought technology to where it is today.

Xbox-Linux is not the ultimate software project for the Xbox; on the contrary, Xbox-Linux is just the beginning of Xbox software hacking. Porting the familiar GNU/Linux development environment to the Xbox enables a larger base of software hackers to join the Xbox hacking project. With GNU/Linux, the Xbox can run a wide variety of application software, from free open-source video games to word processing applications to clustering software for building Beowulf-style computer clusters.

Installing Xbox-Linux

Currently, in order to run Xbox-Linux, you need to install a GNU/Linux boot ROM using an alternate firmware device. This requires opening up the Xbox. The previous chapter, "More Hardware Projects", describes methods for building and installing an alternate firmware device for the Xbox via the LPC interface. Several vendors now offer easy-to-install LPC interface alternate firmware devices. Notably, the Xodus/Matrix device is the first alternate firmware device on the market with an entirely solderless installation procedure. All the tools you need to install the Xodus/Matrix device

Profile: Michael Steil

Michael, can you tell us a little bit more about yourself?

Born in 1979 in Erding/Germany, I'm a student of computer science at the Technische Universität München, I teach Assembly to students in the first semester myself, and I plan to have a MA degree next year. I have been working with computers since I was ten years old; my first computer was a Commodore 64, followed soon by a 386 PC. My main interests were always hardware and operating systems, and I was especially fascinated by the diversity of hardware architectures (Commodore, PC, Amiga, Macintosh, ...) as well as popular embedded systems, such as gaming consoles (did you know the "SEGA CD" has three CPUs, one Z80 and two M68000?). That's why I bought many video game systems for experimentation, such as the Nintendo SNES, the SEGA Genesis or the Nintendo Game Boy. I also had a look at Linux for the SEGA Dreamcast, but I have never seen Linux for the Sony Playstation 2, since the whole set was really too expensive for me, both for experimentation and for real use.

How did you get into Xbox hacking, and in particular, the Xbox-Linux project?

On April 30th 2002, I bought an Xbox, convinced that it would be a great toy for hacking, and well-suited for Linux. After looking at the system software for an hour or two (I bought no game), I unscrewed the Xbox. Looking for information about hacking the box disappointed me at first: I didn't find much more than how to connect the hard disk to a PC, and a site about Xbox Linux with virtually no information on it - so I decided to start my own Xbox hacking site and put information on it I found out by connecting the

continued...

are described in Chapter 1, "Voiding the Warranty", and the Xodus/Matrix device itself comes with some easy-to-follow instructions on how to program and use the alternate firmware device. Keep in mind that Microsoft can and will revise their motherboard layout and security system, so you are well-advised to check with your device vendor for compatibility with your specific system hardware before making a purchase. You will also need an Xbox gameport to USB converter cable if you wish to use a standard keyboard and mouse with the Xbox. Such converters can be purchased through aftermarket retailers such as Lik-Sang (`http://www.lik-sang.com`) or you can build one yourself by following the step-by-step guide in Chapter 4.

Before installing your alternate firmware device, you will need to program it with a ROM image that boots the GNU/Linux kernel. "Cromwell" is an open-source, clean-room (i.e., contains no Microsoft code) boot ROM for the Xbox that is capable of booting GNU/Linux. Significantly, the information contained in the Cromwell source code and binary image cannot be used to bypass any of the native copyright control mechanisms built into

hard disk to a PC.

Xboxhacker.net and the original Xbox Linux mailing list were a great help, they both attracted excellent hackers and published valuable information. Dissatisfied with the original infrastructure of the Xbox Linux Project, I decided to move to Sourceforge on May 23rd. Now every contributor could add anything to the website without having to go through the maintainer. But at this time, everything was still quite theoretical: Without the advent of modchips we couldn't do much more than write code that "should theoretically work". Andy Green's Filtror accelerated everything: This mod made it possible to finish the bootloader and, with Milosch Meriac's help, adapt the Linux kernel within a very short time.

The "anonymous donor" approaching me in June did not only lead to additional publicity of the project and therefore to even more contributors, but also to a personal friendship of mine: Walter Meyer, creator of the BioXX (OpenXbox) modchip happens to live only 20 kilometers away from my place, and, among other things, he helped me a lot modding my boxes, since I'm not really a soldering iron person.

With Linux already running on the Xbox, in December 2002 the Xbox Linux core team (Andy Green, Milosch Meriac, Franz Lehner and me; Edgar Hucek unfortunately couldn't come) met in person for the first time at the Chaos Computer Club Congress in Berlin.

My original motivation for everything was just that it's fun and I could learn a lot by doing it. I didn't start it because I wanted to harm Microsoft - but in the meantime I agree that Microsoft harms their customers by not letting them use the software they want to use on the hardware they bought,

continued...

Profile: Michael Steil, continued...

and that's why especially the Xbox Linux Project is important.

(We're) not "Anti-MS" or "MS-haters". We dislike their market strategy, so we have a rational reason to work against them.

Is there anything more you'd like to say about the $200k prize for Xbox-Linux?

I think that the award didn't attract people that wanted to see some money: Now one month after the deadline, the money still hasn't been distributed yet and still not a single person has sent me a single question about when he will get the money. The award attracted the press, we got more publicity, and this way we got more hackers. But nobody did it because of the money. So we don't want to be regarded as being paid for the job by Michael Robertson. A good proof is that we're still all active after the deadline.

Can you tell us more about your "MIST X-Code hack"?

Some time after Bunnie's original hack, Andy extracted the MCPX ROM completely and Steve, Paul and me started to analyze the code, and I reverse-engineered the X-Code interpreter contained within it. When looking for bugs that could be used to escape the X-Code interpretation loop, I found that a part of the code has already been written with our attacks in mind. This is my original disassembly:

```
cmp     ebx, 80000880h ; ISA Bridge, MCPX disable?
jnz     short not_mcpx_disable
                        ; BUG: too specific: bits 24 to 30
                        ; undefined and ignored by PCI hardware!
and     ecx, not 2        ; clear bit 1 (MCPX ROM will be
                          ; turned off by setting bit 1)
not_mcpx_disable:
mov     eax, ebx
mov     dx, 0CF8h
out     dx, eax           ; PCI configuration address
add     dl, 4
mov     eax, ecx
out     dx, eax           ; PCI configuration data
jmp     short next_instruction
```

I had been working with "PCI configuration" before, therefore I knew that the test for the attack was too specific: Similar codes would do the same, but they pass the test. So the MS developers had a good idea, but the implementation was wrong, thus telling us about their idea this way!

I sent my idea to Andy, Steve and Paul, and they verified after a short time that 0x88000880 worked just as well as 0x80000880 to turn off the MCPX ROM and exiting the interpreter by mapping the interpreter code out of memory!

the Xbox. In other words, it is difficult to argue that Cromwell is any kind of copyright control circumvention tool. Cromwell can be downloaded from the Xbox-Linux website on the Sourceforge.net server at `http://xbox-linux.sourceforge.net`.

After burning the Cromwell ROM to your alternate firmware device and installing the device in the Xbox, you will need to burn onto CD/RW media a GNU/Linux install image that you can download from the Xbox-Linux website (again, `http://xbox-linux.sourceforge.net`). This install image comes as a fairly hefty (100+ MB) "ISO" image, compressed using `bzip2`, and it contains all of the software, interfaces and tools necessary for getting a user-friendly GNU/Linux distribution up and running on the Xbox. When burning this ISO image, you must use the "burn image" option in the CD burner software. Do not copy the ISO image onto the CD as a single large file. ISO images are literal bit patterns for a CD, so an ISO image already contains a complete filesystem description. Burning an ISO image as a regular file, instead of as an image, encapsulates the ISO image in a new filesystem, so the ISO just appears as a "bag of bits" instead of a filesystem with files.

You may also need a second disk burned with the boot program for Xbox-Linux. This boot program comes as a smaller ISO image that should be available from the same place that you downloaded the main GNU/Linux install image. This boot image allows you to boot the Linux installation by simply dropping the boot disk into the Xbox, just like starting a game. You can also copy the contents of this disk onto the hard drive using a third-party dashboard and boot Xbox-Linux directly from the hard drive if you prefer not to deal with a separate boot disk.

Burning a good CD/RW image is perhaps one of the trickiest parts of installing Xbox-Linux. The laser used inside the DVD-ROM drive of the Xbox is not well-suited for reading writeable CD media, so the Xbox is very finicky about the kind of media and the kind of burner as well as the burner settings used to create the CD image. Furthermore, the exact details of how the laser is degraded varies from Xbox to Xbox and is dependent upon the model of drive that happened to be installed. Users have found that few Xboxes can reliably read CD-R media, so CD/RW media **must** be used. In addition, it helps to burn the CD/RW media at the slowest burner setting using either a fresh, blank CD/RW, or a CD/RW that has been fully erased (as opposed to the quick erase that just resets the filesystem and does not actually destroy previously written data). Before committing to a particular type of CD/RW media, try using the regular Xbox Dashboard's WMA ripping tools to copy the contents of a CD/RW that you burned with music to the hard drive. If this works reliably and without errors, then you can probably use that kind of CD/RW media for installing Linux. Many Xbox-Linux installation problems have been traced to problems reading data off of the CD/RW drive. At the time of writing, there are no distributions available in hard-pressed CD-ROM media. There is some talk in the Xbox-Linux community of ordering a set of custom CD-ROM images, since this would solve many of the CD/RW headaches that users have been experiencing. Also note that it is possible to install in your Xbox an aftermarket DVD-ROM drive that has better compatibility with writeable CD formats. This possibility is discussed in the previous chapter.

Keep in mind that Xbox-Linux is an active project, and it is constantly evolving. The most up-to-date instructions for installing GNU/Linux on the Xbox can be found at the Sourceforge Xbox-Linux website, and these instructions have been translated into at least a half-dozen languages at the time of writing. If you are interested in contributing your talents to the Xbox-Linux project, there is a list of projects to-do on the Sourceforge Xbox-Linux website as well as some instructions on how to join the developer's mailing list.

"Project B"

There is a work in progress, referred to as "Project B" by the Xbox-Linux developers, to find a way to install and boot Xbox-Linux without any hardware modifications. The Project B moniker comes from the criteria defined for the awarding of a $200,000 prize offered by Michael Robertson, the CEO of Lindows. The "Project A" prize was $100,000 and it has been awarded to the first group to get Linux running on an Xbox with hardware modifications. The remaining $100,000 will be awarded to the individual or group that completes Project B. The asymmetric division of the prize money hints at the challenge of completing Project B. More details on Project B can be found at the Sourceforge Xbox-Linux website at `http://xbox-linux.sourceforge.net/articles.php?aid=2002354043211`.

There are a number of Project B strategies being pursued by various groups. The most conceptually simple approach is to factor the 2048-bit RSA key used to sign Xbox game disks. This approach is being pursued by the Neo Project (`http://www.theneoproject.com`) using a distributed computing approach. Simply put, if the 2048-bit RSA key is factored to reveal Microsoft's private key, anyone can forge Microsoft's digital signature and create bootable game disks for the Xbox, given that Microsoft never removes from the Xbox kernel the ability to load programs from regular CD or CD/RW media. Significantly, Microsoft ships its games on 2-layer DVD-9 format disks with special security structures. The Xbox firmware could be configured by Microsoft to only boot from disks that have this particular structure, regardless of the digital signature check. Since it is currently impossible to burn 2-layer DVDs using a common DVD burner drive, requiring secured DVD-9 media as the only source for executables would present an impairment to distributing Xbox-Linux through free downloads off of the Internet. The other problem with this approach is that the chance of successfully factoring the Xbox's private key through a brute force search is very, very small. Chapter 7, "A Brief Primer on Security", contains a sidebar on "Very Difficult Problems" that attempts to communicate the computational difficulty of this task. If the private key is successfully recovered within a reasonable amount of time by this approach, it will significantly reduce people's confidence in the RSA algorithm. On the other hand, you can never win the lottery if you don't buy a ticket, and running a free distributed factoring client using the spare cycles on your CPU is much cheaper than a Powerball ticket.

Another approach, related to cracking the RSA-2048 bit key, is to modify an existing, signed Xbox executable in a useful manner without changing its cryptographic hash value. Such a constructive hash collision would make the modified executable look identical to the original as far as the digital signature check is concerned. The hash used in the Xbox's digital signature algorithm is SHA-1. SHA-1 is a 160-bit hash with no publicly known algorithmic weaknesses; since the source of the hash is fixed, about 2^{160} random variations would have to be tried to discover a collision. As a side note, you can't use a birthday attack to reduce the difficulty of the attack to 2^{80} random variations because we are not trying to find two messages that hash to the same arbitrary value. The goal is to generate a specific target hash, or perhaps one of a very limited set of target hashes harvested from the set of all published Xbox game titles. Hence, this approach also falls into the category of "Very Difficult Problems".

An alternative approach to Project B is to find security holes in Xbox softwares and use the holes to seize control of the CPU's instruction pointer. To see how this is helpful, consider this example. Suppose a network-based buffer overrun exploit was discovered in a game that can lead to arbitrary code execution. A program running on a PC connected to the Xbox via the network could then use this exploit to send packets to the

Figure 11-1:

The Xbox-Linux core team at the 19th annual Chaos Computer Conference, held in Berlin, Germany. In the back, Michael Steil; in the front, from left to right: Andy Green, Milosch Meriac, and Franz Lehner.

Photograph courtesy of Gerhard Farfeleder.

Xbox that has the effect of installing a simple bootloader for Xbox-Linux. This bootloader could be something as simple as a program that runs code at a designated location on the Xbox's hard drive or on the DVD drive. Note that any port where the Xbox can accept data is a vector for this kind of attack. This includes the USB and network port as well as the hard drive and the DVD-ROM drive. Corrupted save games or file structures can be imaged onto the hard drive or DVD-ROM drive that cause the Xbox to run user-developed code. To Microsoft's credit, all of the network interactions and save game protocols use fairly strong and well-tested security techniques. In addition, I heard at a presentation about the Xbox by Microsoft at MIT that all game code is inspected by a buffer overrun checker and that Microsoft has contractual remedies against game developers that are found guilty of putting deliberate back doors into their game code. This points to the Xbox code base being more secure than a typical Microsoft product, which makes it all the more of an interesting problem for hackers to work on. If you are interested in participating in hacking on the Xbox as a part of "Project B", I encourage you to first check out the Project B Prize Rules web page at `http://xbox-linux.sourceforge.net/articles.php?aid=20030023081956`.

Recently, a buffer overrun exploit was discovered in the way saved games are handled by Electronic Arts' "007: Agent Under Fire" game. The exploit was first divulged by a hacker known simply as "habibi_xbox" on March 29, 2003 through a posting on the XboxHacker.net BBS. Significantly, the

Profile: Milosch Meriac

Can you tell us a little bit about yourself?

My general history is fairly simple. I was born 1976 in Czechoslovakia. My parents (mother teacher, father civil engineer) escaped during cold war to western germany because of repressions by the communist regime. I was about three years old when we arrived in Germany. In German kindergarden I immediately learned the German language. From this point it was really simple - being ten years old, I got my first computer after some months of whining. Things started to roll.

After school leaving exams and a weird intermezzo at German Federal Armed Forces Military Duty i started studying cybernetics and computer science, but i decided after three years to quit university and to concentrate as a long-term objective on my own company. During my studies i established some valuable business connections, so it was easy to work as a freelancer for various companies in Germany. I did some reverse engineering projects, developed realtime embedded linux systems with small footprint, did some lowlevel programming like realtime extensions for windows systems and developed a software based harddisk safeguard for a famous German company. I now live with my Girlfriend in Berlin and we are having a great time there.

continued...

exploit was identified in an undisclosed number of games, but "007: Agent Under Fire" was the only game explicitly named in the posting. The exploit leverages an unchecked string to run a short segment (few hundred bytes) of code that inserts a series of kernel patches. Various measures were included in the design of the hack to make it very difficult to modify the hack to do anything other than run the intended Xbox-Linux target. For example, the hack patches the original Xbox RSA public key, used for verifying digital signatures, with a new public key, while leaving the digital signature check algorithm unpatched. Only the Xbox-Linux bootloader, provided as part of the hack, is appropriately signed with the corresponding new private key. Other hackers would have to factor the new public key in order to use this hack to run other executables. Also, the "007: Agent Under Fire" game itself performs an independent digital signature check on all saved games, so modifying the exploit code in the hacked savegame file is not trivial. The inclusion of such security measures in the hack is a laudable decision on the part of the hack's implementer, as it helps ensure that the hack is not directly useful for applications such as piracy. Implementing security measures that protect Microsoft's interests may help save the Xbox-Linux project from the wrath of Microsoft and the U.S. Department of Justice.

Looking forward, the success of Project B could spell either a new age for Xbox hacking, or the demise of Xbox hacking. Even though Project B hackers have demonstrated social conscience and good will by trying to

Why do you hack?

After getting more experienced in programming I started to discover that the beautiful and bright entity of the computer world is in fact a fragile patchwork.

In the beginning hacking was like a game for me. You could walk around inside your computer system discovering worlds of new code and possibilities every single day. Occasionally one could challenge the application authors to a duel by trying to analyse and circumvent their copy protections. Sometimes it was like playing chess, some other times it was like a deathmatch.

On one hand I was excited to see my knowledge growing and on the other hand it was naturally a great ego boost for a 14 year old child to circumvent security systems of overpaid godlike hardcore programmers. During my senior high school time I revised this view - while programming tools and applications for some local companies during school vacations I met some genuine programmers - and got disappointed: they were neither gods, nor godlike.

After some time i realized that writing a cool demo, hacking application X or finding a nifty hack for Y doesn't change the world more than a sack of rice toppling down somewhere in china. So I started choosing my realms more wisely - technologies of everyday life like telephones, computers, networks and satellites. I found out that one has the power

continued...

Profile: Milosch Meriac, continued...

to change things by explaining technology to average users or by helping companies to secure their products.

Today I am aware of my power as whitehat hacker. Every person in todays life is affected by information technologies: Surveillance techniques, Data mining, Information Warfare, Digital Millenium Copyright Act, TCPA, Digital Rights Management, new interpretations of Copyright and Patent law are growing like mushrooms after monsoon rain. Like in my past I ache to peek behind this beautiful and bright entities - and hopefully find the bugs and traps before they find us.

Can you tell us about your experience with the Xbox-Linux project?

I joined the Xbox Linux project and helped to get the kernel running – this was tricky, because the Xbox architecture has some traps and differences compared to a personal computer. I created the early Linux distributions for Microsoft's Xbox. This was important because we had only 1 MB flash available to store the complete distribution and the kernel - and the harddisk wasn't unlocked yet. I also provided a console driver for Andy Green's filtror device, so we were able to see the kernel boot messages and got a linux console by using his device as some sort remote interface. This distribution already included network drivers, soundcard drivers, mp3 support, a telnet server, webserver, NFS support and a broad range of standard linux tools. This enabled us to get rid of our custom-made hardware and allowed hundreds of people to join the project, either as code contributors or as test persons. We had no screen output yet, so I added a framebuffer interface to the Xbox Linux kernel and made many other contributions.

The number of contributing developers started to grow enormously. We get awesome help from all over the world to make Xbox Linux possible – some stay hidden because they are afraid of legal uncertainties like the DMCA in United States - others can contribute freely.

Do you have any other comments you would like to share?

Some people may ask why full-grown people like me fiddle about with this Xbox toy. Every person certainly has his own reasons - my reason is to improve my skills and to learn more about recent technologies. The Microsoft Xbox for instance is the predecessor of a TCPA/Palladium protected computer - with all the technical and social implications. It's a fine playground for my research on more secure computer systems without pressing users.

One of the main reasons is our community. It's really fun and a great pleasure to work together with all this bright geeks - online and especially offline in a pub with pints of fine beer. I am amazed every day by the growing strength of our community. Thanks to all for making this possible!

protect Microsoft's interests, it is impossible to prevent less scrupulous hackers from reverse engineering the hack and eventually figuring out how to reproduce the technique in some less Microsoft-friendly form. The end result could either be a harsh crackdown by Microsoft upon all hacking activity, or Microsoft exiting the video game business altogether since their revenue stream would be cut off like Sega's in the Dreamcast piracy debacle. Or, Microsoft could just elect to plow more money into the business and release a redesigned console that incorporates patches and countermeasures for known security holes. The outcome will depend heavily upon how events unfold in the next few months. However, with deep price cuts on the horizon for the Xbox and rumors of a thoroughly redesigned "shrink" version of the console floating around, it seems that Microsoft's near-term strategy is to focus its energies on storming the market instead of stemming fair-use or piracy. After all, every Playstation2 or Gamecube sold probably has a worse effect on Microsoft's business than every Xbox converted to run GNU/Linux, or even an Xbox converted to run pirated games.

OpenXDK

Many interesting and useful projects for the Xbox, such as the XboxMediaPlayer and MAME-X (Multiple Arcade Machine Emulator for the Xbox), have been developed for the native Xbox gaming platform. Unfortunately, these programs were developed using unauthorized versions of the Microsoft Xbox SDK (Software Development Kit). Microsoft's Xbox SDK is supposed to be available only to approved, licensed developers. However, the SDK was leaked even before the console was launched, and since then many have used the leaked Xbox SDK for creating their own Xbox programs. While the proprietary Xbox SDK is convenient and easy to use, it is also technically illegal to use. The lack of a legal SDK for the native Xbox platform makes it difficult to attract a large base of open-source developers.

The OpenXDK project was created to address the need for a legal alternative to the Xbox SDK. OpenXDK's stated goal is to create a legal development kit for creating Xbox Executables (XBEs). OpenXDK will allow users to create native XBE files that, when signed with the appropriate digital signature, could run on a vanilla Xbox. Since this appropriate digital signature is as of yet unknown, this work is done in anticipation of a legal technology that enables interoperability with programs developed using the OpenXDK. Despite its utility, the OpenXDK project is still in its nascence and is looking for developers. More about the OpenXDK project can be found at `http://openxdk.sourceforge.net`. OpenXDK's project managers are Dan Johnson (also known as SiliconIce, the creator of the XboxHacker BBS) and Aaron Robinson, (also known as caustik; caustik is also leading the CXBX executable relinker and the CXBE Xbox emulator projects).

CHAPTER 12

Caveat Hacker

Reverse engineering and intellectual property law has some tricky legal interactions. On one hand, innovation deserves its just reward. The right of inventors or authors to exclusively produce or sell the fruits of their labor must be protected. On the other hand, a free and competitive market place is also required to preserve innovation and to ensure fair markets. The study of the design principles embodied in existing products and the ability to produce improved derivative products are an important part of a competitive market place.

This chapter provides an overview of intellectual property law, and some of the more important bits that you need to know about as a hacker. Ignorance is not a valid defense, and there are some severe penalties prescribed by the law for those who ignore the laws that govern reverse engineering and intellectual property rights. Some acts of intellectual property violation are punishable as felonies along with hefty fines.

The majority of this chapter was written by Lee Tien, a Senior Staff Attorney with the Electronic Frontier Foundation. Lee (and Joseph Liu) were my counsel during the period when I was trying to publish my findings on the Xbox security system. Chapter 6 has a sidebar titled "The Legal Challenges of Hacking" that describes my fight with MIT to get my paper published.

The content of this chapter is presented with the intention of providing an informational resource for hackers. If you think you may be in a legally compromising situation, there is no substitute for contacting an attorney and getting proper legal advice on your specific situation.

Profile: Lee Tien

Lee Tien is a Senior Staff Attorney with the Electronic Frontier Foundation, specializing in free speech law, including intersections with intellectual property law and privacy law. Before joining EFF, Lee was a sole practitioner specializing in Freedom of Information Act (FOIA) litigation. Mr. Tien has published articles on children's sexuality and information technology, anonymity, surveillance, and the First Amendment status of publishing computer software. Lee received his undergraduate degree in psychology from Stanford University, where he was very active in journalism at the Stanford Daily. After working as a news reporter at the Tacoma News Tribune for a year, Lee went to law school at Boalt Hall, University of California at Berkeley. Lee also did graduate work in the Program in Jurisprudence and Social Policy at UC-Berkeley. [1]

The Electronic Frontier Foundation

The Electronic Frontier Foundation (EFF) provided me legal counsel during the period when I was trying to publish my paper on the Xbox security system. The following paragraphs introduce what the EFF does, and who they are.

Imagine a world where technology can empower us all to share knowledge, ideas, thoughts, humor, music, words and art with friends, strangers and future generations.

That world is here and now, made possible with the electronic network — the Internet — with the power to connect us all. And future developments in technology will enable us to access information and communicate with others in even more powerful ways.

But governments and corporate interests worldwide are trying to prevent us from communicating freely through new technologies, just as when those in positions of power controlled the production and distribution of — or even burned — books they did not want people to read in the Middle Ages. But only by fighting for our rights to speak freely whatever the medium — whether books, telephones, or computers — can we protect and enhance the human condition.

The Electronic Frontier Foundation (EFF) was created to defend our rights to think, speak, and share our ideas, thoughts, and needs using new technologies, such as the Internet and the World Wide Web. EFF is the first to identify threats to our basic rights online and to advocate on behalf of free expression in the digital age.

Based in San Francisco, EFF is a donor-supported membership organization working to protect our fundamental rights regardless of technology; to educate the press, policymakers and the general public about civil liberties issues related to

continued...

technology; and to act as a defender of those liberties. Among our various activities, EFF opposes misguided legislation, initiates and defends court cases preserving individuals' rights, launches global public campaigns, introduces leading edge proposals and papers, hosts frequent educational events, engages the press regularly, and publishes a comprehensive archive of digital civil liberties information at one of the most linked-to websites in the world: http://www.eff.org.[2]

[1] From the EFF website, http://www.eff.org/homes/lee_tien.html

[2] From the EFF website, http://www.eff.org/abouteff.html

Caveat Hacker: A Primer on Intellectual Property by Lee Tien

Reverse engineering is the process of extracting know-how or knowledge from an artifact; in the marketplace, it's been called the "time-honored technique of figuring out just what makes a competitor's product tick."[1] But anyone who studies mass-marketed products today should be aware of the legal minefield surrounding reverse-engineering. The anti-circumvention provisions of the Digital Millennium Copyright Act (DMCA),[2] contractual terms prohibiting reverse-engineering, and the Economic Espionage Act[3] are a few of the dangerous legal areas that technologists should know about. This chapter will briefly survey these areas to give hackers a rough idea of the issues.

There are two general issues here. First, is the reverse engineering lawful? Second, even if you may reverse engineer the product, can you publish what you learn from the reverse engineering?

Classical Intellectual Property Law: An Overview

Intellectual property law traditionally meant copyrights and patents. Both are created and limited by federal statutes based on the Constitution's intellectual property clause: "Congress shall have the Power . . . To promote the Progress of Science and useful Arts, by securing for limited Times to Authors and Inventors the exclusive Right to their respective Writings and

[1] Joel Miller, *Reverse Engineering: Fair Game or Foul?*, IEEE Spectrum, Apr. 1993, at 64, 64.

[2] 17 U.S.C. § 1201-1204.

[3] 18 U.S.C. § 1831-39.

Discoveries."[4] Computer programs are typically protected as copyrighted "literary works," but they can also be patented.[5]

People have recently come to think of trade secrets as another kind of intellectual property. Trade secrets were originally protected by courts under case law, but they are now the subject of both state and federal states as well. Unlike copyrights and patents, trade secrecy law is historically grounded in unfair competition principles.

In the United States, authors and inventors don't have "natural rights."[6] Instead, their rights are based on a notion of public welfare. Society will benefit if authors and inventors get some protection, because they won't have adequate incentives to create if others can freely use their work. But that protection is limited in order to assure that the public ultimately benefits.[7] For example, copyright and patent rights are only for "limited times"; eventually, protected works must enter the public domain.[8] In short, intellectual property law sets the terms for a "bargain" between the public and authors or inventors.

Copyright

Copyright law protects original works of expression that are "fixed" in a tangible medium and gives the author (or assignee) exclusive rights over reproduction, distribution, adaptation, public display and public performance of the work. It does not protect against independent creation.

Works are not the same as copies or phonorecords (copies of sound recordings). When you buy a book, you own a copy, but the copyright owner retains the rights to the work itself. Note, by the way, that the "first sale" doctrine allows lawful owners of copies to sell or transfer these lawfully owned copies,[9] with certain exceptions.[10]

There are many different types of works, with many different rules for each

---

[4] U.S. Const. Art. I, §8, cl. 8. When the Constitution was written, the word "science" was often used as a synonym for "knowledge."

[5] See *Diamond v. Diehr*, 450 U.S. 175 (1981); *In re Alappat*, 33 F.3d 1526 (Fed. Cir. 1994).

[6] In Europe, copyright has traditionally been viewed as protecting an inherent inalienable personal right of the creator of a work.

[7] " The economic philosophy behind the clause empowering Congress to grant patents and copyrights is the conviction that encouragement of individual effort by personal gain is the best way to advance public welfare through the talents of authors and inventors in 'Science and useful Arts.'" *Mazer v. Stein*, 347 U.S. 201, 219 (1954).

[8] *Feist Publications, Inc. v. Rural Tel. Serv. Co.*, 499 U.S. 340, 348-49 (1991) ("This result is neither unfair nor unfortunate. It is the means by which copyright advances the progress of science and art.").

type. So copyright law is quite complex, and technology hasn't simplified matters. Consider a copyrighted song. The song or musical composition (MC) is protected by copyright, typically held by the songwriter. To record the song, one needs permission from the MC copyright owner.[11] Once recorded, there is an independent copyright in the sound recording (SR), which protects the actual recorded sounds including the singer's interpretation of the underlying song as well as the efforts of the producer and sound engineers. Record companies usually own SR copyrights. As a result, if you want to use a copyrighted sound recording of the song in a TV commercial, you need permission of both the MC copyright owner and the SR copyright owner.

Most of the copyright owner's rights are fairly obvious, but some of them are not — especially when computers are involved. For instance, computers load programs into RAM, creating a copy for copyright purposes. The copyright act contains a specific exemption that permits the owner of a copy of a computer program to copy the program into computer memory.[12] This illustrates the general strictness of copyright law: that one can't use a copyrighted work for its intended purpose without making a copy doesn't mean that making the copy isn't copyright infringement. The implications of this strictness for the Internet are serious, since Internet dissemination generally involves the making of copies.

The right over adaptation can also be confusing. Adaptations, or "derivative works," are works based on a copyrighted work: foreign-language translations, movies based on books, and so on. In one much-criticized case, a court found that cutting pictures out of lawfully owned copies and mounting the pictures onto ceramic tiles created infringing derivative works.[13] Most courts disagree with this result.[14]

---

[9] See 17 U.S.C. Sec. 109. "The whole point of the first sale doctrine is that once the copyright owner places a copyrighted item in the stream of commerce by selling it, he has exhausted his exclusive statutory right to control its distribution." *Quality King v. L'Anza Research Int'l*, 523 U.S. 135, ___ (1998).

[10] For instance, phonorecords and stand-alone computer programs are treated differently than books under Sec. 109.

[11] Under current copyright law, the MC reproduction copyright is controlled by compulsory license provisions, which means that you automatically get permission by paying a statutory rate.

[12] 17 U.S.C. § 117 (permitting making of copy or adaptation copy or adaptation "as an essential step in the utilization of the computer program in conjunction with a machine.").

[13] *Mirage Editions, Inc. v. Albuquerque A.R.T. Co.*, 856 F.2d 1341, 1344 (9th Cir. 1988), cert. denied, 489 U.S. 1018 (1989).

[14] See, e.g., *Lee v. Deck The Walls, Inc.*, 925 F. Supp. 576 (N.D. Ill. 1996), aff'd sub nom. *Lee v. A.R.T. Co.*, 125 F.3d 580 (7th Cir. 1997) (rejecting reasoning of *Mirage Editions*); *Precious Moments, Inc. v. La Infantil, Inc.*, 971 F. Supp. 66, 68-69 (D.P.R. 1997) (denying claim against one who purchased fabric and then incorporated it into bedding); *Paramount Pictures Corp. v. Video Broadcasting Sys., Inc.*, 724 F. Supp. 808 (D. Kan. 1989) (distribution claim barred by first sale doctrine, distinguishing *Mirage Editions*).

Copyright protection begins automatically when a work is created and generally lasts for the life of the author plus 70 years.[15] Works become free for all to use, i.e., enter the public domain, once the copyright term expires.

There are many exceptions to copyright. The rule that copyright protects expression means that it doesn't bar anyone from using the ideas or facts revealed in the work. "Ideas" includes the plots of stories. More generally, copyright doesn't protect the utilitarian aspects of a work, so you can write a computer program that does the same thing as another program so long as you don't copy its expression.

Facts are considered "outside" copyright because they are discovered, not authored. This would include, for instance, the discovery of new prime numbers. But you can have a copyright in the selection, sequence or arrangement of facts or anything else that is not itself copyrightable. The classic example is an anthology of public-domain poetry. You can have a copyright to the compilation even though the individual pieces are unprotected if the selection, sequence or arrangement is sufficiently original. The alphabetical arrangement of facts in the typical telephone "white pages" directory fails the constitutional originality requirement. You don't get any protection merely because you invested money, time or effort into collecting the phone numbers.

Copyright doesn't cover many "ordinary" uses of the work. In itself, reading a book isn't subject to copyright, because it doesn't infringe any of the copyright owner's rights. Singing a song in the shower is a performance, but the copyright owner only has a right over public performances. Here again, however, the Internet has changed things. When you read a document in your web browser, a copy of the document was probably made by your computer. Thus, many formerly ordinary uses now entail the making of a copy, which raises copyright issues.

Today, there's a lot of controversy about "fair use." Fair use is a defense to copyright infringement that was intended to allow people to make some unauthorized use of copyrighted works. Fair use allows book reviewers to quote from books. It's a very complicated area of law; whether a use is "fair" depends on factors like the purpose, nature, amount, and economic effect of the use.[16]

Patent

Patent law protects inventions and gives the inventor (or his assignee) the right to exclude others from making, selling, or using the invention for 20 years from the date of the filing of the patent. Unlike copyright, patent law protects against independent invention by another person.

The bargain here is that in return for the patent, the inventor must provide enough information in the patent application to enable one "skilled in the

[15] Under the first copyright act, protection lasted for only 14 years.

[16] 17 U.S.C. § 107

art" to create the invention without much experimentation. Once a patent is awarded, the application is made public. By making the information public, the patentee contributes to society's store of knowledge.

A patent confers no affirmative rights, however; if you patent an improvement to someone else's invention, you can't practice the improvement without infringing on the underlying patent. If you invent and patent a new drug, you may still need regulatory approval before you can sell the drug.

To be patentable, an invention must be useful, novel, and "nonobvious" to one "skilled in the art." The novelty and nonobviousness requirements mean that the invention must be a sufficient development in technology before the right to exclude is given. Developments that do not meet these high standards are denied protection.

Trade Secrets

A third area of law — trade secrecy — is also considered part of intellectual property law, although it is not really property. A trade secret is commercially valuable business or other information known to the user but not to competitors. Secrecy, although not absolute secrecy, is the essence of a trade secret; one must take reasonable precautions to protect the trade secret against disclosure.

There's an obvious relationship between patents and trade secrets, because both protect useful information. If the useful information isn't patentable at all, there's no choice. But one might not want patent a patentable invention for several reasons. You might not want to disclose information in the patent application. Also, if you don't expect the technology to be valuable for very long, it might not be worth getting a patent that lasts 20 years.

The main downside of trade secrecy is that it provides no protection against independent invention or against reverse-engineering. Trade secrecy is therefore unwise if the secret can be figured out from the product. If, on the other hand, the invention is a process used in making the product, it might be hard to reverse-engineer. Even though Coca-Cola has been on the market for many years, apparently no one has figured out how to duplicate it.

The Constitutional Copyright Bargain

Intellectual property rights are a means to an end — to promote the progress of knowledge and technology. As the Supreme Court once said, "the monopoly privileges that Congress may authorize are neither unlimited nor primarily designed to provide a special private benefit."[17]

[17] *Sony v. Universal City Studios* 464 U.S. 417, 429 & 432 (1984).

The above passage indicates that intellectual property law has long been concerned about limiting the potential monopoly power conferred by copyright and patent law. For instance, the first-sale doctrine prevents patent and copyright owners from controlling the market once patented products or copies of copyrighted works are sold.

Also, copyright law has long been interpreted by courts and crafted by Congress to preserve a balance with freedom of speech. Doctrines like the idea/expression dichotomy, the fair use doctrine, and copyright's limited term are generally viewed as reducing the potential conflict between copyright and freedom of expression.[18]

Interestingly, concern about monopolies is historically linked to the concern for free speech. English copyright law had long functioned as a kind of state-sponsored cartel; in return for private monopolies over writings, the publishers agreed to act as policemen of the press in the service of government censorship — in particular, the Bible and other religious works.[19]

Similarly, copyright law's idea-expression dichotomy ensures that uncopyrightable facts and ideas and unpatentable functional principles remain in the public domain for future creators to build on.

The Traditional View of Reverse Engineering

Historically, reverse engineering has always been a lawful way to gain information embodied in mass-marketed products. For many technology firms, reverse-engineering competitors' products to study their innovations is a standard practice. Indeed, U.S. courts have also treated reverse engineering as an important factor in maintaining balance in intellectual property law, and the Supreme Court has called reverse engineering "an essential part of innovation."

The law recognizes three main purposes of legitimate reverse engineering. Competitive reverse-engineering is intended to create a direct substitute. Compatibility or interoperability reverse-engineering is aimed at figuring out how to make a product that works with the reverse-engineered product. And of course, researchers often reverse-engineer products in order to gain knowledge with no commercial purpose.

Trade Secrecy and "Improper Means"

In general, a trade secret is misappropriated only if a person or firm misuses or discloses the secret in breach of an agreement or confidential relationship,

---

[18] See generally Neil Weinstock Netanel, *Locating Copyright Within the First Amendment Skein*, 54 Stan. L. Rev. 1 (2001).

[19] See generally L. Ray Patterson, *Free Speech, Copyright, and Fair Use*, 40 Vand. L. Rev. 1 (1987).

engages in other wrongful conduct (e.g., bribery, coercion, trespass) to obtain the secret, or acquires the secret from a misappropriator knowing or having reason to know that the information was a misappropriated trade secret.

Most states, like California, explicitly provide that reverse engineering is a lawful way to acquire a trade secret. Several reasons support reverse engineering as a sound principle of trade secret law.[20] Buying a product in the open market generally gives the buyer personal property rights in the product, which include the right to take the product apart, measure it, subject it to testing, and the like. The law also regards sale of a product in the open market as a publication of innovations it embodies and a dedication of them to the public domain unless the creator has obtained patent protection for them.

The vulnerability of trade secrets to reverse engineering is part of the overall constitutional scheme. In *Bonito Boats v. Thunder Craft Boats*, the Supreme Court struck down a Florida law that forbade manufacturers of boats from using existing boat parts as "plugs" for a direct molding process that yielded competing products because the law "prohibit[ed] the entire public from engaging in a form of reverse engineering of a product in the public domain."[21] The court explained that reverse engineering is "an essential part of innovation," likely to yield variations on the product that "could lead to significant advances in technology." Indeed, "the competitive reality of reverse engineering may act as a spur to the inventor" to develop additional patentable ideas.

In cases like *Bonito Boats*, the question is whether a state law is "preempted" by federal law. When federal and state law conflict, either directly or as a matter of federal policy goals, the state law loses under the doctrine of "conflict" preemption. This stems from the Constitution's Supremacy Clause, under which federal law generally trumps state law.[22] Copyright law also contains a specific preemption clause, discussed below.

Copyright Law and the Problem of Intermediate Copying

Until recently, copyright law didn't need to worry about reverse engineering, because there was little reason to reverse engineer books, art, or music. Now that computer programs are "literary works," things are much different. Since many computer programs are distributed only in object code, the reverse engineering process commonly requires an initial decompilation into source code — which entails making a copy.

---

[20] See generally Pamela Samuelson & Suzanne Scotchmer, *The Law and Economics of Reverse Engineering*, 111 Yale L. J. 1575 (2002).

[21] The Court went on to say that "(w)here an item in general circulation is unprotected by a patent, '(r)eproduction of a functional attribute is legitimate competitive activity.'"

[22] U.S. Const. art. VI, cl. 2.

U.S. courts have found that copyright law does not necessarily prohibit reverse-engineering, because copying incidental to reverse engineering can be a "fair use": "The Copyright Act permits an individual in rightful possession of a copy of a work to undertake necessary efforts to understand the work's ideas, processes, and methods of operation."[23] This can be true even when the ultimate goal of the reverse engineering is commercial. The courts generally rely on the Constitutional purpose for copyright protection: "the promotion of 'the Progress of Science….'" [24] The fair use doctrine advances this Constitutional objective by "encourag[ing] others to build freely upon the ideas and information conveyed by a work."[25]

The key case here was *Sega Enterprises Ltd. v. Accolade, Inc.*[26] Accolade disassembled Sega game programs in order to get information necessary to make its games compatible with the Sega Genesis game console. Accolade then sold its own games in competition with games made by Sega and its licensed developers. Accolade raised a fair use defense to Sega's claims that the disassembly copies were infringing. The court accepted Accolade's defense for the reasons described above. It also noted that if Accolade could not dissassemble Sega's code, Sega would get "a de facto monopoly over [the unprotected] ideas and functional concepts [in the program]," which is only available under patent law.[27]

The court's holding, however, was limited to reverse engineering undertaken for a "legitimate reason," such as to gain access to the functional specifications necessary to make a compatible program, and then only if it "provides the only means of access to those elements of the code that are not protected by copyright."[28]

Patent Law

There is no general fair use defense or reverse-engineering exemption in patent law. In theory, you shouldn't need to reverse-engineer a patented product, because the patent specification should inform the relevant technical community of the best way to make the invention.

Some reverse engineering activities will not infringe a patent. The buyer of a machine embodying a patented invention, for example, is generally free to disassemble it to study how it works under patent law's first-sale principle. Buying the product means that you have the right to use it, and simply studying it doesn't infringe the patent owner's exclusive rights to make or sell the invention. Nevertheless, courts sometimes enforce contractual restrictions on reverse engineering.[29]

---

[23] *Atari Games Corp. v. Nintendo*, 975 F.2d 832, 842 (Fed. Cir. 1992); *see Sony Computer Ent. Corp. v. Connectix Corp.*, 203 F.3d 596 (9th Cir. 2000).

[24] Id., quoting U.S. Const. Art. I, §8, cl. 8.

[25] *Feist Publications, Inc., v. Rural Telephone Serv. Co., Inc.*, 499 U.S. 340, 350 (1991).

[26] 977 F.2d 1510 (9th Cir. 1992).

[27] Id. at 1526-1527.

[28] Id. at 1518.

Also, one who tries to make a patented invention to satisfy scientific curiosity may have an "experimental use" defense. Under U.S. law, this defense is narrow and probably does not include research uses that may lead to development of a patentable invention or a commercial product.[30]

The clash between these three areas can be seen if we look again at the *Sega* situation. Suppose Sega had a patent on an algorithm used in all of its game programs. By disassembling Sega programs, Accolade arguably "makes" or "uses" the patented algorithm, even if it did so inadvertently. In short, the intermediate copying problem reappears in the patent context.

New Challenges for Reverse Engineers

The importance of reverse engineering has only grown with the rise of commercial cryptography in mass-marketed products, because it is impossible to make systems more secure without trying to break them. Ironically, the growing use of encryption has contributed to laws against reverse engineering. The entertainment industry, for example, now relies on encryption and other technologies to protect digital information like music on CDs and movies on DVDs against unauthorized copying. Unsurprisingly, new laws have been enacted to prevent people from "circumventing" encryption and other forms of security.

Legal encroachments to reverse engineering haven't been limited to encryption. In the 1970s and 1980s some states forbade the use of a direct molding process to reverse-engineer boat hulls.[31] In the late 1970s and early 1980s, the semiconductor industry sought and obtained legislation to protect chip layouts from reverse engineering to make clone chips.[32] A major international agreement on intellectual property rights says nothing

[29] See *Pioneer Hi-Bred Int'l, Inc. v. DeKalb Genetics Corp.*, 51 U.S.P.Q.2d (BNA) 1797 (S.D. Iowa 1999) (enforcing a "bag tag" prohibiting purchasers of PVPA-protected corn seed from using the seed for breeding or research purposes).

[30] See *Roche Prod. v. Bolar Pharmaceutical Co.*, 733 F.2d 858, 858-63 (Fed. Cir. 1984) (defense does not permit "unlicensed experiments conducted with a view to the adaptation of the patented invention to the experimentor's business," as opposed to experiments conducted "for amusement, to satisfy idle curiosity, or for strictly philosophical inquiry"); Rebecca S. Eisenberg, *Patents and the Progress of Science: Exclusive Rights and Experimental Use*, 56 U. Chi. L. Rev. 1017, 1023 (1989).

[31] These state laws were struck down by the Supreme Court in *Bonito Boats*.

[32] Semiconductor Chip Protection Act, Pub. L. No. 98-620, 98 Stat. 3347 (1984) (codified at 17 U.S.C. § § 901-914 (1994)). We will not discuss this statute except to note that it contains a specific reverse-engineering privilege that permits the copying of protected chip designs in order to study the layouts of circuits, and also the incorporation of know-how discerned from reverse engineering in a new chip. Interestingly, reverse engineers must engage in enough "forward engineering" to develop an original chip design that itself qualifies for SCPA protection.

about reverse engineering.[33]

The Digital Millennium Copyright Act and the Problem of Unauthorized Access

The DMCA is one of the most important laws that now regulate reverse engineering. One part of the DMCA — its "anti-circumvention" provisions — gives legal protection to technical measures that effectively control access to or prevent copying of a copyrighted work. Unfortunately, the DMCA is extremely complex; for instance, the DMCA makes it unlawful to bypass "effective technical protection measures" without clearly specifying what that term means.

Unauthorized Access

The DMCA essentially creates a new right of "access" for copyright owners. Spokesmen for the copyright industry liken the act of circumventing a technical protection system to "breaking and entering" a home.

One simple example is censorware programs used by schools and libraries to prevent children from viewing inappropriate images. These programs often contain encrypted "blacklists" of censored websites, which vendors typically treat as trade secrets. Suppose a researcher finds that a particular program blocks sites that are wholly appropriate for children, and wants to read the blacklist in order to figure out how many appropriate websites are being wrongly blocked.[34] Because the vendor has encrypted the blacklist in order to prevent people from gaining access to its content, and the list is arguably a copyrighted compilation of facts, the encryption is a technical protection measure applied to a copyrighted work and unauthorized decryption would be an unlawful act of circumvention — except that the DMCA currently has a temporary exemption for decrypting censorware blacklists.

Another example: the movie industry uses an encryption scheme called Content Scrambling System (CSS) to protect movies on DVDs. In the *2600* case,[35] CSS was held to be a technical measure that "effectively" controls access to movies. Bypassing CSS without the copyright owner's authorization is an unlawful "act of circumvention" under the DMCA. Note that the courts have not found that the fair use doctrine applies to the DMCA (as opposed to copyright law). Thus, if the use of CSS prevents you from fast-

---

[33] Agreement on Trade-Related Aspects of Intellectual Property Rights (TRIPS), Apr. 15, 1994, Marrakesh Agreement Establishing the World Trade Organization, Annex 1C, Legal Instruments—Results of the Uruguay Round vol. 31, 33 I.L.M. 81 (1994). The trade secrecy provision of the TRIPS Agreement is Article 39, 33 I.L.M. at 98.

[34] See, e.g., http://www.sethf.com.

[35] *Universal City Studios v. Reimerdes*, 111 F.Supp. 294 (S.D.N.Y. 2000), *aff'd* 273 F.3d 429 (2d Cir. 2001).

forwarding through the commercials on a DVD movie – it is still unlawful to "circumvent" that restriction.

Note here that the notion of "effective" here is not connected to cryptographic efficacy. Even weak encryption is "effective" under the DMCA because the ordinary person could not defeat it.

Circumvention Technologies

The DMCA protects technical measures in a second way: its "anti-device" provisions outlaw the manufacture and distribution of technologies that enable circumvention.[36] Continuing the "breaking and entering" metaphor, spokesmen for the copyright industry liken circumvention technologies to "burglars' tools," which are illegal in many states.

Section 1201 of the DMCA states that "[n]o person shall manufacture, import, offer to the public, provide, or otherwise traffic in any technology, product, service, device, component, or part thereof" if it has one or more of the following three characteristics: (1) if it is "primarily designed or produced for the purpose of circumventing [technical] protection," (2) if it has "only limited commercially significant purpose or use other than to circumvent [technical] protection," or (3) if it is "marketed by that person or another acting on its behalf with that person's knowledge for use in circumventing technical protection."

Note that these provisions apply not only to the new right of "access control," but to the rights of copyright owners generally. Thus, technologies that would circumvent copy-protection measures for CDs can be unlawful under these provisions.

Recall the two examples just given. In the *2600* case, at issue was the DeCSS program, which enables people to decrypt DVD movies protected by CSS. DeCSS was found to be a prohibited circumvention technology. In the censorware example, the DMCA exemption permits the act of decryption, but it says nothing about whether a censorware researcher can make available the computer program used to decrypt the encrypted blacklist, or even the details of the method of decryption.

Navigating the DMCA's Exemptions

Just as you can't reverse-engineer object code without decompiling or dissassembling it, you can't reverse-engineer a technical protection measure without circumventing it. Moreover, you often need a technological device or tool to actually perform reverse engineering, so the ban on circumvention technologies also restricts reverse engineering.

[36] The DMCA covers two different kinds of technologies based on what they protect: technologies that "effectively control access to (copyrighted) works," Sec. 1201(a)(2) and technologies that "effectively protect() a right of a copyright owner . . . in a work or a portion thereof." Sec. 1201(b)(1).

In combination, these DMCA provisions create major barriers to cryptographers and security researchers who want to analyze the security measures used in real, mass-marketed products. A commercial reverse engineer who discovers a problem with another firm's technical measure and offers suggestions about how to improve it is at risk of being indicted on criminal DMCA charges.

Even an academic reverse engineer is at risk of being sued for publishing a paper about the weaknesses in a firm's security measures, because such a paper could be labeled a "tool of circumvention."[37] One example is Princeton professor Edward Felten, who assembled and entered a team of scientists in the music industry's "SDMI Challenge," a contest to crack digital watermarking and other technologies being considered by the Secure Digital Music Initiative for protecting digital music. Felten and his team entered the contest with the intent of using the SDMI Challenge as a real-world security case study, and they eventually authored a peer-reviewed academic paper that was to be presented at a conference. Before the paper was actually presented, the Recording Industry Association of America (RIAA) sent Felten and the conference organizers a letter warning him that publishing the paper would violate intellectual property laws, including the DMCA.

The DMCA also contains several exemptions relevant to reverse engineering: circumvention of a technical protection system when necessary to achieve interoperability among computer programs; circumventions conducted in the course of legitimate encryption research; and circumvention for purposes of computer security testing. Unfortunately, each of these exemptions is both complex and narrow. Even when the act of reverse-engineering is allowed, the DMCA strictly regulates what can be done with the resulting information.

1201(f): reverse-engineering for interoperability

This exemption allows the circumvention of technical protection measures for interoperability reverse engineering. It also allows, to a very limited extent, the dissemination of information gained from reverse-engineering. Note that 1201(f) would not have exempted Felten's attack on the SDMI watermarks, because it had no relation to interoperability.

The *2600* case, mentioned earlier, concerns the publication of a computer program known as "DeCSS" on the website of 2600 Magazine. DeCSS can be used to bypass CSS, the technical protection measure used to control access to DVD movies. EFF, which represented 2600 Magazine, argued that DeCSS qualifies for the interoperability privilege of 1201(f). DeCSS was designed, we argued, to enable people to build software that would enable them to play legitimately purchased DVD movies on their platform of choice, namely, Linux computer systems.

The courts rejected this argument, saying that 1201(f) only permitted circumvention for purposes of achieving program-to-program

[37] While this seems odd, consider that many academic papers in the security include computer program code.

interoperability, whereas DeCSS enabled program-to-data interoperability that 1201(f) did not cover. This ruling is dubious, because there are computer programs as well as data on movie DVDs.

While 1201(f) seems to follow *Sega* in permitting interoperability reverse-engineering, it is more restrictive in several ways: interoperability is the only legitimate purpose for which reverse engineering may be done; only program-to-program interoperability qualifies, even though circumvention may be needed to achieve hardware-to-program interoperability or program-to-data interoperability; and the information resulting from reverse engineering cannot be freely published.

1201(g): encryption research

The DMCA also contains an express exemption for encryption research. Unfortunately, it is also very narrow. For one thing, this exception only applies if the cryptographer has asked (even if he or she has not received) permission from the copyright owner to engage in an act of circumvention before the circumvention is accomplished. Second, the statute emphasizes the need for a cryptographer to be an expert in order to qualify for this exemption, even though some of the most brilliant minds in the field of cryptology lack formal training. Third, the statute permits a cryptanalyst to make tools to bypass access controls, but is silent on whether tools to bypass use or copy controls are permissible (that is, it contains an exception to one but not both of the anti-device rules). Fourth, it regulates the cryptologist's ability to disseminate the results of decryption.

Consider again Prof. Felten's SDMI research: it would not be exempted by 1201(g) because digital watermarks are not encryption.

1201(j): security research

The DMCA's security research exemption has a similar structure: it applies only if the tester asks in advance and likewise allows making tools only to bypass access controls, not copy or use controls. Like 1201(g), it too regulates the tester's dissemination of the results of the testing.

Even in this narrow form, it is not clear whether Felten's research would be covered. Sec. 1201(j) only permits making a tool to bypass an access control. Is a digital watermark an access control or a copy control? The answer to this question depends to a large extent on how the watermark is used. EFF argued that, as contemplated by the RIAA, the SDMI watermark technologies were both access and copy control technologies.

End-user License Agreements and Contractual Prohibitions on Reverse-Engineering

Intellectual property isn't the only obstacle to reverse engineering. It's common for software licenses to prohibit reverse engineering. A typical license clause might say: "You may not, and you may not permit others to,

(a) disassemble, decompile or otherwise derive source code from the Software, (b) reverse engineer the Software, (c) modify or prepare derivative works of the Software, (d) copy the Software, except as expressly permitted in this Agreement, (e) rent or lease the Software, or (f) use the Software in any manner that infringes the intellectual property or other rights of Licensor or another party."

Companies argue that such provisions legally bind purchasers not to reverse engineer their software. If they do so anyway, they have breached a contract and can be sued for damages. The problem, of course, is that the anti-reverse-engineering provision gives the copyright owner rights beyond those it would have under, say, the *Sega* decision.

Whether this kind of contractual prohibition is enforceable is a hotly disputed issue. Courts have sometimes rejected reverse engineering defenses in trade secrecy cases because this activity exceeded the scope of licensed uses of the software.[38] Courts have sometimes refused to enforce software shrinkwrap license restrictions against reverse engineering because of a conflict between the clause and federal intellectual property policy. In *Vault Corp. v. Quaid Software Ltd.*,[39] the maker of copy-protection software tried to enforce an anti-reverse-engineering clause under Louisiana law against a firm that had reverse-engineered its copy-protection scheme. The court held that federal law preempted the contractual clause as a matter of federal policy, the same argument used in *Bonito Boats* to override the Florida boat hull law.

In addition, Section 301 of the Copyright Act preempts state-created or state-enforced rights "that are equivalent to any of the exclusive rights within the general scope of copyright ...." As might be expected, there's a debate about what "equivalent" means. Courts have said that contract provisions enforceable under state law are "equivalent" to federal copyright when the conditions for infringement are the same. But if infringement of the state-created right requires an "extra element," it is not "equivalent."

---

[38] E.g., *Technicon Data Sys. Corp. v. Curtis 1000, Inc.*, 224 U.S.P.Q. (BNA) 286 (Del. Ch. 1984) (holding that a consultant to a hospital used improper means to obtain trade secret interface information by wiretapping the hospital's licensed software system to study the manner in which the server software exchanged data with the client software because this use had not been authorized by the hospital; stating further that even if the use had been authorized, the action would have breached restrictive terms in the license); see also *DSC Communications Corp. v. Pulse Communications, Inc.*, 170 F.3d 1354 (Fed. Cir. 1999) (holding that there was a triable issue of fact as to whether Pulsecom's use of a "snooper board" at a telephone company to get access to interface information about DSC's software resulted in a misappropriation of a trade secret in view of restrictions in the telephone company's license to use DSC's software).

[39] 847 F.2d 255 (5th Cir. 1988).

Such a contractual clause was recently found enforceable. In *Bowers v. Baystate Technologies, Inc.*,[40] an inventor marketed a patented computer-aided design (CAD) software "toolkit" with an anti-reverse-engineering license clause. Baystate, a competitor, reverse engineered Bowers' software and then marketed a competing CAD toolkit. After some complicated litigation, the court eventually held, among other things, that Baystate breached its contract with Bowers.

The court held that the license wasn't preempted because a contract has an "extra element" — the parties must agree.[41] It follows that federal copyright law can never preempt a contractual prohibition. The problem with the *Bowers* decision is that it focuses only on the specific preemption clause of the Copyright Act and completely ignores constitutional "conflict" preemption.[42]

The Uniform Computer Information Transactions Act (UCITA) is a state legislative atttempt to address these issues, but it is also mired in controversy.

Trade secrets and the Economic Espionage Act

The Economic Espionage Act (EEA)[43] created the first federal cause of action for trade secrecy misappropriation. But it has no reverse engineering defense. This is troubling because rights granted under the EEA arguably implicate certain reverse engineering activities previously thought to be lawful. In particular, it's unclear whether decompilation and disassembly of computer programs may violate EEA rules that forbid duplicating trade secrets.

The Responsible Hacker: Ignorance is no Defense

In general, there are two ways you can violate intellectual property laws. Direct infringement means that you actually infringed. Indirect infringement means that you facilitated actual infringement by someone else. For example, in the Betamax case, the issue was whether Sony, by selling VCRs, could be found liable for its customers' copyright infringement.

---

[40] 302 F.3d 1334 (Fed. Cir. 2002).

[41] The court relied on an earlier case, ProCD, Inc. v. Zeidenberg, 86 F.3d 1447, 1454. (7th Cir. 1996) ("A copyright is a right against the world. Contracts, by contrast, generally affect only their parties; strangers may do as they please, so contracts do not create 'exclusive rights.'").

[42] EFF has submitted an amicus brief supporting Baystate's petition for rehearing en banc in the case. (add cite)

[43] Economic Espionage Act of 1996, Pub. L. No. 104-294, 110 Stat. 3488 (codified at 18 U.S.C. § § 1831-1839 (Supp. V 1999)).

Civil and Criminal Offenses and Penalties

The legal theories we've talked about carry a broad range of potential penalties. The main concern is civil liability, either economic damages or an injunction against the activity or both. Damages are usually tied to the amount of harm caused by the infringement.

In patent law, for example, the usual basis for damages is that of a "reasonable royalty." The court will calculate how much you should have paid the patent owner in royalties if you had contracted for a license. Damages can also be based on the infringer's profits or the patent owner's lost profits.

"Willful" infringement is treated more harshly. The patent statute permits a court, in its discretion, to increase damages up to three times the base damages (and also to pay the patent owner's attorney's fees) if the infringer knew about the patent and did not consult with competent patent counsel.

The current trend in intellectual property law is toward greater attention to criminal penalties. Under the first federal copyright act in 1790, copyright infringement was a purely civil matter. It was not until 1897 that Congress added criminal penalties to the copyright act, and criminal copyright infrngement was classified as a misdemeanor.[44] Moreover, criminal copyright infringement was rarely used.

Today, the risk of criminal prosecution appears considerably higher, and the criminal penalties are much greater. Amendments to the copyright act in 1982 and 1992, for instance, classified certain kinds of infringement as felonies. Even then, however, criminal infringement had to be undertaken willfully and for commercial advantage or private financial gain.

The 1997 No Electronic Theft Act (NET Act) criminalized the reproduction or distribution of one or more copies of copyrighted works that have an aggregate retail value of over $1,000 during any 180 day period, regardless of how those copies are created or distributed. It retained the willfulness requirement, but eliminated the requirement that the defendant's infringement be motivated by profit or commercial gain.

The DMCA also contains criminal provisions, which were invoked in the prosecution of Dmitry Sklyarov and the company he worked for, ElcomSoft. Elcomsoft produced and distributed software that can be used to convert digital books from Adobe's eBook format into Adobe's PDF format. In the course of the format conversion, the use restrictions imposed by the eBook format are stripped away. It was undisputed that the Elcomsoft software can be used to facilitate noninfringing uses of eBooks (e.g., fair use excerpting, or to facilitate automated translation into Braille for blind readers). Sklyarov himself was never accused of infringing a copyright, or assisting in the infringing activities of any third party. Nevertheless, for

[44] See generally Lydia Loren, *Digitization, Commodification, Criminalization: The Evolution of Criminal Copyright Infringement and the Importance of the Willfulness Requirement*, 77 Wash. U. L.Q. 835, 840 (1999).

his part in developing the software, the FBI arrested him and held him in custody for 3 weeks.[45] He and Elcomsoft were indicted by a grand jury; based on the indictment, Sklyarov faced a maximum of 25 years in prison and a fine that could exceed $2 million.[46] ElcomSoft and Sklyarov eventually were found not guilty of violating the DMCA.

Reverse Engineering as "The Freedom to Tinker" and other Legal Issues

Edward Felten, a computer science professor at Princeton University, views reverse engineering as a part of the "the freedom to tinker," which should include the freedom to "take them apart, to discuss them, to explore how they work, to modify them, to make them better." Felten argues that "as more and more of our world is experienced through electronic devices, and communications and culture are more and more mediated by these devices, it becomes increasingly important that we be able to tinker with them, to be able to understand this part of our world."

The freedom to tinker should also include the right to talk about tinkering. But as we've seen, many of the new intellectual property rules limit the right of reverse-engineers to share what they learn from tinkering. These limits not only raise serious First Amendment free-speech issues, they go to the heart of the constitutional basis for copyright and patent law: progress in the arts and sciences. One of the major issues raised by the DMCA is its chilling effect on scientists.[47]

---

[45] *See* Professor Larry Lessig, "Jail Time in the Digital Age," *N.Y. Times* (July 30, 2001) (available at <http://www.nytimes.com/2001/07/30/opinion/30LESS.html>); Declan McCullagh, "Hacker Arrest Stirs Protest," *Wired News* (July 19, 2001) (available at <http://www.wired.com/news/politics/0,1283,45342,00.html>); Jennifer 8 Lee, "U.S. Arrests Russian Cryptographer as Copyright Violator," *N.Y. Times*, July 18, 2001.

[46] *See* Brad King & Michelle Delio, "Sklyarov, Boss Plead Not Guilty," *Wired News* (Aug. 30, 2001) (available at <http://www.wired.com/news/politics/0,1283,46396,00.html>).

[47] See generally Electronic Frontier Foundation, *Unintended Consequences: Four Years under the DMCA* (2003) (cite to EFF website)

CHAPTER 13

Onward!

The state of the art in Xbox hacking is constantly advancing. Thousands of hackers are constantly researching, innovating, discovering and sharing new methods and techniques for making the Xbox a more useful and valuable piece of hardware to the end users. Keeping abreast of the latest developments in hacking can be overwhelming. Hopefully, reading this book has given you the faculties to understand the latest posts and news on various websites and web fora dedicated to Xbox hacking. This chapter discusses where you can go to find out more about the latest hacks, where to ask for help, and how you can contribute your unique abilities and perspective to the community. This chapter also discusses some of the larger challenges that will face hackers in the future, namely the trusted PC initiatives.

The Hacking Community

Xbox hackers are an anarchistic community that works mostly underground, keeping in touch and sharing information through various Internet fora (fora is the plural of forum, as data is the plural of datum). Most of the Xbox hacking community keeps a low profile, and hackers often use pseudonyms to protect their identities. The reasons for using pseudonyms varies, but in general anonymity carries the benefit of greater operating freedom. Hackers are more inclined to share their results and findings if they know they can back away unscathed in case things get ugly. The use of pseudonyms also levels the playing field. Hackers judge each other primarily on the basis of the quality and frequency of their contributions, and little else. The fact that you may be young does not detract from your first impression or street credibility, as it might in other situations. Likewise, many hackers have no qualms about being blunt when you've made an error, and they have even less patience for stupidity presented as erudition or rude assertions. On the other hand, many hackers are more than happy to extend a hand to those who have made an honest effort to read the FAQs, search the web and generally try their best to check and make sure that the question hasn't already been answered.

Hacking Fora

The Xbox hacking community has many civic fora for sharing their results and airing their concerns. The most popular fora are web-based BBSes such as `www.XboxHacker.net` and `www.xbox-scene.com`, and IRC channels such as #xboxhacker. Web-based BBSes typically feature news logs, FAQs and useful links to information. More importantly, BBSes include fora where people can share information and post questions. Through these fora, you can tap the collective knowledge of all the hackers that frequent these BBSes. The logged history of these fora also contains a wealth of Xbox hacking information (and misinformation). I encourage readers who have unanswered questions from this book to check out these fora for answers.

One of the first Xbox hacking fora to be created was the XboxHacker BBS (`www.xboxhacker.net`). Many of the best and brightest Xbox hackers have contributed to its fora. For example, one of the forum threads document, in real-time, the adventures of Andy Green (known as numbnut on the XboxHacker BBS) as he hacked the version 1.1 security scheme of the Xbox. I have learned much from reading the forum postings of the XboxHacker BBS. I have also met some of the most interesting people through the BBS fora. The founder of the XboxHacker BBS, Dan Johnson (also known as SiliconIce) tells his story in the sidebar "Profile: Dan Johnson".

Another resource for finding more information about the Xbox in general is the web search engine Google (`www.google.com`). As more hackers become involved with the Xbox, Google is becoming an increasingly important tool for casting a wide net and discovering the latest tools and techniques. For example, at the time of writing Google started indexing a number of resources for replacement Xbox components. This can be useful for those who do not want to go through the trouble of adapting an ATX power supply to work with the Xbox.

Try to use keywords that are as specific as possible when searching with Google. Typing "Xbox hacking" into Google will return a large number of links related to the general topic of Xbox hacking, but few specifics. For example, today's top hit on Google for "Xbox hacking" is a LWN.net article titled "LWN: Lindows CEO funds Xbox hacking contest (News.com)". This seems fairly removed from information about how to install a new hard drive or the details about the Xbox security system. When narrowing down your search, try to figure out what the de facto jargon and spelling is for your concept. Suppose you are looking for information on the new Xbox security system. If you search on "new Xbox", you hardly get any technical information. However, if you search on "xbox v1.1", the search returns many more useful technical results. One of the best ways to harvest the current jargon and acronyms is by browsing the hacking BBSes.

Making a Contribution

If you are looking for a way to contribute to the Xbox hacking community, keep in mind that most hackers have a unique skill or strength that typically correspond to his or her area of greatest interest, and that most hackers hack for fun. For example, I really enjoy hardware, especially when it requires building something. Also, while I can write code, I don't particularly enjoy it. Thus, my contribution to the hacking community is primarily through hardware projects. Likewise, I have a hard time motivating myself to engage in software projects. So, most of the time I just sit back and enjoy watching what other people are doing on the Xbox. It is both educational and entertaining. When trying to think about what you can do for the Xbox hacking community, don't worry yourself about trying to jump in quickly and rush into a project that you aren't in love with, or that you aren't comfortable executing. You will know when your time has arrived: the project will just shout your name, and you will naturally be compelled to hack.

Profile: Dan Johnson (a.k.a. SiliconIce)

Can you tell us a little bit about yourself, and how you got into hacking?

For some time, I had been interested in electronics hacking, though for the most part my interest had been limited to merely reading about such feats. Hacked devices such as Sega's Dreamcast and the Netpliance I-Opener had caught my attention from time to time. However, my first real experience with electronics hacking came with the "ePods", a discontinued internet appliance/web-tablet device. I read about these interesting devices online and found my way to Ken Segler's I-Appliance BBS (`http://www.linux-hacker.net`), home of the famous I-Opener hacks. After reading about the neat things people were doing with these tablets, I was intrigued and spent a good deal of my saved up money at the time ($200) on one of the units. After receiving my new toy, I spent a lot of time performing many of the documented hacks, mostly software based. This was to be my first glimpse into the world of electronics hacking. After the ePods, I moved on to another internet appliance, the Gateway Connected Touchpad. A slick-looking 10" touchscreen with a 400MHz Crusoe and 96MB RAM housed behind it, it looked like a great deal and perfect for a fun project. The device ran a custom build of Linux for AOL off of a 32MB CompactFlash card. I swapped this out with a Microdrive and after much swapping of this disk between laptops and USB readers and the Gateway, the device booted a pared down version of Windows using "98Lite." The device seemed perfect for use as a finger-operated, network-attached mp3 jukebox (among other

continued...

Profile: Dan Johnson, continued...

things) so I began working on a custom player that would allow easy operation via the touchpad. The whole Gateway experience made for a neat summer project between my Junior and Senior years of high school.

How did the XboxHacker BBS come about?

It was during this time period that I got the idea for XboxHacker.Net. To me, the Xbox seemed to have the potential to be the ideal computing device for under the TV...as soon as it could be programmed. The hardware was most impressive for the time, and more than adequate for what I hoped would be accomplished on the device. Unlike other consoles, the Xbox also was to have a hard drive and ethernet port built in. Once hacked, the Xbox could be used to emulate old consoles such as NES, SNES, N64, and even PSX, to conveniently play back any type of media file, such as mp3s or DivXs, on your home entertainment system, to play streamed media from a home network, or even to double as a basic PC. Some argued that the cost of the device at $299 made it out of range to bother hacking, as a PC with similar specs could be constructed without the need for hacking for not much more in cost. However, the Xbox had the advantage that it could also play Xbox games and was already designed to sit with your TV. The hacks would just be added value. After my short foray into the world of electronics hacking, I thought that hacking the Xbox could be an interesting project to help organize as I was intrigued by the possibility of having a convenient box for my TV to perform the tasks mentioned above. It was not until many months later that I would actually acquire the XboxHacker.Net domains.

How was your experience growing and running the XboxHacker BBS?

From the beginning, XboxHacker.Net focused on a few primary goals: providing and spreading technical information about the Xbox, and providing a place for fellow hackers to discuss technical information related to hacking the Xbox. Though due to my limited technical knowledge and experience I could do little in the way of actual hacking to contribute to the effort, I knew plenty enough to help facilitate the effort by collecting and distributing relevant information and moderating a discussion board. Not long after the site launched, we were fortunate enough to receive some links from such high-profile websites as Mike Magee's *The Inquirer* and Van Smith's *Van's Hardware*. The XboxHacker.Net BBS quickly became one of primary places on the internet to discuss any material related to hacking the Xbox and the XboxHacker.Net news page had the most up-to-date news on the status of the Xbox. A few weeks after the site came online, it received mention in an article on CNET, and from then on the activity level steadily increased. It wasn't long before XboxHacker.Net had outgrown the small shared server we were on, so the site moved to a much larger account which was also outgrown in a matter of weeks. Traffic to the forums continued to increase

continued...

Trusted Computing

Trust is the cornerstone of security, and in order to have faith in your security system, you need to have faith in the hardware and software you are running. The trusted computer is a machine that has been architected to be resistant to attacks that could compromise the trustability of the machine. There are many approaches to building a trustable computer, from the Automated Teller Machine model of physical security and tamper-resistance, to less hardware intensive solutions such those used in the Xbox. The Xbox fits into the broader picture of trusted computing since it is one of the first high-profile, widely-deployed trusted PC implementations. In a way, the Xbox gives us a hint of what we might expect down the road for trusted computing,

Trusted computing is a potentially disruptive emerging technology. The rise of trusted clients in an ad-hoc network like the Internet harbors the promise of enabling safe and private on-line financial transactions, of reducing or eliminating the occurrence of computer viruses, and of reducing or eliminating spam email. Trusted PCs can also be used to securely store sensitive data, such as your medical and financial records and your naughty or embarrassing secrets. Another application of trusted PCs is to reliably enforce digital content access rights and management policies upon users. The digital rights management (DRM) aspect of trusted computing could fundamentally change the way we use computers today; many of us enjoy the benefits of pseudo-free content and flexible copyright implementations. The fundamental problem is not the existence of content management policies – indeed, content management policy can be beneficial for consumers. The real problem is when the policies which govern your rights can be set unilaterally by content providers. In the current trusted PC proposals, the user is not trusted to have control over certain key secrets inside their machines. Instead, the attestation information (information required to establish trustability) of a user's machine is partially maintained by a third party. Can we rely on a non-elected, unregulated third party with business interests to determine who can do business, send emails, and otherwise be recognized as a trustable entity?

Trusted computing is like a gun. It's great to have one as long as you're the one controlling the trigger. Unfortunately, many trusted PC opponents fear that in practice, systems will be deployed with preset rights, policies and third-party trust affirmation resources pointed in the wrong direction for consumers. A company, during good times, may set the privacy and security policy in favor of users to attract a larger customer base, but once Chapter 11 comes knocking, or the company is sold or otherwise changes hands, these policies can and will shift. What is to prevent businessmen from promoting trusted computing initially with user-friendly policies, and then suddenly shifting into a wallet-squeezing DRM mode? Ethics?

Profile: Dan Johnson, continued...

rapidly, so I made the decision to move the site to its own dedicated server where we could have room to grow and not worry about every few MBs of bandwidth usage or how many concurrent forum users were online.

It didn't take long before the activities of XboxHacker.Net captured the attention of Microsoft. Early in the site's history, I was contacted a couple of times with requests to remove materials. The first instance was of a screenshot of a developer tool I had received without much explanation that showed "security sectors" on the disks. The second instance was a request to remove a link someone had posted in the forums to a BIOS image of the Xbox. Aside from these few minor incidents, contact between Microsoft and XboxHacker.Net was virtually non-existent. It was made a policy early on to steer clear from issues of questionable legality such discussion about backing up of games, linking to copyrighted materials, or posting Microsoft code from the BIOS.

In the beginning, though interest was high, progress seemed to be relatively slow...there was not a lot that could be done with the Xbox before the security was broken. There were many individuals who contributed notably early on. Some of the earliest contributors the XboxHacking world were Andy and Luke, whose page contained a plethora of information on file formats and (need to find caches of their pages). Steve "SurferDude" Gehlbach contributed to the design of a VGA converter circuit for the Xbox and Ken Gasper improved on this to create a true VGA adapter for the Xbox. Bunnie's early analysis and hardware info page generated interest in XboxHacking as well after its appearance on Slashdot. Indeed, there are numerous others who made their mark as well. Privileged to count such skilled hackers among the contributing members on the boards, XboxHacker.Net grew into a hub for technical Xbox information, discussion, and news.

The crown jewel of XboxHacker.Net has no doubt always been the XboxHacker BBS. The site was centered around the forums and activities of our members. Often, the latest XboxHacking news would simply be links to forum topics and clips from posts made by our members. The purpose of the forums was to enable the diverse, multi-national group of people interested in hacking the Xbox to work together towards this common goal. The forums provided a great place to share information and discuss ideas with fellow hackers and also served to bring together many talented hackers who may otherwise have had no means of collaborating. It was a great feeling to watch the progress that the forums enabled. One particular discussion that comes to mind took place over the course of several days. A number of members were discussing the new security system in the second generation Xbox, looking for flaws and ways around it. It was exciting to watch the events unfold as hackers got closer to the solution and eventually broke the security on the revised Xbox. Our hundreds of contributing

continued...

Taking a Step Back

There is a problem with the phrase "trusted computing": it has become synonymous with cryptographically secured trusted computers. Let's take a step back and just talk about alternative approaches to building trusted computers.

Trustability has always been important in computers. However, back in the early days of computing, machines were so expensive that the hardware necessary to enforce strong trust policies was not within the reach of consumers. For example, many early machines shipped with a socket for a hardware Memory Management Unit (MMU) chip. The MMU was one of the first steps toward trustable hardware memory models; part of an MMU's job is to enforce page-level memory access protections. MMUs were sold as an option because they were quite pricey at the time. Unfortunately, the move toward trustable hardware stopped at the MMU, partially because computer networks didn't exist in any major form until relatively recently. In a non-networked world, data needed to be protected only from programmer errors and from access by a few select users with physical access to the machine. Today, computers need something stronger than just an MMU, something that can provide trust in the face of viruses and remote attackers attempting to exploit subtle software weaknesses to run malicious code.

The natural extension to the MMU's hardware-enforced paged virtual memory model might be address capabilities with a tagged memory model. A memory tag is a set of bits that record the type of data or code stored in a memory location. In a tagged memory model, every memory location has a set of tag bits, kind of like how every memory location in a conventional error-correcting memory implementation is associated with some ECC bits. Tag bits help the hardware enforce data type management policies; for example, a memory location tagged as piece of data can never be accidentally or intentionally executed as code. A capability is a pointer granted by a trusted kernel that cannot be forged. The unforgeability property is preferably enforced by hardware through tag bits. Many architectures also include the ability to enforce access boundaries as part of a hardware capability[1]. Capabilities and memory tags are not new ideas; in 1961, the Burroughs B5000 used capabilities (then called descriptors) and tagged memory to guard, in hardware, against buffer overflow attacks, and to isolate code from data[2]. The MIT PDP-1, Intel i432, IBM System/38, and the Mach and Amoeba operating systems also implemented capabilities in some form, and this is by no means a complete list of systems that have used capabili-

[1] An efficient, high performance hardware implementation of precise object boundaries using tagged capabilities can be found in a tech note titled "A capability representation with embedded address and nearly-exact object bounds" by Jeremy Brown, J.P. Grossman, Andrew Huang and Tom Knight. http://www.ai.mit.edu/projects/aries/Documents/Memos/ARIES-05.pdf

[2] "The Architecture of the Burroughs B5000 - 20 Years Later and Still Ahead of the Times?" by Alastair J.W. Mayer. http://www.ajwm.net/amayer/papers/B5000.html

Profile: Dan Johnson, continued...

forum members were in large part responsible for the success of XboxHacker.Net and the progress of the XboxHacking world in general.

Besides the activity on the XboxHacker.Net BBS, there were no doubt many other groups working to hack the Xbox in secret. One such group I knew of on IRC contained contributing forum members as well as others from the electronics hacking underground. Names here will go unmentioned. Many bits of information from independent groups or individuals were relayed to me for reporting over time. However, despite the growing interest in XboxHacking and the number of people involved in the effort, it would be some time before any major breakthroughs became public knowledge.

The XboxHacking scene picked up pace fairly rapidly after the public availability of modchips near summertime 2002. By this time, the Xbox security system had been cracked by multiple groups and it was only a matter of time before modchips were readily available to the public. At this point, the work shifted away from hardware hacking for the most part and more towards software development. A sister site to XboxHacker.Net, XboxDeveloper (`http://www.xboxdeveloper.net`) was started to help catalog the software that became available for the Xbox, though it never took off to the level that XboxHacker.Net did. Using leaked copies of the Microsoft Xbox SDK, programmers began writing and porting various applications for the Xbox, including media players and emulators such as MAME. The Xbox-Linux project (`http://xbox-linux.sourceforge.net/`) under the leadership of Michael Steil, successfully allowed the Linux operating system to run on the Xbox. I pushed to start the OpenXDK project (`http://sourceforge.net/projects/openxdk/`), an open source developer kit that would allow development of software for the Xbox unhindered by legal issues, though that project has met with only mixed success. It is now under the leadership of "Caustik" (Aaron Robinson), a CS student at Case Western University. Due to the more accessible nature of software development compared with hardware hacking, the number of contributing members to the general XboxHacking effort increased rapidly. The amount of "homebrew" software available for the Xbox today is amazing and includes everything from media players, console emulators, and utilities to originally written games.

ties or tagged memory. The security properties of capabilities have also been demonstrated in many academic studies, such as the EROS (Extremely Reliable Operating System)[3]. Unfortunately, capabilities and tagged memory never made their way into the heart of mainstream PC architecture. Security and reliability has always taken a back seat to cost, backward-compatibility and performance.

[3] Originally conceived at the University of Pennsylvania by Jonathan Shapiro. `http://www.eros-os.org/`

This brief history lesson demonstrates that trusted computing does not *require* the cryptographic approach that is being proposed today by Palladium and the Trusted Computing Platform Alliance (TCPA). In fact, cryptography on its own does not provide any security. Secure key management is really what provides all the security in Palladium/TCPA. Cryptographic algorithms simply transfer the security of the key into the user's domain.

This being said, one can draw an analogy between a capability and a cryptographic key. Both require a trusted OS to manage their creation, dissemination and destruction. Both are equally weak if the system cannot protect against forged keys or capabilities. The big difference is that if a secret key leaks, all security is lost, eternally; on the other hand, capabilities are created and destroyed dynamically, so the leakage of a capability might lead to a security breach, but the scope and duration of the breach is limited. To this extent, capabilities provide a more robust solution for computer security.

Note that relying solely on cryptographic techniques for hardware security still leaves machines open to classic buffer-overrun style attacks and security holes due to programmer errors. "Measurements" of the software's state helps mitigate this weakness by detecting code alternations before executing security-critical operations, but measurements are not a perfect solution. On the other hand, buffer-overrun attacks are impossible in systems using hardware enforced capabilities with bounds checking.

Memory tags can also be used to implement security features that are not feasible using a purely cryptographic approach to trusted computing. One example is the trustable concurrent processing of compartmentalized secrets[4]. In this example, multiple threads with varying levels of security clearance are operating on a single processor. The hardware enforces a policy where all threads impress their security level upon the data that they access. In other words, every computation simultaneously operates in two domains: the conventional arithmetic domain, and the security domain. Suppose an unclassified thread adds two unclassified numbers and creates a piece of data named *foo*. *foo*'s security tag is also computed in parallel with the add arithmetic operation. In this case, the security tag's result is "unclassified". Now, suppose a top-secret thread touches *foo*: *foo*'s security tag now changes to "top secret". Unclassified threads can no longer read *foo*, even if the unclassified thread has a valid pointer to *foo*. *foo* must be explicitly reclassified before it can be read again by unclassified threads. Such a strictly compartmentalized security system can be used, for example, to ensure that no internal kernel structures are ever accessible to user processes, even in the presence of bugs and memory leaks (including scenarios where kernel memory is deallocated and re-assigned to a user process without a memory clearing step). This scheme can also be used to establish security audit trails. Audit trails help programmers trace down the root cause of a security breach, and audit trails are also useful as a damage control measure in the

[4] More about security systems like this can be found in a tech note titled "A Minimal Trusted Computing Base for Dynamically Ensuring Secure Information Flow" by Jeremy Brown and Tom Knight. `http://www.ai.mit.edu/projects/aries/Documents/Memos/ARIES-15.pdf`

case of a security breach.

To be fair, an advantage of the cryptographic approach to trusted computing is that if a rogue did get a hold of data through some hardwares means — eavesdropping on the hardware, stealing a hard drive — the data cannot be deciphered. However, users can elect to use cryptography for data protection in any computer implementation, including those using hardware capabilities and tagged memory. The problem of secure key management is still a difficult problem, but perhaps the problem can be solved in part by integrating cryptographic smart card readers into PCs.

There is no essential reason why a trusted PC implementation *must* use the cryptographic techniques proposed in Palladium and TCPA. The techniques reviewed in this section, namely capabilities and tagged memory, can be used to implement a secure, trustable PC in a manner that does not involve the risk of users losing the ability to set their own access policies. Users would be in full control of their machine and their secrets at all times.

Palladium versus TCPA

There is much confusion these days about the current trusted PC proposals, namely Microsoft's Palladium and the Trusted Computing Platform Alliance (TCPA). There are enough similarities between the two proposals that many people think they are one in the same, but the goals of each initiative is different. The TCPA is a multi-corporation alliance to create computers with some nominal amount of trust. Significantly, much of the TCPA's specifications can also be applied to non-PC platforms. In TCPA the trust is planted in a secure hardware module called the TPM (Trusted Platform Module). The TPM contains features to ensure that the secrets contained within the module are never leaked through software attacks, and it also contains features, such as secured system "measurements", that attempt to transfer the trust contained within the TPM to the host machine. Palladium, on the other hand, is a whole-system PC-centric security concept created by Microsoft alone. One of the components of Palladium is a TPM-like security module, but Palladium also calls for sweeping changes to the hardware chipset and the way I/O ports are implemented. The chipset is required to enforce memory security policies from all potential DMA sources, such as the graphics card. Palladium also calls for the I/O to the keyboard and video subsystems to be encrypted.

This requirement for cooperation between chipset vendors, OEMs and Microsoft is a potentially large flaw of Palladium. There isn't enough margin in the commodity PC hardware industry today to support the overhead of an extensive cryptographic security overhaul. In addition, many chipset vendors do not have any experience with implementing secure systems. On top of the language barrier faced by many overseas chipset vendors, chipsets are usually developed on a short fuse and with a keen eye on the pocketbook. Can chipsets developed under these conditions be expected to protect sensitive secrets?

The Xbox is an example of what can go wrong when security policies are defined by one body and implemented by another very different organization. Microsoft wrote a specification for a trustable piece of hardware, namely, the Xbox. Strong cryptographic algorithms are used liberally in the Xbox, and the master key for the system is locked deep inside a complex piece of silicon. However, experience has demonstrated that the Xbox's security system can be bypassed using a combination of an unsecured debug port, a flaw in the hardware initialization scheme, and a bug in the handling of a boundary case of the instruction pointer in the CPU. These three minor oversights, committed by three independent parties (the assembly contractor, the Xbox firmware designer, and Intel), conspired to provide a convenient method for defeating Xbox security.

Each of these oversights on their own did not represent a significant security problem, which leads to the disconcerting question of how many security breaches in a particular Palladium implementation will be caused by the stacking of multiple benign flaws. Every complex consumer electronics system has minor bugs or design oversights, especially when systems are composed of components built by multiple independent entities whose primary interest is turning a profit. In the consumer electronics industry, one can either ship a perfect product, or one can make money. Products that don't make money are quickly cancelled. Thus, it is very rare to find a consumer product that is technically perfect in all respects. As a result, the only practical way to guarantee the security of consumer electronics system as complex as Palladium is to throw it into the wild, and let the hackers have their way with it for many years until all of the big security holes have been discovered and plugged.

On the other hand, the TCPA's TPM is a device created to solve a certain set of problems that is smaller in scope than Palladium's. Thus, the TPM is not as exciting from a market perspective, but it may be more practical and serviceable for its intended purpose. Both the TPM and Palladium are weak to hardware attacks, but the TPM doesn't attempt to extend security requirements as far into third-party system design territory. The TPM is primarily a secured key management module that has the capability of detecting most modifications and intrusions to the host system. The software layers built on top of this substrate do the rest of the heavy lifting, *caveat emptor.*

Hacking the Trusted PC

The current proposals for the trusted PC are weak against some fairly simple hardware attacks, even in the absence of any integration oversight or bug-related back doors.

The first attack is one that I call the "**S**urre**p**titious B**IOS**", or SPIOS (pronounced "Spy OS") attack. SPIOS can be used to defeat DRM policies that rely on the cryptographically sealed storage feature of the trusted PC to prevent unauthorized user access to data. The basic idea behind is to boot the PC with an unmodified BIOS into trusted mode and extract all the desired data into system RAM. Then, a warm reset of the system is performed while swapping the BIOS image. The modified BIOS image can be used to read out the desired data from system RAM. The desired data may be a session key stored in memory, or the actual decrypted data itself, depending upon how the program structures and caches its data in memory. Since the current trusted PC specifications call for an LPC bus based BIOS, inexpensive alternate firmware devices similar to those used on the Xbox can be used to execute this attack. There are techniques that application programmers can use to complicate this attack, such as only decrypting a single block of data at a time into system memory, but many of these techniques come at the price of severely degraded system performance. The degradation of system performance may be especially pronounced if file caching and prefetching is disabled.

Another attack is one that I call the "**S**urre**p**titious R**AM**", or SPAM attack. The goal of this attack is to spoof the trusted routines responsible for measuring the fitness of the system state. A device, such as an FPGA or ASIC, is installed on the plug-in memory cards in between the DRAM chips and the memory connector. This device monitors the pattern of addresses going by, or perhaps it has an extra connector that sniffs the state of the wires connected to the I/O pins of the cryptomodule that is responsible for authenticating the system. Either way, when a system measurement is in progress, the SPAM device presents a memory image that is consistent with an unmodified, trusted system state. However, during all other operating modes, the SPAM device presents a memory image that is modified to do whatever the user pleases. This modification can be very subtle: just a couple of bits flipped at the right locations is all it takes to modify key branch instructions in the security kernel. This device is more powerful than the SPIOS, since it works on a system that is powered-up and supposedly trustworthy. It can be applied to effectively defeat a wider range of DRM schemes as well as some authenticated transactions between the local machine and the server. SPAM alone cannot be used, however, to falsely identify a system as another registered, trusted system, since SPAM lacks the secret shared between the tamper-resistant secure cryptomodule in the local machine and the authentication server. False system identification would require either extracting the key from a tamper-resistant secure cryptomodule – possible, but not trivial and most likely destructive to the module – or somehow tricking a secure cryptomodule from another registered, trusted machine into providing the falsified identity.

The SPAM device can be manufactured for relatively little, as high performance FPGAs can cost as little as $50 today in single quantities. It can also be very easy to install. It can be either integrated directly into a memory module, in which case it functions as both a trust violation device and as a memory expansion device, or it can be provided as a device that is installed in a stacked configuration in between the motherboard's memory slot and the existing memory device. In some memory card configurations, particularly ones that employ heat shields, it may be possible to hide the SPAM device and pass the module off as a regular memory expansion device. While elaborate, this may be a worthwhile attack against a large corporation or bank that stores high-value secrets on a trusted PC-based server.

Looking Forward

When considering the prospect of trusted computing, we need to first consider if the currently proposed schemes will offer all the benefits that they promise, and then weigh those against the potential harm to consumers' rights and the potential benefits to criminals (enhanced privacy can be used for both good and ill). If trusted computing could provide perfect security for on-line businesses, then that might be worth the potential risks. However, the scenarios outlined in this chapter indicate that the trusted PC's security may be less than perfect. Consider the Xbox. The Xbox is a trusted PC implementation that can be hacked with just a $50 solderless module. This places a fairly strong bound on the value of secrets that can be trusted to an Xbox. Hardware modchips are so inexpensive that they pay for themselves with the cost of a copied game title, or two games if you elected to pay someone to install the chip for you. Of course, there are always the moral and social implications of stealing content, and new legislation such as the DMCA aims in part to make such acts a crime. Unfortunately, the current trusted PC proposals on the table are also weak in the face of similarly inexpensive hardware attacks. Thus, it is unlikely that the current trusted PC initiatives will provide the level of security required for high-value or very embarrassing secrets.

The fact of the matter is that hacking technology will be developed whether or not is illegal, and whether or not the intention is good or evil. Thus, it is in the best interest of consumers and companies to educate the population about hacking, and for everyone to understand the limitations of their "trusted PC". The worst-case scenario would be if billions of dollars were invested in trusted computing, only to have a net result of no greater safety or privacy for consumers, while consumers' rights are severely curtailed by poor content policy implementations.

The good news for trusted PC proponents is that shrinking feature sizes in integrated circuits is driving greater integration throughout the PC. Within a decade, today's PC will fit on a single piece of silicon. Once the RAM and the BIOS are fully integrated into a single piece of silicon, hacking a system becomes much more difficult – but not impossible. Focused Ion Beam (FIB) machines, a tool used by chip designers and failure analysis labs, are capable of cutting and jumpering nano-scale features. Another upside for for trusted machine designers is that public key processors could become so small and cheap to integrate into a chip that individual chips, especially memory chips, could start using strong crypto to authenticate and encrypt their I/O. Another technology that could aid the implementation of trusted PCs is integrated tamper-resistant or tamper-detecting features. For example, a time-domain reflectometer (TDR) could be built into a chip's I/O cells. A TDR can detect the presence of an eavesdropper on a wire by recognizing certain changes to the electrical properties of the wire. In addition to the ability to detect eavesdroppers, integrated TDR devices are desirable for high performance I/O since they can be used to calibrate the drive impedance and equalization/pre-emphasis filters required for multi-gigabit speed communications.

Concluding Thoughts

This book has taken you through a whistle-stop tour of Xbox hardware hacking, from the basics of soldering and disassembling to the latest projects and techniques. This book also introduced you to the social aspects of Xbox hacking: the people who hack, and the interplay between society, law and hacking. While the details of how to install a blue LED in an Xbox may be irrelevant in a few years, the skills you learned executing the installation will last a lifetime. Moreover, the social and legal issues confronting hackers and consumers will extend beyond the Xbox and into every part of our emerging information-centric way of life.

The material in this book is just a starting point; there is a world of hardware out there waiting to be explored. Please check out the appendices, they contain a little advice and a few hints on topics relevant to hardware hacking. I hope this book has provided the novice readers with a strong starting point for becoming an explorer, fixer and innovator in a world increasingly filled with, controlled by and dependent upon electronics.

Happy hacking!

— bunnie@xenatera.com

APPENDIX A

Where to Get Your Hacking Gear

A significant psychological barrier to getting started in hardware hacking is the perceived unavailability of hacking tools. While Radio Shack stocks a small supply of components and tools, the components are expensive and most of the tools are difficult to use with today's miniaturized components. This appendix lists a few of the component and tools vendors that have a solid selection for reasonable prices. This appendix also includes Jameco order numbers for the basic tools required to do the projects in this book. You can enter these order numbers directly into Jameco's secure ordering website to help get you started quickly.

Vendors for Hobbyists

There are a wide variety of component and equipment distributors, from those that cater primarily to large businesses, to those that service individuals, hobbyists and repairmen. You may experience some frustration when dealing with a distributor that caters to large businesses. These distributors service high-volume accounts, so accounts are serviced by a designated sales representative. As a result, it may be difficult to get a comprehensive catalog of parts or pricing and inventory information for small orders. The vendors listed in this section are friendly to individual orders and the their collective inventory will stock most of the parts you will ever need.

Vendor Name	*Vendor Contact Info*	*Specialties and Notes*
Digi-Key	www.digikey.com 1-800-344-4539 (phone) 1-218-681-3380 (fax)	Wide selection of original manufactured components. Hobbyist-friendly, prompt service. $5 handling charge on all orders under $25. Excellent website features real-time inventory and pricing check information, data sheets and parametric search tools.
Jameco	www.jameco.com 1-800-831-4242 (phone) 1-800-237-6948 (fax)	Economical hobbyist-friendly vendor. Components are a mixture of original and surplus stock. Good selection of tools at a reasonable price. $5 handling fee on all orders under $20. A wide selection of do-it-yourself kits available.
MCM Electronics	www.mcmelectronics.com 1-800-543-4330 (phone) 1-800-765-6960 (fax)	Specialty consumer electronics service/repair tools and parts as well as common tools and components. Sells hard-to-find security bits and replacement parts. $2.95 flat handling charge, no minimum order requirement for internet purchases.
Mouser	www.mouser.com 1-800-346-6873 (phone) 1-817-804-3899 (fax) orders@mouser.com	Tools and component vendor that stocks a good selection of original components. Hobbyist-friendly, no minimum order, no handling charge.
Newark	www.newark.com 1-800-463-9275 (phone)	Larger, traditional component distributor. Broad component selection but not all components are stocked; you may have to wait some weeks for certain orders to get filled. A good place to go for components you cannot find at other hobbyist-friendly distributors. $5 handling fee on all orders under $25.
Fry's Electronics	www.frys.com	Retail electronics store that stocks a reasonable selection of components and tools. A great place to go and browse if you do not like catalog shopping. Only found in California, Texas, Oregon and Arizona.
McMaster Carr	www.mcmastercarr.com	Vendor of mechanical hardware, metal stock and machine tools. A place to get raw sheet metal and fasteners to finish off a project. Website is comprehensive and helpful.
FindChips	www.findchips.com	Automated parts search engine. Search dozens of distributors for parts. Most hobbyist-friendly vendors are listed in this search engine.

Table B-1:
Table of vendors of components and equipment.

Prepared Equipment Order Forms

This section contains a selected list of tools sold by Jameco that you can order to get you geared up for hacking. The "basic" order form contains all the bits and drivers necessary for opening up an Xbox, as well as some basic soldering tools. The "advanced" order form contains a set of tools and utilities that are useful to have on hand, but are expensive enough that those on a budget may consider ordering them only as they require them.

In addition to the tools in these order forms, you will need a few small parts for the projects described in part I. Please refer to the introduction of each respective chapter for a list of parts that you will require.

Basic Order Form

The table below lists the basic tools that you will need to do the projects described in this book. You can order these parts by going to Jameco's website, `www.jameco.com`, and clicking on the yellow "Quick Order" button on the left hand side. Enter in the Jameco part numbers listed here and get started hacking!

Description	*Jameco Part Number*	*Price*
16 to 30 Watt Variable Soldering Iron	116572	$18.95
1/32" Conical Bevel tip for soldering iron	35326	$4.49
Small pack of 60/40 Kester flux core solder	73576	$2.59
2 oz Kester rosin paste flux	73584	$1.59
Desoldering Wik	175986	$2.49
Soldering iron tip cleaner and conditioner	132986	$4.95
26-Piece SAE Hobby Tool Set	170069	$14.95
Wire stripper, 22-30 gauge	127870	$4.95
Total price		$54.96

The 26-piece SAE Hobby Tool Set includes all of the bits, drivers and screwdrivers necessary to disassemble an Xbox, including the T-10, T-15 and T-20 torx bits. I have included the 1/32" conical bevel tip in the order form above because the soldering iron comes with a horrendously large 1/8" chisel tip. A 1/8" tip is useful for soldering together small countries and creating solder shorts all over your fine-pitched components. Conical bevel and chisel tips feature a flattened region that enables rapid heat transfer, and thus are easier to use than conical sharp tips. I also included some soldering iron tip cleaner and some rosin paste flux. They are a little bit pricey, but they will make your life a lot easier, trust me.

Advanced Order Form

The table below lists a few tools that are nice to have around, but are pricey enough that you probably should only get them if you anticipate doing a lot of hacking.

- The soldering iron stand and sponge are a must if you plan on doing even a moderate amount of soldering. The stand safely stows the hot soldering iron tip, reducing the chance of burns and fires.
- Try soldering with the 1/32" semi-chisel tip. You may find that you like it better than the conical bevel tip.
- The anti-stat wrist-strap is always a good idea to have on hand, especially if you tend to wear clothes and shoes that tend to generate static electricity.
- The SMT removal kit comes in handy when trying to remove smaller SMT components.
- The multimeter is a great all-purpose test, measurement and diagnostic tool to have on hand at all times that has applications all around the house or dorm. Many models of multimeters are available, the one listed here offers the most features for the lowest price. I have tried it out and it works well.
- The wire stripper and crimping tool listed here are very helpful for the power supply replacement project. The crimping tool is sold by Digi-Key, not Jameco. The crimping tool is a bit on the pricey side but it features shaped crimp dies for higher-quality solderless crimps than the sub ten dollar tools.

Description	*Part Number*	*Price*
Soldering iron stand	36329	$4.25
Sponge for soldering iron stand	134631	$2.99
Semi-chisel 1/32" tip	35078	$4.49
Adjustable anti-stat strap	159257	$7.95
SMT component removal kit	141305	$21.95
Multimeter (volts, ohms, amps, farads, temperature, frequency, dide/transistor)	177480	$49.95
Wire stripper, 16-26 Gauge	127861	$4.96
Crimping tool (order from Digi-Key)	WM9999-ND	$36.19

APPENDIX B

Soldering Techniques

This Appendix will explain the basics of soldering as well as some more advanced surface-mount soldering techniques. You will get the most out of this Appendix if you experiment with the soldering techniques as you read along. Jameco Electronics (`www.jameco.com`) sells a wide range of project kits that require through-hole assembling that you can use for basic soldering practice. Companies such as TopLine (`www.topline.tv`) offer economy practice kits using component blanks if you want to practice your SMT assembly techniques, and MCM Electronics (`www.mcmelectronics.com`) offers a practical Surface Mount Solder Practice Kit. I highly recommend that you practice your SMT soldering skills before trying to attach an SMT component that you care about.

Introduction to Soldering

The basic technique for soldering is fairly easy: wedge the tip of your soldering iron into the space between the component lead and the circuit board pad to heat both pieces up. Once they are sufficiently hot, gradually feed some solder wire into the joint until a nice, smooth solder fillet is created. In reality, however, soldering requires a bit of practice and experience before one reaches the level of being able to solder a typical board with over a thousand joints without any bad solder joints.

In order for a good solder joint to be created, the hot liquid solder must "wet" the subject pieces in order for a connection to be made. Thus, the real art of hand-soldering is understanding how to guarantee solder wetting.

You can tell when liquid solder is wetting a piece of metal by looking at it. A wetted joint looks like the molten solder has lost all surface tension; the liquid solder is shiny and it flows smoothly over the work area. In the opposite situation, the solder has a dull sheen to it, and it tends to ball up around the soldering iron tip instead of flowing outward.

Use Flux

Solder fails to wet the subject metal because oxygen in the air or dirt and grease have reacted with the metals. In this case, you can apply a *flux* to your workpiece to break down these foreign compounds. The word flux comes from the Latin *fluxus*, which means flowing. Most solder comes with a core of flux built into them to enhance solderability. If you look at a cut piece of solder carefully, you can see the flux core surrounded by the solder alloy. Always use solder with a flux core, or you will be in a world of pain trying to get the solder to wet. Almost all solders made specifically for electronics have a flux core, but there are solders that you can accidentally purchase in a hardware store that are made for purposes such as joining pipes where they have no flux in them. When you heat a flux-core solder, a small puff of vaporized flux smoke will rise up. A small fan placed near the work area will blow the fumes away and prevent inhalation.

A common novice mistake is to have too much faith in flux-core solder. Frequently, the flux contained in a flux core solder is not enough to get the solder to wet. In this case, you will need to apply extra flux. Raw flux comes usually as a liquid or a paste, so application is easy. In liquid form, a single drop of flux can be applied with half of a toothpick. Break the toothpick in half, leaving the break slightly jagged. Dip the broken end of the toothpick into the flux, and a small drop will cling to the end. Applying liquid flux to a large area can be done with a fine-tipped artists brush, but be sure to clean the brush when you are done or it will end up gummy and unusable in a couple of days. A flux dropper is also handy, but expensive. A flux dropper is a bottle with a thin capillary needle on top; when you invert the bottle, flux slowly drips out of the capillary. In paste form, flux can be applied by dipping any piece of scrap, such as a toothpick or a piece of solid wire, in the flux paste. Finally, flux pens are handy for beginners because they combine flux storage and dispensing in a convenient and inexpensive package. Flux pens don't have the accuracy or quality of other flux application techniques, but they are convenient and good for occasional use.

Many fluxes require clean-up after use. Fluxes will either harden with time, making repairs difficult in the future, or they will slowly attack the board, or they will absorb water and become conductive. The traditional soldering flux is a resin flux. Resin fluxes require the use of strong solvents that are flammable and toxic. As a result, I tend to recommend water soluble fluxes or no-clean fluxes. Water soluble fluxes can be removed by just washing down the board with water. It is better to use distilled deionized water, but I have found that most warm tap water is pretty effective as well. When I have to clean a large batch of boards, I throw them into a dishwasher (with the food trap cleaned and no detergent!). After the boards are washed, set them on a conductive, clean cookie sheet or aluminum foil, and put them into an oven on low heat (around 200 degrees F) to bake for about an hour or two, or until all the water is driven away. Be sure not to turn the oven too hot, or else water trapped inside the pores of components will turn into steam and cause them to crack or explode. Most parts are designed to be "process sealed" so washing them with water is fine. Be careful with connectors and switches, however. You may need to tape over them with a piece of Kapton tape to prevent contamination with water.

Warning

Do not use acid-type flux on circuit boards. They will attack the board and components and cause failures with time. Acid fluxes frequently plague novices who use solders and fluxes that are intended for pipe soldering.

Starter Tips

Components with many leads need to be aligned and tacked in place before soldering. If the component is a surface-mount type of component, it can be held in place by soldering down two pins on opposite corners of the device. After tacking the component in place, re-inspect the alignment in case the component drifted during the tacking process. If the component is a through-hole type of component, you will need masking tape to hold the component in place while you turn the board over. Tack the corner leads of the component in place, and check that the component is level to the board before soldering all of the leads. Masking tape has a bit of play in it and frequently you will have to heat one of the tacked corners while pressing down on the component to level the component with the board.

Kapton tape is a fairly handy thing to keep around the workbench. Made by DuPont, Kapton can withstand temperatures up to 500°F, well above the melting point of solder. It is handy for masking off nearby regions where you do not want solder. However, Kapton tape is expensive so use it only in situations where it will come in contact with hot solder.

Solder fails to wet metal that is too cold. This is a common problem when soldering large joints, or when soldering joints attached to large sheets of copper. In these cases, the connected metal conducts enough heat away so that the junction never reaches the melting point of solder. The solution to this is to either use a more powerful soldering iron (but be careful—the heat of very large soldering irons can also cause the board traces to fall off), or to leave your soldering iron in contact with the junction for a longer period of time before applying the solder. One trick to heating up the work area faster is to feed just a touch of solder into the tip of the iron where it is heating things up. Even though the solder will not wet on the board, the liquid solder on the iron's tip increases the effective contact area between the iron and the board, and heat will be transferred more rapidly into the board. Sometimes you will have to rotate the iron, maintaining contact at the joint, after applying the solder to the tip in order to get the molten solder in contact with the board.

You can tell when a component lead or a board pad is sufficiently hot by carefully observing the way light reflects off of it. Component leads and pads on a circuit board typically have some kind of plating on them, usually made out of solder. This solder plating has a slightly dull sheen under normal conditions. When made sufficiently hot, however, the sheen goes from dull to almost perfectly reflective. To get a feel for what this looks like, try heating up a large square pad with your soldering iron, using the technique described above. You can usually watch the melting front propagate across the pad as the soldering iron heats the board.

Warning

If you are using a non-temperature controlled soldering iron, use the lowest wattage soldering iron you can to get the job done. This will help prevent board damage, as excess heat can cause the copper traces to delaminate from the board.

Surface Mount Soldering

Mastering the skill of surface mount soldering requires a bit of patience, practice, and good tools. The basic tools that are required beyond the basic soldering kit are tweezers and a magnifying lens.

A good pair of fine-tipped tweezers is an essential soldering accessory for surface mount components. Tweezers are required for the safe handling of surface mount components during soldering, as small components will rapidly heat up and become hot enough to burn your finger. Tweezers are also necessary to hold small components in place because they will be pulled around by the surface tension of the liquid solder as it melts and cools. The point on the tweezers should be small enough to fit in between the pins of the finest surface-mount part that you intend to work on. This way, you can use the tweezers to manipulate individual pins during soldering and inspection. There are many grades of tweezers. The grading is based on the sharpness, quality and durability of the tips, the alignment of the tips, and the spring action of the tweezers. High-grade tweezers are a little bit pricey, but well worth the investment if you intend to do a lot of surface mount soldering. Distributors that have a focus on production supplies, such as Future-Active Electronics (`www.future-active.com`), sell a reasonable selection of good tweezers.

The biggest challenge in surface mount soldering is being able to see what you are working on. Your hands have the ability to easily and repeatedly manipulate objects smaller than the naked eye can see. The ideal magnifying solution for soldering is an optical stereoscope, like the kinds used for the inspection of biological specimen. Unfortunately, these microscopes are very expensive, with the better models priced around the same cost as a used car. A more economical solution is to use a tabletop magnifying lens. Many drafting/art supply stores sell these kinds of lenses, and most office supply stores sell at least one model of lamp with an integrated magnifying lens.

These magnifying lenses will help assembly, but they lack the power to do a thorough inspection of your soldering job. A high-power loop magnifier, such as a jeweler's loop or a proofing magnifier, should be used to inspect finished solder joints.

Technique for Simple Components

Simple surface mount components, such as resistors, capacitors, inductors and small semiconductor devices such as transistors and diodes, are easy to mount on a circuit board. Let's look at the technique for mounting these components thorugh an example.

The first step is to place a blob of solder on one of the component's pads. Then, place and align the component over its pads using a pair of tweezers. Once you feel comfortable with the component's placements, apply heat to

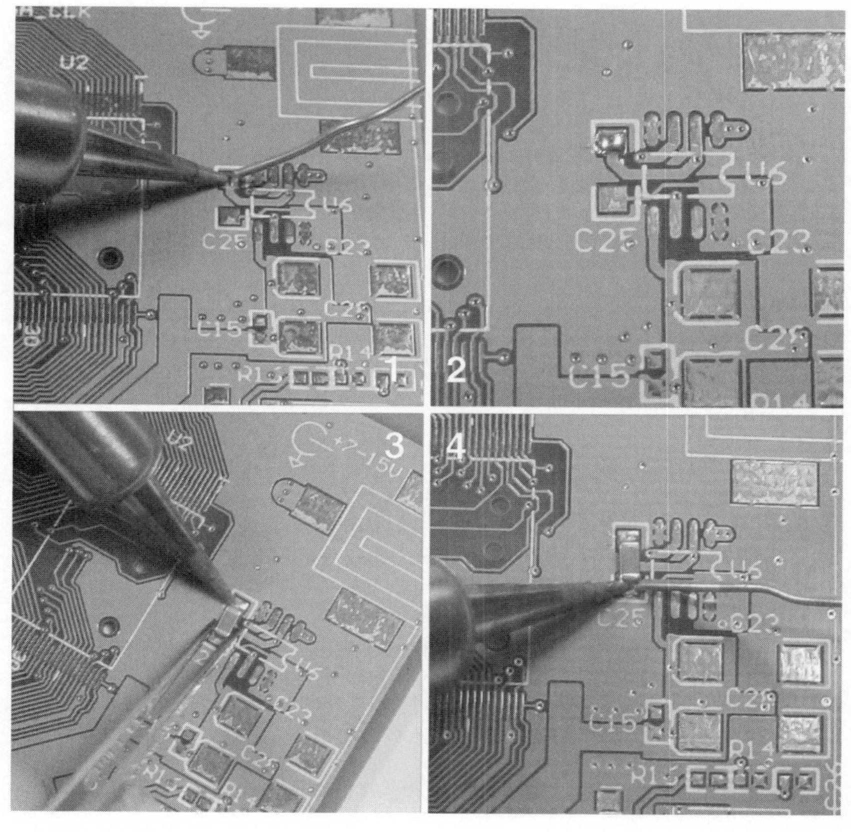

Figure A-1:

(1) Apply a touch of solder to one of the target component's pads. In this case, the target component is C25. (2) Picture of the solder blob after application. (3) Use tweezers to align the target component and then apply heat with a soldering iron until the initial solder blob has flowed around the component's leads. (4) Solder the remaining component pads.

the blob of solder until it melts and the component sinks into place on its pads. Keep applying the heat whilst you adjust the alignment of the component. Remove the heat, and wait for the solder to cool down and solidify. Double-check the alignment of the component, and then solder the rest of the component's contacts to the board. If the first solder joint looks dull or weak, re-heat it with a touch more solder once all the other pins have been soldered down. Figure A-1 illustrates this process.

This technique works for components with two or three pins, or multi-pin components with a wide pitch, such as the 50-mil pitch small outline IC packaged devices.

The most difficult situation for soldering down these components is when one or more of the component leads are attached to a large area of copper, such as a power plane. In this situation, a large amount of heat must be applied to the PCB pad before the solder will wet and adhere to the circuit board. Beware when this happens, as the solder will oxidize and ball up and make a poor electrical contact with the board. Add a touch of solder flux if this situation occurs to help enhance the wetting action of the molten solder.

Tip

A "dry" soldering iron tip will have trouble heating large patches of copper, or pads that are connected to power planes. One way to increase the rate of heat transfer from the soldering iron is to start the iron out with a blob of molten solder on the tip, and touch the iron to the board through the molten solder blob. This blob will spread out and locally heat the board and establish a good thermal connection that more effectively transfers heat. This will ultimately lead to a better solder connection after more solder is added.

Technique for Complex Components

Most integrated semiconductor components today are available in some kind of a fine-pitch surface mount package. This kind of packaging can be intimidating at first, but a few simple techniques and tips with a little bit of practice is all it takes to attach these parts with a high degree of confidence. The process of attaching a fine-pitch surface mount component is very similar to that of attaching a simple surface mount component, and it should not take more than a few minutes for a typical mid-sized surface mount package.

The first step is to tack the component on the circuit board by soldering down only two corner pins on the chip. If the alignment is not correct on your first try, it is easy to correct by just heating one of the two corners while pushing the chip in the desired direction for alignment. This process is illustrated in Figure A-2. Be very mindful of the accuracy of this alignment. A misaligned chip will lead to no end in frustrations while trying to solder the chip down.

Figure A-2:

First, solder down one pin on each of two opposite corners of a chip. The arrows on this diagram indicate the corners used in this example.

The next step is to apply a thin film of solder flux around the chip. This solder flux will enhance the wetting action of the solder on the chip pins and cause the solder to wick onto the component pads, instead of in between the leads causing a short. Figure A-3 illustrates this process.

Tip

When laying out a board, use extra-long pads for fine-pitched surface mount components. The extra length will make hand-soldering easier, at the trade-off of making routing a little bit more difficult and slightly growing the board size. The extra pad length acts to wick away excess solder from the chip leads, thus making solder bridges less likely.

Once all of the leads have been uniformly coated with the soldering flux, load the tip of a soldering iron with a tiny ball of solder, and press this ball up against the unsoldered leads. The ball of solder will wick into the space underneath and around the component leads. Repeat this process until all of the leads have been coated with solder. Do not worry at this point if excess solder bridges multiple pins. Once you are finished soldering all the pins, use a copper desoldering braid (solder-wick) to remove any solder bridges. This process is illustrated in Figure A-4.

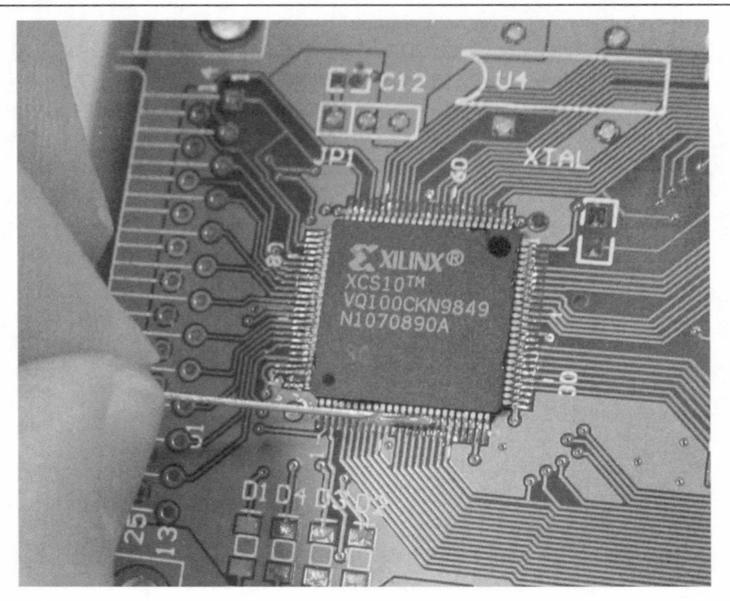

Figure A-3:
Apply a thin film of solder flux to the pins around the chip. In this illustration, a paste flux is being applied using a scrap piece of wire that is frequently dipped in the flux container.

You are almost done. The final thing to do is to make sure that all the pins are firmly soldered down. It is difficult to do this inspection visually without a microscope. Instead, pull on the pins with a needle or the tips of a tweezer. Drag the tweezer along the pins as illustrated in Figure A-5 using a firm, steady motion. Pins that are not soldered in place will move slightly. Repair these pins by pushing them back into place, if necessary, and applying a touch of solder to the pin.

Caution

Always check for power shorts after soldering a circuit board. Some solder bridges can be microscopic dendrites, and some solder bridges will form behind the pins underneath the chip. Check for power shorts using a multimeter set to measure resistance. Do not use the audible continuity mode, as large, high speed computer boards usually have a low (few ohms) resistance between power rails, which is low enough to register a short on many continuity meters. Also, when measuring the resistance between power lines, wait a second or two for the measurement to settle. The initial resistance between power rails will be very low while the large capacitors that sit on the power lines charge up.

Once your component has been soldered down, clean up the excess flux using a mild solvent, such as Isopropyl alcohol, and a cotton swab as illustrated in Figure A-6. Clean-up is important because it makes visual

Figure A-4:

(1) melt a small amount of solder onto the tip of a hot iron. (2) Transfer this solder onto the pins of the component. Repeat steps (1) and (2) until all pins are soldered. (3) Solder bridges, indicated with arrows, will have formed across many pins. (4) Remove the solder bridges using a piece of copper desoldering braid.

inspection easier, and it also makes it easier to probe the chip pins during debugging. It is also important because many fluxes have a tendency to crust over and trap contaminants with age, and this will hamper repairs in the future.

Technique for Removing Components

There are many techniques for removing surface mount components, and many of them require special tools, such as tong-style soldering irons or hot air guns. Tong-style soldering irons are good for removing smaller surface mount components, especially on boards that are densely packed. They are fairly quick and efficient, and a proper tong-style soldering iron will leave the pins of the component in relatively good condition. However, tong-style soldering irons are fairly expensive and they require a bit of practice in order to figure out the right timing and pressure to use when removing a chip. An

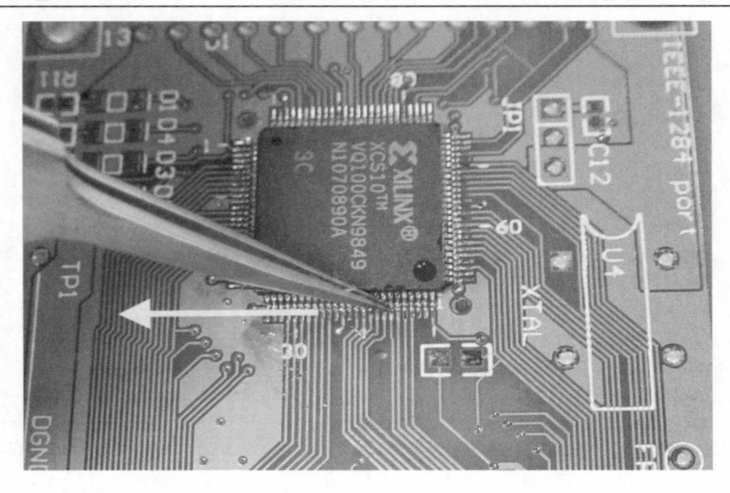

Figure A-5:
Stroke the pins along the side of the chip using a pair of tweezers or a needle using a firm, steady force. Pins that are not soldered well will bend slightly. The arrow indicates the direction of motion.

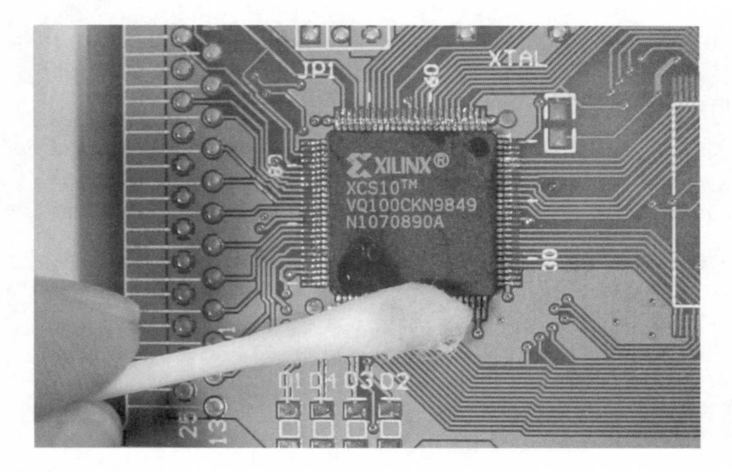

Figure A-6:
Clean up the flux residue using a cotton swab dipped in a mild solvent.

easier and cheaper solution is to use a heat gun, like the kinds sold in hardware stores for removing linoleum floor tiles. The heat gun will heat the entire region of a board, and components will float right off of their pads with minimal damage to their leads. The downside of this technique is that it is not very precise, so it is not an ideal solution for removing chips on boards that are going to be used again. As a result, heat guns are most effective for salvaging good chips from broken boards. The other problem with using heat guns is that the heat can warp boards or cause destructive failures in chips that have absorbed moisture into their packages. This failure mode, called "popcorning", happens when moisture trapped inside a chip boils but cannot escape, causing a pressure buildup that culminates in a destructive release event. Chips and boards operating in a humid environment or that have been washed in water should be baked in an oven at around 200-250 °F for a few hours before desoldering with a heat gun.

Another option that is particularly appealing for hobbyists is to re-alloy the solder joint so that it melts at a very low temperature, below 300 °F. A company called Chip Quik (`www.chipquikinc.com`) holds the patent on this technique, and removal kits can be purchased from many vendors, including Jameco (order number 141305). This technique is appealing because it requires no special equipment, and it is easy and fairly safe, as illustrated in Figure A-7. First, coat the chip pins with soldering flux. Then, melt the chip removal alloy onto the pins of the component to be removed. This will create a large bead of low melting temperature alloy all around the chip. Next, heat the entire bead by dragging the tip of the soldering iron through the bead. The stored heat in the chip and the alloy will keep it molten long enough for the whole chip to be easily slid off its pads. Finally, clean up the low melting temperature alloy by heating it with a soldering iron and then wiping it away with a cotton swab. The alloy will wipe off fairly easily from both the board and the chip. This re-alloying technique preserves the integrity of the removed chip's pins as well as the pads on the circuit board. The downside of this technique is that cleaning up the alloy can be a bit messy, and tiny particles of alloy can get caught between the pins of neighboring chips. A little bit of caution while cleaning up will prevent this problem. The other downside is that removing chips consumes the removal alloy, so removing large numbers of chips with this alloy can become expensive in the long run. Fortunately, chip removal is a fairly rare occasion for most hobbyists.

Note

A type of surface mount package that is becoming increasing popular due to its high electrical performance and density is the "ball grid array" (BGA) package. These packages are attached to a board through a large array of solder balls underneath the package. Clearly, this kind of package cannot be soldered using a conventional soldering iron. In addition, BGA packages are very difficult to inspect because most of the solder connections are buried deep underneath the package. The only viable method for attaching these components is to use an oven that heats the whole board and the component to the point where all the solder balls melt. Typically, the alignment of these BGA packages is accomplished with the aid of a machine of some kind, and the inspection of these BGA packages is accomplished with either X-rays or ultrasonic imaging.

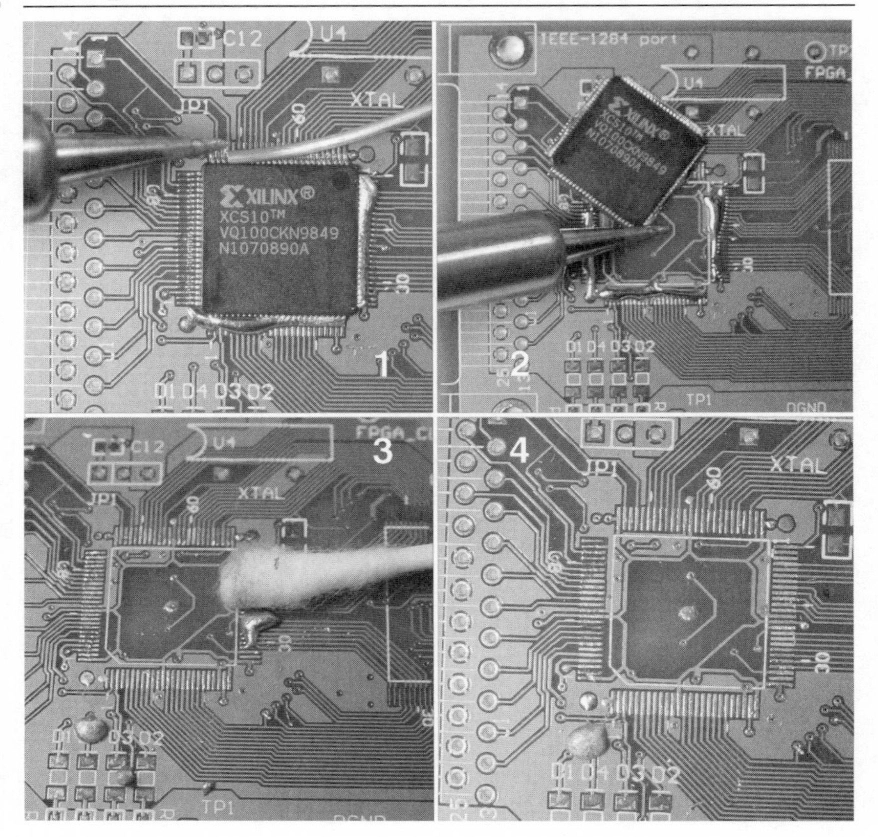

Figure A-7:

Removing a chip by realloying the solder joint. Prepare the chip pins with soldering flux before starting this process. (1) Melt the realloying compound onto all of the chip pins. The realloying compound comes in wire form. (2) Heat the blobs of metal around the chip by dragging a soldering iron through the metal. All the realloyed solder will become molten, at which point the chip can be pushed off its pads. (3) Clean up the realloying compound from the board and the chip by heating it and wiping it away with a cotton swab. (4) The result, a clean chip removal.

APPENDIX C

Getting Into PCB Layout

This appendix will introduce you to the PCB design and layout process. Additionally, this appendix surveys available tools on the market that you may need to achieve your design goals, featuring products and techniques for those on a shoestring budget. This appendix concludes with the presentation of some simple designs intended to get you started in your hardware adventures.

Philosophy and Design Flow

Printed circuit boards are the canvas of the hardware hacker, and CAD tools are the brushes. Like any engineering or artistic discipline, building a proficiency in printed circuit board design and layout takes practice. Fortunately, the advent of inexpensive PCB prototyping services and free (or near-free) CAD tools have made PCB design and layout an inexpensive and accessible hobby.

The design and the layout of PCBs are two intimately coupled tasks. Trade-offs give and take throughout the design and layout phases. Sometimes a component may not fit, or maybe a part is not available, and you'll have to change the schematic design to accommodate for this shortfall. Other times, you may have a high-level design change or you may catch a bug, and the PCB will have to be updated to reflect these changes. In my experience, the key to rapidly cranking out a successful PCB design is being flexible on all design fronts.

Refining your Idea

The PCB design process always starts with your idea, and the first thing you need to do is get a very clear vision of what you are trying to build. The more specifics you have up front, the easier you will find the design process. You should have an idea of how big you want the final board to be, how much it should cost, and of course what it should do. I always find it helpful to draw sketches and, in the case of large projects, write design documents that help me organize and record my thoughts. For the first few designs, nailing down an idea will be one of the most difficult steps because you do not know what kinds of components are available to implement your idea, and what sorts of real-world constraints you will have to design around. The best way to get started is to find an existing idea that is very similar to yours and model your idea after it. Many chip manufacturers offer free application notes and design samples that form a great starting point. Another source of information for defining your ideas is from existing products: if you want to build an alarm clock, take an existing clock apart and see how it was done.

Schematic Capture

Once you have your idea, you need to create a schematic diagram. A schematic is a symbolic representation of your idea, expressed as a collection of part symbols and virtual wires.

Most schematic capture software tools come with a library of parts to help accelerate the schematic capture process. If you do not find the part you need in the library, you will have to build your own schematic symbol. All schematic symbols are linked to a PCB component footprint. A footprint is the pattern of copper on a PC board that mates to a component. A common source of errors is not checking the link between the symbol and the footprint: a 16-pin DIP footprint does not fit a 16-pin in-line surface mount connector, and most design tools cannot tell the difference between the two. Therefore, you must check to make sure that your footprint assignments are all correct. For this reason, double and triple checking the schematic symbol is highly recommended. In particular, always check and re-check power pins, since they can cause the most difficult and destructive kind of errors. Perhaps a friend can help double checking the symbols as well, to avoid repeating errors or allowing errors to pass unknowingly. This amount of redundancy may sound silly for simple parts, but it becomes absolutely essential for hundred and thousand-pin parts where your brain becomes mush halfway through the checking process.

Attention to detail is the most important skill for capturing a schematic. As we saw in the last section, errors can sometimes be very elusive, so having attention to detail initially can save you from frustrating bugs later on. Every pin on every component is there for a reason, and if any pin is left unconnected, you should understand why that is okay (or not okay). To this end, it is advisable to read the product data sheets, including every

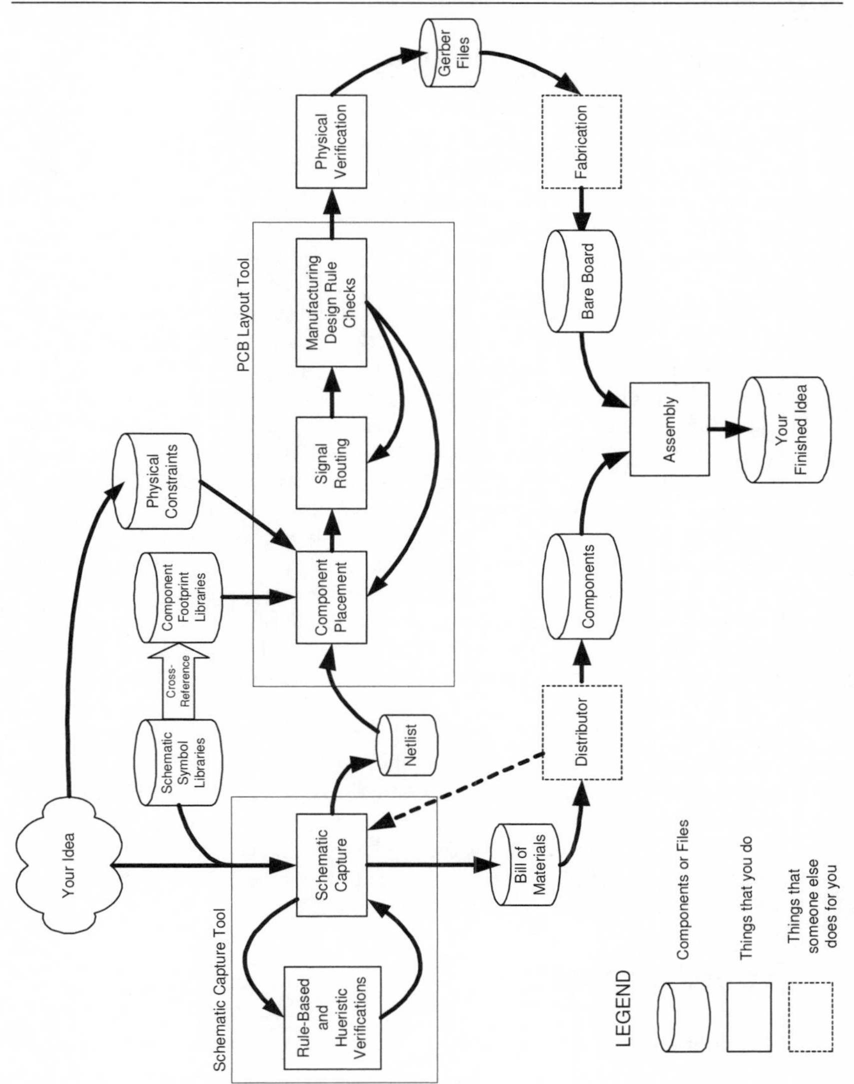

Figure C-1:
Board design process, from idea to finished product.

single page and footnote. A common source of frustrating bugs is ignoring the fine print that requires a pull-up resistor to set startup conditions, or a capacitor to filter noise or stabilize the system.

Design rule checkers are helpful in finding some errors in schematics. The checks performed by these tools are usually quite elementary, and thus catch only the grossest of errors. A typical set of checks performed by a design rule checker include catching duplicate part designators, dangling nets, and floating inputs.

In addition to conventional design rule checkers, simple checks can devised by the user. One check that many design tools *do not* perform are netlist parity checks which can be generated fairly easy using a perl script or a spreadsheet program. Netlist parity checks are heuristic checks where a tally is taken of how many components are connected to each netlist, then the tally is sorted by number of connections. At the top of the sorted list will be all the "single-pin nets". A single-pin net is almost always an indication of a typographical error (misspelled netlist name) during schematic capture. It can also be useful to browse through the whole sorted list briefly, and check that all groups of signals have the same number of connections. Most signal busses have the same number of connections to every signal in the bus. A tool that enables netlist connection tally checks for your schematic capture program can be created in an afternoon, and will undoubtedly save countless hours of effort and money from the bugs that it will catch.

Before exporting the schematic to the board layout tool, it is recommended that you order all of the parts in the schematic's bill of materials. Often times, critical parts will be in shortage and the schematic capture will have to be redesigned accounting for the shortage. Frequently, a change in a component footprint assignment is the only redesign necessary. Modifying to the schematic design to account for manufacturer's shortages avoids the difficult task of making the change on a finished board layout.

Board Layout

The input to a board layout program is a netlist that is annotated with component footprint information. A netlist is an intermediate representation of every component, pin and their connectivity. Netlist extraction is a well-automated process, but the correlation of schematic symbols to PC board footprints is not always well-managed. The difficulty of symbol-to-footprint correlation stems from the availability of multiple packaging options for a single part. For example, the symbol for a transistor could equally imply a tiny SOT-23 packaged device or an enormous TO-3 packaged device, and it is up to you to ensure that the proper package is chosen during netlist extraction. A good habit to have is always checking the implied footprint *at the time the component is placed in a schematic*, rather checking all at once during the netlist translation, or worse yet, during placement or final design review. Once you have a finished netlist, you are ready to do the board layout.

The other external input to a board layout program are the design rules. Design rules are set by the board fabrication company and include specifications for the minimum trace width and minimum trace to trace spacing, minimum hole size, minimum through-hole annulus, and the number of power and routing layers. The exact design rules depend on the process you choose; which in turn is driven by what you can afford. The best processes offer traces as fine as 2 mils (a mil is 1/1000th of an inch or 25.4 microns) and laser-drilled blind/buried vias with a diameter of about the same, but the price for fabrication is well outside the typical hobbyists' budget of less than a hundred dollars. A more typical hobbyists' process features 6 mil trace/space design rules with 15 mil minimum finished hole sizes, with either two or four layers of copper. A list of board fabrication companies is provided toward the end of this Appendix.

Board layout consists of two phases: placement and routing. An intelligent parts placement will greatly simplify the routing task. In general, the goal is to place all parts so that connections are kept as short as possible, with as few vias as possible so as to minimize noise, delay and signal losses. The placement of some parts, such as connectors, switches and power components are well-constrained, leaving you little choice in their placement. For the remainder of the parts, an understanding of the design will help prioritize which parts should get the best placement.

Once your placement is finished, print the design at a scale of 1:1 and verify that the components fit in their respective footprints by populating the printed layout with the actual components. If you intend to use a socket with a component, be sure to use the socket for verifying the 1:1 plot, as sockets require more space than the component itself. This check guarantees that you have all the components in the correct package type, and it also guarantees all your component outlines are correct and there is sufficient clearance between each component to facilitate easy assembly. Another important thing to check on the 1:1 plot is the orientation and pinout of all the connectors. It is very easy to invert a connector or to have used the wrong gender's footprint on the circuit board. Be careful when handling chips, especially those with fine-pitch surface mount leads. Do not bend the leads, and observe proper static electricity control protocol.

General Placement and Routing Guidelines

Here is a short list of some placement and routing guidelines. Remember, these are just general suggestions and there will be situations where they do not apply.

Leave Space for via Fanouts on Surface Mount Devices

Surface mount devices offer a great density advantage when compared to the older through-hole componentry that used to be the de-facto standard. However, surface mount components still require through-hole vias for route-ability, especially in complex and/or auto-routed designs. These routing vias are referred to as "fan-out" vias for SMD pads. Figures C-2 and C-3 demonstrates the use of fan-out vias on a surface mount part.

Decoupling Capacitors fit Nicely Underneath SMD Pads

The most common passive component in a typical digital design is the decoupling capacitor. These tiny capacitors are everywhere, and they can consume valuable routing and via fan-out space if they are not properly placed. If you are willing to do a double-sided surface-mount board, decoupling capacitors can be placed on the board side opposite the target component's pads. By placing these components underneath the component's pad space, you are not consuming any via fan-out area. In fact, a well-placed decoupling capacitor can share the power via used by the

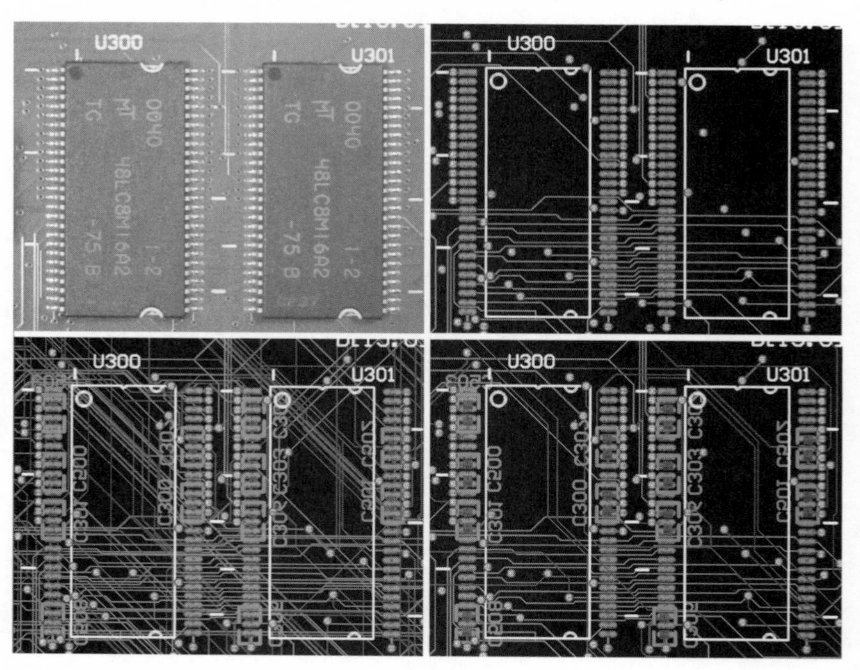

Figure C-2:
Four views of a circuit board layout. From the top left, clockwise: fabricated circuit board with components; top-layer circuit board view in PCB layout program; all-layers circuit board view in PCB layout program; top and bottom only layers view demonstrating two-sided SMT layout.

component's power pins. The view in the lower left hand corner of Figure C-2 provides a clear illustration of this technique. There are some special cases where you may not want to do this, as noted in the next section.

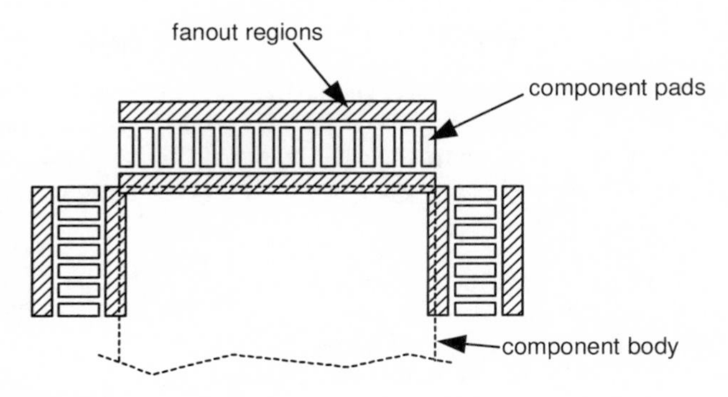

Figure C-3:
Fan-out regions around an SMD component's footprint.

Know your Special Traces

The good news about laying out digital circuit boards is that most traces require little thought, unlike a typical analog board. The bad news is that if you don't do the rest of the traces correctly, your board will exhibit strange, and frustrating to debug behavior. As a result, routing these special traces is a little bit of a black art. This section gives just a few guidelines for coping with these special traces, but I encourage interested readers to find a text dedicated to board layout to really learn and appreciate these techniques. Two texts that I recommend are "Digital Systems Engineering" by William J. Dally and John W. Poulton, and "High Speed Digital Design: A Handbook of Black Magic" by Howard W. Johnson and Martin Graham.

Typically, the kinds of traces that require special attention when routing a circuit board include:

- Power traces
- Timing reference (clock) traces
- High speed traces
- Analog/mixed signal traces

As a general rule, power traces need to be thicker than your average signal trace, especially if you are using one of the higher-end fabrication processes that offer narrow (~ 5 mil) trace widths. Power traces need to be thickened to counter both resistive heating and parasitic inductance. Narrow power traces, especially near the key power distribution points, will act like resistors and heat, dropping the supply voltage to a level that causes indeterminate malfunctions in your circuits. The proper sizing of a power trace depends upon the thickness of the copper. Typical boards use "1-oz copper" that is 1.35 mils thick (one square foot of 1.35 mil thick copper foil weights one ounce). An exterior 12 mil wide trace in 1 oz copper is required to pass 1 ampere of current with a 10 degree Celsius temperature rise. Thicker traces are required for buried layers for a similar current handling capacity.

When routing power traces between layers, remember that vias have resistance as well. A single via is insufficient to connect critical power traces between layers. Critical power traces should have multiple vias connecting them between layers to keep parasitic resistances and inductances down. Distributed power planes on multiple layers should also have vias generously distributed throughout in order to ensure that a common potential is preserved.

Note that in high performance or low noise applications, placing a via in between a decoupling capacitor and the power pin may carry too high of an electrical integrity price for the routing convenience. Vias disrupt the propagation of high-speed (hundreds of megahertz) electrical waves and thus, the optimal location of a decoupling capacitor in these applications is between the component pin and the power via.

Timing reference signals include clocks and strobes. Many memory devices require asynchronous control strobes that have sensitive timing requirements. These signals should be properly terminated and routed in a manner consistent with the termination strategy that typically implies a "daisy chain" route. Daisy chain routes have no branches, so there is only one path for the wavefront of the signal to travel.

Electric signals travel at about 1/4 the speed of light on a circuit board, or about three inches in a nanosecond. Thus, it is critical that high speed traces have matched lengths, or else signals can arrive significantly out of phase with respect to the timing reference. Trace lengths are matched by extending shorter traces to the length of the longest trace. Trace length extension is accomplished using serpentine traces that meander and increase the effective length of a trace without changing the placement of the trace's endpoints.

Analog and mixed-signal routing is well beyond the scope of this Appendix. In an average hobbyists' digital design, most of the analog circuitry will be isolated to the power supplies. Any special layout requirements for a particular power supply component is typically well-documented in the component's datasheet Also, keep in mind that electrical signals are lazy and promiscuous: signal current will always follow the path of least resistance, and signals will couple into adjacent traces. Furthermore, current must be conserved, so every signal current path must have a return current path, whether it is explicit or not. Keep these simple rules in mind as you layout any analog sections on your circuit board.

Circuit Boards Make Fine Heatsinks

When routing high-power components, such as power regulators and high-performance microprocessors, keep in mind that the copper in a circuitboard is an excellent conductor of heat. You can save yourself a heat sink under certain conditions by simply laying out a large region of copper connected to the heat slug or ground pins of the target part. If you are using a multi-layer board design with power planes, use multiple vias to help conduct heat into the internal layers.

The heatsinking capabilities of a circuitboard can also be a nuisance during hand-assembly. The good thermal conductivity of copper makes it difficult to heat up a component pin that is also connected to a large region of copper. When connecting low-power components to the power planes, consider using vias with thermal reliefs. A thermal relief is a set of small gaps in a via connection to a power plane that reduces thermal conductivity without significantly impacting the electrical performance of the connection. Note that a large group of densely packed thermally relieved power vias around a region of copper can result in unconnected or poorly connected islands of copper.

Establish Preferred Routing Directions for Each Layer

Establishing a dominant routing direction for each layer can simplify the routing of dense boards. For example, make the top layer the horizontal routing layer, and the bottom layer the vertical routing layer. If you need to route a signal between two components located diagonally across the board, first run a horizontal trace on the top and then a vertical trace on the bottom to connect the two components. The alternative strategy of just running a trace diagonally across the top layer of the board, for example, reduces the overall routability between the two halves of the board by one-half: the only way to get from one half to the other is now to go on the bottom.

Exceptions to this rule are acceptable, especially if you have to make a signal integrity versus routability trade-off.

Stack a Board with Orthogonal Layers

After establishing the preferred routing directions for each layer, stack the layers such that no two layers have parallel preferred routing directions. This orthogonality helps keep the interference of signals between layers to a minimum. If you have power layers, try to stack them in between layers. This also helps shield interference between signal layers.

On Two-Layer Boards, use Fingers to Bus Power

On a two-layer board, it is often tempting to just run power and ground as a ring around the outside of the board. This is not an ideal situation, because the ring starves the heart of the board and also increases the potential for large parasitic current loops that will degrade circuit performance. Instead, use interdigitated and/or stacked power fingers.These fingers will establish the dominant routing direction of each layer, and should be laid out before routing any signals.

Hints on Using an Auto-router

Auto-routers are a mixed blessing: they can save hours of routing time, but they can also cause hours of frustrating problems. The first rule of using an auto-router is to never allow an auto-router to work on your only copy of a circuit board design file. Instead, create a copy of your design and let the auto-router perform its magic on the copied design.

The second piece of advice is to learn the auto-router's bugs using simple test designs before applying the auto-router to your final design. Auto-routers frequently have critical bugs or limitations that need to be understood before using the tool. When learning an auto-router's bugs, particular attention should be paid to how the auto-router handles locked traces, poured polygons and awkward trace sizes. Some auto-routers will actually remove locked traces (traces laid down by hand and marked as unmovable), while others ignore or do not function in the presence of locked traces. This can be particularly frustrating if you have spent hours laying out the critical power and timing nets before turning on the auto-router.

Finally, don't count on an auto-router to fully route a complex board. Auto-routers are great for quickly routing the first 90% of a board, but they really slow down as the board gets more congested. Note that subtle changes in component placement can make or break an auto-router. Many auto-routers will not recognize busses or straight-through connections without special annotation or ideal component placement.

CAD Tools

Board design tools have dropped in price significantly over the past few years. The tool I use most frequently for board design is Protel 99SE. There is a newer version, Protel DXP, but I have not yet purchased the upgrade. Protel is a highly integrated tool, featuring schematic capture, simulation, library management and board layout with design rule checking and auto-routing, all integrated into a single tool. It seems like every software release some new feature is integrated into the design environment, for better or for worse. You can download a 30-day free fully functional demo of the Protel software from their website at `www.protel.com`. While a full-fledged license for the product is in the thousands of dollars, this still compares favorably against many other software packages that offer the same depth of functionality and number of features. Other high-end PCB CAD vendors include Mentor (PADS), Cadence (OrCAD), and Altium (P-CAD). Interestingly, Altium also owns the Protel software suite.

For those who are just starting out and want to do some casual board layout, some board fabrication companies offer full-function captive design tools for free. ExpressPCB (`www.expresspcb.com`) offers a free schematic capture and PCB layout tool for clients who use their fabrication service. Their tool is functional, but a little limited in terms of the design rule checks and the practical complexity for which you can realistically use it. ExpressPCB is a great starter tool for beginners, however, and is capable of implementing almost any weekend hardware project.

Before submitting any finished design for production, previewing your exported files with a third-party file viewer is a good idea. This will help protect your fabrication investment against bugs in your design tools. The most common file format used for board fabrication is the "Gerber" file format. A good, free Gerber previewer that I trust is made by Graphicode. You can download the previewer at `http://www.graphicode.com/`.

Board Fabrication Companies

Board fabrication companies come in as wide a range of capabilities as the CAD tools. Some companies only do large production orders, while others earn their bread and butter servicing the quick-turn prototype and hobbyist market. Here are a few of my favorite board fabrication companies, along with a brief description of their basic offerings.

Sierra Proto Express

Located in San Jose, Sierra Proto Express offers some of the most competitive quick-turn prototype rates. At the time of writing, Sierra Proto Express offers a line of "No Touch Product" processes. These fabrication processes have strict design rule requirements, but they are very affordable. For example, you can have a 2-layer circuit board fabricated in 4 days for $34/board (min. order of 2 boards), or you can have a 4-layer circuit board fabricated in 4 days for $51/board (min. order of 2 boards). The technology offered at these prices is a 6 mil trace/space design rule with 15 mil finished hole sizes. Sierra Proto Express also offers faster turn-time processes with trace widths down to 5 mils and 10 mil finished hole sizes. For more information, visit `www.sierraprotoexpress.com`.

Data Circuit Systems

Data Circuit Systems is also located in San Jose, California, and they are my vendor of choice for designs that require aggressive design rules or special processing options that don't fit well with the cheaper quick-turn companies' offerings. Data Circuits Systems has a comprehensive Process Capabilities Survey available for download at their website. Their capabilities survey is comprehensive and clearly written, so it takes a lot of guesswork out of interpreting the design rules. Data Circuits Systems also does a fairly rigorous set of factory checks on your submitted design. Their checks often catch subtle layout errors that can cause problems later down the road. I have also found their staff to be competent and friendly. Their prices are slightly higher than most engineering prototype manufacturers, but their well-documented process and design rule checks help reduce the risk of aggressive designs, and in the end the extra cost is probably worth it. Data Circuit Systems' website is `www.datacircuits.com`.

Advanced Circuits

Advanced Circuits is located in Aurora, Colorado. Their website (www.4pcb.com) features an instant quotation feature. This feature alone makes them a good choice for intermediate-complexity boards that do not fit any of the discount quick-turn process guidelines. You can use the instant quote feature to optimize your choice of implementation technology for price. In addition, Advanced Circuits frequently offers discount quick-turn specials, such as their current $33/board (min. order 3) promotional for two layers at 6 mil trace/space design rules (no hole size rule given on the website, unfortunately).

Alberta Printed Circuits

Alberta Printed Circuits (AP Circuits) is one of the original quick-turn prototype PCB houses, and they are located in Alberta, Canada. Despite being in another country, their service is prompt, thanks to NAFTA. The P1 process offered by AP Circuits is a basic process, with no soldermask or silkscreen. As a result, it is difficult to execute fine-pitch surface mount designs because during the assembly phase, solder tends to get everywhere. However, AP Circuits will fabricate and ship your board in the P1 process in just one day for an unheard of price, and there is no minimum order requirements. Pricing fluctuates due to the currency exchange rate, but the base fee for a production run is $46 at the time of writing, with a $0.65 per square inch charge on top of the base fee. The technology is an 8 mil trace/space with a minimum drill size of 20 mil (28 mil if you want to stick with the cheapest process option). AP Circuits is great for boards that have to get done in a pinch and on a strict budget, especially if you are using through-hole or coarse SMT components that are easy to assemble without a soldermask. Their website is www.apcircuits.com.

Starter Projects

In Chapter 5, Replacing a Broken Power Supply, you are instructed on how to replace an Xbox power supply with a standard ATX power supply. The one problem is that the polarity of the power on signal is inverted between the Xbox and the standard ATX supply. The hack solution proposed in the chapter is to always leave the supply on, and to instead switch the Xbox on and off by first turning on the power supply and then pressing the Xbox's power button.

It is fairly easy to design and layout a board that enables you to invert the polarity of the power signal so that you can control the power state of the Xbox from just the front panel of the Xbox. You can also properly regulate the standby power supply, instead of using two diodes. Such a board would consist of an inverter chip, such as the 74HCT04, and a regulator, such as the LM317K. The LM317K is an adjustable regulator that can be set to reduce the +5V standby voltage provided by the ATX supply down to the +3.3V standby voltage demanded by the Xbox. An example schematic diagram of this board is shown in Figure C-4.

The choice of connectors to this board is up to you. The simplest solution would be to just use holes and solder the wires through the holes. There are only five connections on this board. Three go to the power supply: the +5VSB (violet) wire, a ground (black) wire, and the power on output (green) wire. The remaining two, +3.3VSB (pin 6 on the power connector) and power on input (pin 11 on the power connector), go to the Xbox.

Be sure to test the voltage output of the regulator before installing your finished board. It is fairly easy to get a resistor value wrong or a pin swapped, and both of these conditions could lead to dangerously high voltages going into the Xbox. Also, when installing the board permanently, be sure to insulate the bottom and top of the board from accidental contact with the Xbox case or other Xbox components.

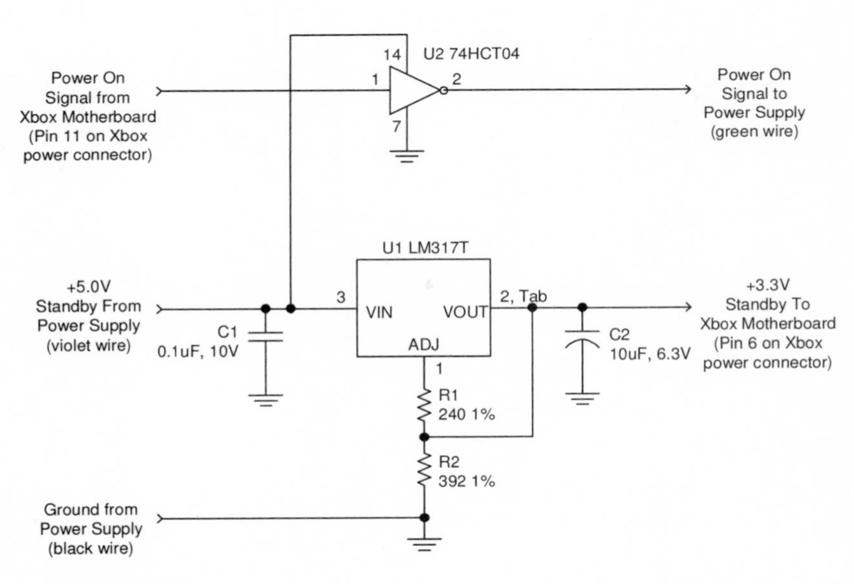

Figure C-4:

Example schematic diagram of the ATX power supply replacement adapter board. Resistors R1 and R2 program the output voltage of the voltage regulator, U1, to be +3.3V.

APPENDIX D

Getting Started with FPGAs

Integration is the bane of hardware hackers. We like to take things apart, modify them and improve them, but the trend has been to cram everything into one or two ASICs (Application Specific Integrated Circuit). This kind of integration is out of the reach of mere mortals, as the cost of a set of masks used for defining the features on chips is rapidly approaching a million dollars. A millions dollars *per unique revision* of the chip. If a mistake was made that requires a new mask set, you have to spend yet another million dollars to fix it. Fortunately, a million dollars of up-front cash for a chip is too much even for many corporations, and this has created a market for FPGAs — general-purpose, programmable ("reconfigurable") hardware devices that can be used in the place of an ASIC in many applications.

What is an FPGA?

FPGA stands for "Field Programmable Gate Array". In other words, it is an array of gates that can be programmed in the field, i.e., by end users. You can think of them as custom silicon that you can build in the comfort of your own home, although the trend toward partial reconfigurability and context-sensitive reconfiguration adds a dimension to FPGAs that is not found in ASICs. While ASICs are cheaper per unit in volume and ASICs can have much higher clock speed performance, FPGAs have established themselves as the tool of choice for low to moderate volume applications and for prototyping.

The basic architecture of an FPGA is an array of hardware primitives embedded in a flexible routing network. The power of the FPGA comes from the fact that complex computations can be broken down into a sequence of simpler logic functions. These simpler functions can each be broken down in turn, until the entire computation is described by nothing more than a sequence of basic logic operations that can be mapped into the FPGA's hardware primitives. Thus, the same FPGA can be used to implement a microprocessor or a video controller or a tic-tac-toe game just by changing the configuration of the hardware primitives and the routing network.

The kinds of hardware primitives implemented by an FPGA architecture strongly influence the implementation efficiency of the FPGA for a given target application. Modern FPGAs provide designers with mostly one bit wide primitives: a 4 or 5 input to 1-bit output lookup table, and a single bit of time-synchronized storage known as a flip flop. Lookup tables are used as the logic primitive because they can be programmed to perform any logic operation with as many terms as there are inputs to the lookup table. These primitives are then wired into a vast programmable network of wires; a typical high-end FPGA might have many tens of thousands of these primitive elements.

It turns out that while single bit-wide structures are very general, they can be very resource-inefficient in applications where the natural data width is large. In particular, the area dedicated to the actual logic primitives is around 1% in many cases, with the remainder being configuration memory and interconnect. All of this wire is required to handle the multitude of permutations of routing that you might require for single-bit wide applications. In order

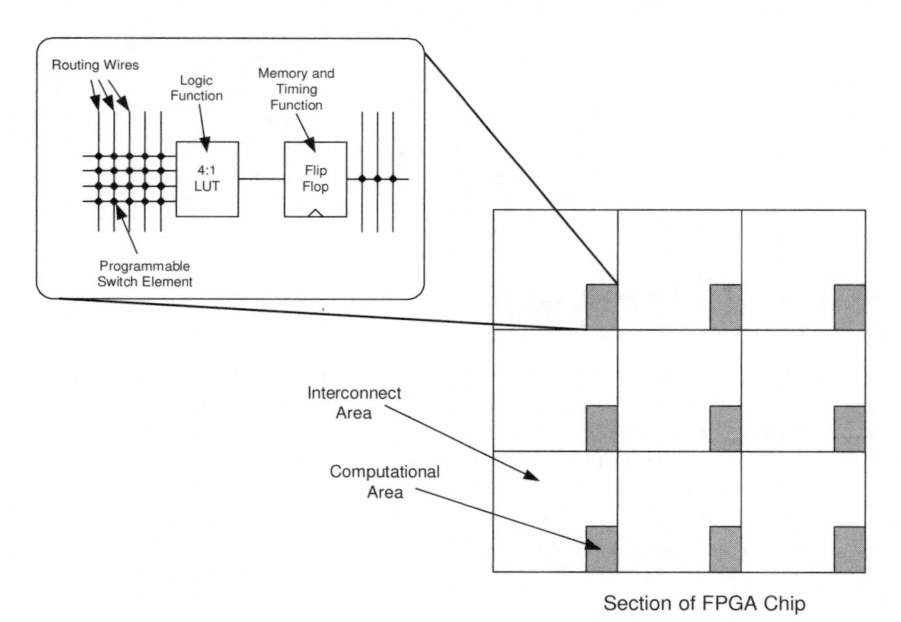

Figure D-1:
Block diagram of a typical FPGA structure, illustrating the disparity between the amount of wire on an FPGA versus the amount of computational logic. A typical modern FPGA will contain several tens of thousands of these basic cells.

to boost area efficiency, many FPGAs also include a few coarse-grain primitives, such as chunks of RAM or a multiplier block. Xilinx's Virtex II-Pro FPGAs even include several PowerPC cores on-chip. While this sounds impressive, the actual area consumed by such a core is surprisingly small: a PowerPC processor probably consumes a little more than $1mm^2$ of silicon area, whereas the area of the FPGA is hundreds of square millimeters.

The most recent FPGAs on the market have very flexible I/Os in addition to having very flexible computational hardware. A typical FPGA can interface to all of the most popular high-speed signaling standards, including PCI, AGP, LVDS, HSTL, SSTL, and GTL. In addition, most FPGAs can handle DDR clocked signals as well. In case those acronyms didn't mean anything to you, the basic idea is that an FPGA can be used to talk to just about any piece of hardware you might find on a typical PC motherboard, such as the Xbox. This is extremely good news to hardware hackers, because it means that an FPGA can be used to emulate or monitor almost any chip found in a PC. Of course, the PC may have to be down-clocked in the cases where the FPGA cannot keep up with the speed of the PC.

Designing for an FPGA

You have a number of design entry options to choose from for a typical FPGA design flow. If you prefer to think graphically, most design flows support a schematic-capture tool. Schematic capture is often more intuitive for hardware designs, but they can be more difficult to maintain and modify. For example, changing all instances of a net name can be tedious if you have to click on every wire and type in the new name. Furthermore, the size of any single level of design hierarchy is limited to the size of a schematic sheet, so a complex design will require a good deal of planning and forethought for just the schematic capture. As a result, hardware Description Languages (HDLs) are the tool of choice for implementing complex designs. HDLs look very similar at first glance to normal programming languages. For example, the syntax of Verilog looks very similar to that of C or Java. However, the semantics of the language can be a bit of a challenge to understand. Hardware has an inherent parallelism that procedural languages such as C cannot express. If you think about it, every gate and every flip flop on an FPGA can compute in parallel, whereas in a C program, a single thread of execution is nominally assumed. As a result, HDLs represent hardware as a collection of processes that operate in parallel; it is up to the coder to group all the functions into the correct processes so that the compiler can understand how to turn a process into gates.

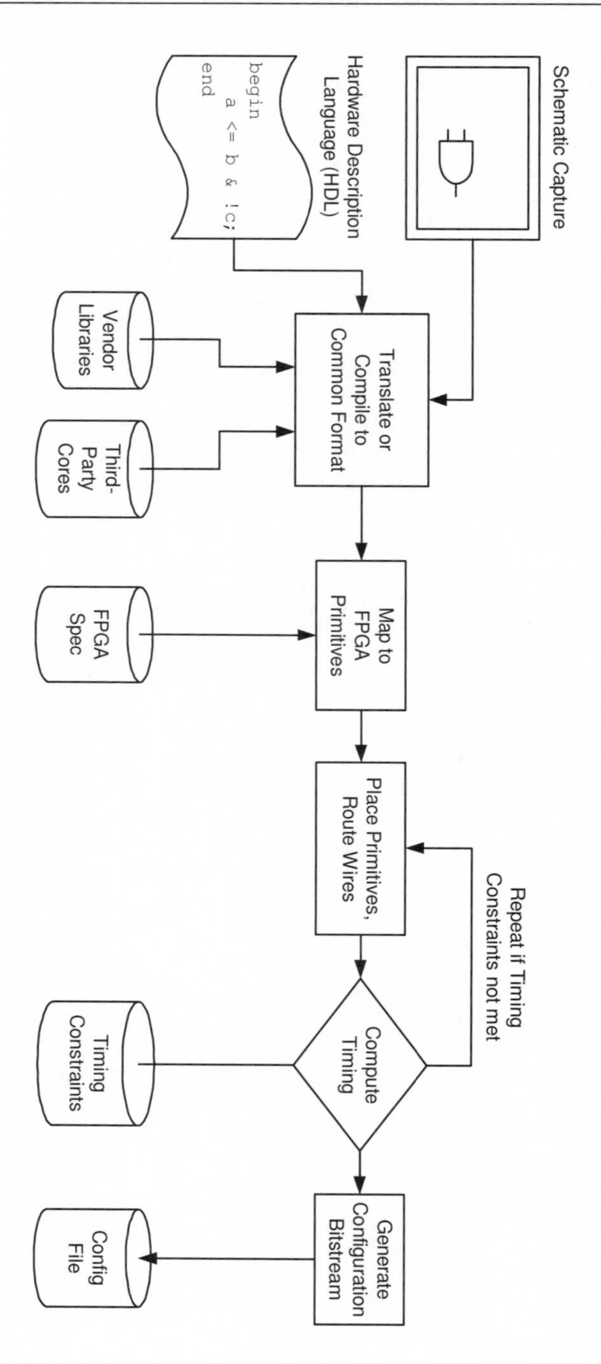

Figure D-2:
Typical FPGA design flow.

For example, a single clocked storage element (a flip-flop) in Verilog is a "process" that typically has a structure similar to this:

```
input inData;        // declare your inputs and outputs
input clock;
reg   bitOfStorage;  // declare the storage bit as a reg
type

always @(posedge clock) begin
  bitOfStorage <= inData;
end
```

This code takes the value on input port `inData`, and on every rising clock edge, stores `inData` in a flip flop whose output is called `bitOfStorage`. Multiple processes delimited by `always @( ... ) begin ... end` syntax can exist in a single design, and all processes execute in parallel.

Combinational logic can also be expressed as a process. For example, the following Verilog code implements a two-input multiplexer that has no clock:

```
input  a;
input  b;
input  select;
output out;
reg    c;
always @(a or b or select) begin
  if( select == 1'b1 ) begin
    c <= a;
  end else begin
    c <= b;
  end
end

assign out = c;  // assign statements can contain logic
                 // functions as well
```

In this example, the contents of the parenthesized block following the `always` keyword contains a *sensitivity list* that includes all of the inputs that might affect the output. Leaving a parameter out of the sensitivity list means that the output will not change, even if that parameter changes. For example, if you omitted `a` and `b` from the sensitivity list, then the only time the output would change would be when `select` changed: you would have built a latch that stores either `a` or `b` depending upon the state of `select`. However, the desired operation of a multiplexer is to relay changes on either `a` or `b` to the output at all times, even when `select` does not transition, so `a` and `b` must both be part of the sensitivity list.

There are a number of subtleties when learning an HDL that are beyond the scope of this book, but the two code segments above should give you a flavor for what to expect. A skilled software programmer may have more trouble adjusting to an HDL than a novice, because many software tricks that are taken for granted translate very poorly to direct hardware implementation. Arrays, structures, multiplication and division primitives are all taken for granted in the software world, but each of these constructs translate to potentially large and inefficient blocks of hardware. Furthermore, in a hardware implementation, all possible cases in a `case` statement exist whether or not you intend for it; neglecting to fully-specify a `case` statement with a `default` case often means that extra hardware will be synthesized to handle the implicit cases. Numerous tutorials and syntax reference manuals for Verilog are indexed in Google; `verilog syntax` and `verilog tutorial`

Overclocking FPGA Designs

It is worth noting that the timing models used for an FPGA are quite conservative. This means that it is quite likely that an FPGA will operate properly at frequencies much higher than the timing analyzer will admit. In fact, careful hand-layout of an FPGA's logic can stretch the performance of the FPGA much further than its stated specifications. For example, the FPGA (Xilinx Virtex-E) used to implement the Xbox Hypertransport bus tap is only specified to handle data rates of around 200 Mbits/s/pin, but the application demanded 400 Mbits/s/pin. The reason I could pull this off is that the actual logic and storage elements themselves can run very fast, but most of the performance is burned off in the in the wires and repeaters that carry the signals between logic elements. Specifically, some wires will have so much delay at 400 Mbits/s that they effectively store data for a single clock cycle. I determined which wires were slower than the rest by capturing a sequence of data and comparing it against a pattern that I had previously discovered using an oscilloscope. Once the slow paths were identified, I inverted the clock and/or inserted flip-flops on channels that had too little delay. The end result was a set of signals that were time-skew corrected. These signals could then be trivially demultiplexed to a lower clock rate where conventionally compiled HDL design techniques could be used. While this technique is very powerful, it is not generally applicable because the amount of delay caused by a wire varies from chip to chip and can depend on parameters such as the ambient temperature and the quality of the power supply voltage. However, for one specific chip under controlled circumstances, I was able to get 2x the rated performance. Another important difference between this application and a more general application is that bit error rates on the order of 1 error in a few thousand was tolerable, since I could just take three traces and XOR them to recover any information lost to random noise sources. However, 1 in 10,000 bit error rates are not acceptable for normal applications; unrecoverable error rates better than 1 in 10,000,000,000,000 are more typical. This all goes back to a saying that I have: "It is easy to do something once, but doing something a million times perfectly is hard".

are both good sets of keywords to start out with when searching for syntax references or tutorials. Xilinx's website also has a good Verilog reference for FPGA designers, and Sutherland HDL, Inc. has a free Verilog quick reference guide at `http://www.sutherland-hdl.com/on-line_ref_guide/vlog_ref_body.html`.

Another advantage of the HDL design entry approach is the availability of free and paid "softcores". Websites such as `www.opencores.org` offer general-public licensed HDL cores for functions such as USB interfaces, DES and AES crypto-engines, and various microprocessors. In addition, almost every standard function is offered by third-party vendors who will sell you cores for a fee.

After design entry, it is highly recommended to simulate your design before compiling it into hardware. Trying to track down bugs by twiddling code, pushing it to hardware and probing for changes is very inefficient. Simulation allows you to probe any node of the circuit with the push of a button; in addition, the effort required to simulate a code change is very small, especially when compared to the effort of pushing a change all the way through to hardware.

Once the design has been entered and simulated, it needs to be compiled or translated into a common netlist format. This netlist format is fed into a program that maps the netlist primitives into the target FPGA hardware primitives. Then, the mapped primitives are placed and routed. The resulting design is analyzed for compliance with a set of constraints specified by the designer. If the design does not meet the specifications of the designer, then the design is iteratively refined through successive place and route passes. Once the design passes its design constraints, it then goes to a configuration bitstream generator where the internal representation of the FPGA gets translated into a binary file that the FPGA can use to configure itself. All of these steps happen fairly seamlessly at the touch of a button in the later versions of the FPGA design tools.

Project Ideas

Now that you know a little bit about what an FPGA is and how you can program them, what sorts of things can you do with them? It turns out that FPGAs have enough logic capacity and performance these days to accomplish a very impressive range of tasks. The obvious industrial application of FPGAs is in the emulation of designs intended for hard-wired silicon. The cost of building a custom chip has been skyrocketing, and it will soon be the case where a single critical mistake can cost hundreds of thousands of dollars, if not millions, to fix. On the other hand, fixing a mistake made in an FPGA HDL description pretty much only costs time and design effort; you don't throw away any parts, and you don't have to buy any new parts. Thus, many companies have adopted the strategy of fully simulating a mock-up of the design in FPGAs before taping out the final silicon. A side benefit from this approach is that the software and hardware teams that are users of the custom silicon can begin validating their designs using the FPGA mock-up while the custom silicon is being fabricated, a process that can sometimes take a couple of months.

For hackers, FPGAs are sort of a panacea for all kinds of complex projects. FPGAs are excellent choices for implementing cryptographic functions if you are interested in doing brute-force keysearches or encrypting large amounts of data quickly. They are also very useful for implementing signal processing functions, especially given the existence of free multiplier and digital filter cores. FPGAs can achieve higher performance for less power than a DSP, and thus they have a unique niche in applications such as battery-powered robotics. FPGAs are also useful for embedded controller applications. A small microprocessor core, equivalent to or better than a PIC, can easily fit in an FPGA today. Add all your custom hardware peripherals, such as a serial port and PWM timing generators, and you're in business.

FPGAs are also useful in situations where the focus is not big number crunching. An FPGA makes a great piece of glue logic in a tight spot. A well-place FPGA can save you from having to ever add a wire jumper to patch a board due to a logic design error. They also make a cheap logic analyzer alternative for those of us who cannot afford a $10,000 Tek TLA mainframe. The high-speed I/O capabilities of the latest FPGAs combined with large autogenerated FIFO-configured embedded memories makes short work of designing a signal capture and analysis system.

Finally, FPGAs have applications in mixed-signal situations that are not immediately obvious. The most common mixed-signal application is probably using an FPGA to drive the analog signals of a VGA monitor. A couple of resistive dividers or a well-chosen output driver type is all you need, and all the timing and logic necessary to generate color images can be handled with logic inside the FPGA. FPGAs can also be trivially used as PWM D/A converters, or even as part of a sigma-delta D/A or A/D converters.

Where to Buy

You're probably thinking that any tool this versatile and powerful has to cost a fortune. This was true about a decade ago, but today you can buy 100,000 gate FPGAs for well under $50, and the design tools are often free for educational users and/or hobbyists. Of course, an FPGA on its own is not so useful; it needs to be mounted to a board with the proper connections to be used. To this end, a company called XESS (`www.xess.com`) makes a line of fairly affordable FPGA starter kits. Their product line shifts as new FPGAs are introduced, but the current entry-level FPGA board is the XSA-50 board that comes with a 50,000 gate FPGA for about $150. The board also includes a few megabytes of RAM, a parallel port, a VGA port, a PS/2 keyboard port, and a few other essential items.

The other option is to build your own board from scratch, if you feel bold. Other appendices in this book describe how to get into board layout and fabrication and how to attach fine-pitched FPGA devices to your boards. It is actually quite a rewarding experience to try and build your own boards, and I recommend giving it a try; the cost of fabricating a board is well below $100 these days, so you don't loose too much even if your board doesn't work in the end. If you are making your own board, you will need to buy your FPGA from a Xilinx distributor. The Xilinx webpage (`www.xilinx.com`) has the most up-to-date links to distributors. As of the time of writing, one of the more convenient distributors is NuHorizons (`www.nuhorizons.com`), as NuHorizons gives product availability and pricing information on their webpage without requiring registration or a special customer account.

FPGA development software can usually be acquired at a low price or free. For example, Xilinx offers a free development environment for its Virtex-II (up to 300K gates), Spartan II-E and CoolRunner lines of parts. The development environment is called the Xilinx ISE WebPACK, and it is available for download after registration at `www.xilinx.com`. This free environment sports an impressive list of features, including schematic and HDL input, HDL synthesis, a flooplanner, timing driven place and route, timing analysis, and power analysis tools. Xilinx also offers a version of its software called "Xilinx Student Edition" through Prentice-Hall. This software comes bundled with a number of tutorials and documentation that can help you get into FPGA design. Xilinx also offers a wide variety of helpful tutorials and lectures on the their website under the "Education" tab.

APPENDIX E

Debugging: Hints and Tips

Don't Panic!

Developing your debugging skills is as important, if not more important, than developing your design skills. The most important single piece of advice is to never panic: randomly tweaking and changing things will introduce more uncertainty and bugs than it will fix.

Debugging is simple when given total visibility into a system and total knowledge of the expected state of a properly working system. Simply comparing the observed state against the expected state will elucidate what went wrong. Unfortunately, the world rarely works this way. Chips are black boxes, and the only visibility into the internal state of the chip is through its pins. Many signals are also too difficult to directly measure or record. Also, the specifications provided by manufacturers are often vague or difficult to interpret. Thus, the real art of debugging is in tracing a set of symptoms to a root cause despite a lack of visibility and total system knowledge.

Understand the System

Trying to debug a system without first understanding what you are trying to debug is like trying to read a Japanese comic without any knowledge of Japanese. You can figure out at a superficial level who is the bad guy and who is the good guy, but you get really lost as to exactly what the floating cat has to do with all of it. In order to fully understand the plot, you need a Japanese dictionary and a lot of time and patience. Similarly, basic electronics principles and intuition will get you to the point where you know roughly what to expect, but enlightenment only comes after you have read the component data sheets. The more you understand about a system, the easier it will be to figure out why things went wrong. Keep notes as you read more about the system, and think to yourself about ways problems might express themselves if something did go wrong. It also helps to have seen other systems that are similar to the one you are trying to fix, and it helps to have an understanding of the theory of operation.

Observe Symptoms

Bugs manifest themselves through symptoms, and it is up to you to deduce the root cause by observing several symptoms and deducing the culprit. A blank screen on a TV that should be showing the video output of your console is an example of a symptom. There are many reasons why your TV screen could be blank, such as a broken video cable, a broken TV, a broken video connector, a broken video source, blank media in the video source, or even lack of power to the system. As a general rule, you should observe at least two, preferably three, symptoms that are consistent with a cause before concluding that you have found the root cause. Keep in mind that the most telling symptoms are often not outwardly obvious, and will require a measurement or an experiment to find them. In the example of our blank TV screen, our measurements are as simple as seeing if the power light on the TV turns on, or if sound comes out of the TV without the video.

The basic strategy for debugging is to start with an obvious symptom and isolate various parts of the system to determine which part is the immediate cause of the symptom. An immediate cause is defined as something that directly impacts the observed symptom. Immediate causes for video failure on a TV are lack of a signal to the TV, a broken TV, or lack of power; non-immediate causes would be a hardware failure in your video source or the phase of the moon. In other words, given symptom A, think of all the possible immediate causes X, Y and Z. Then, test X, Y and Z to determine which is the actual cause. Once you have isolated the problem to one of X, Y or Z, think about what might have caused X, Y or Z to fail and repeat the process until you have discovered the *root cause.*

Isolating the cause of bugs can be facilitated by the use of known good references. In our example, you can eliminate the TV as a source of failure by feeding it a signal from a known good DVD player. In order for a known good reference experiment to be valid, you must keep everything constant except for the piece you are replacing with the reference. Plugging the good DVD player into a different input from the consoles' on the TV will only tell us that the display part of the TV works. The path from the console input to the TV is not tested. A proper execution of the experiment would plug the DVD player into the video input used by the console.

This kind of paranoia or inherent mistrust of the system becomes very important when tracing down subtle hardware bugs. Do not take any factor for granted that could affect the system you are observing, and never, ever ignore inexplicable or inconsistent behaviors, even if it is intermittent. For example, sometimes a system will work properly or break if you touch a certain location on the circuit board or wave your hand near a certain area; sometimes a system will demonstrate different behavior for a brief moment after power-on. It is tempting to write off such observations as anomalies or trivial occurrences, but the fact is that they did happen and there must be an explanation. One specific example is touching a circuit board and observing a change in the state of the system. Where did you touch? How did you touch it? Are your hands sweaty or dry? When you touch a circuit board, your body acts like a small capacitance and a large resistance. This can slightly slow down signals or discharge high-impedance nodes such as an unconnected digital input. If you pressed firmly on the board, you could be flexing the board in such a way that changes the electrical properties of a cracked trace or a bad solder joint.

There are also some symptoms that are often times incorrectly interpreted as causes. A burned-out trace or a damaged component is usually a symptom and not a cause of the problem. In other words, a malfunction elsewhere in the circuit is usually responsible for the failure of a component. Spontaneous component failure is a relatively rare occurrence. Suppose you are debugging a broken stereo. You smell something burning coming from the stereo, and you see a large resistor that is blackened from overheating. Chances are that if you just replace that resistor, the replacement will just burn out again. The real cause might be a shorted transistor or a damaged power supply circuit, but these do not manifest themselves as obviously as the burned out resistor.

Another potent observation technique is comparison against a known good system. If you are trying to debug a broken device, find a working one and compare voltages and other operational characteristics between the two. If you are trying to debug your own home-brew system, construct a simulation of the circuit if possible, or find a circuit with a similar design. You can use these known good systems to quickly isolate anomalous behavior. Furthermore, you can induce failures in the known good sample in a controlled fashion to check if you have really found the root cause of the problem. This technique is particularly applicable to simulated systems.

Common Bugs

The most common source of hardware bugs in home-brew projects are poor solder joints and improperly installed polarized components, such as capacitors, diodes, ICs, and connectors. Also, connectors are particularly notorious sources of failures because they are subjected to the most physical abuse and it is typically difficult to determine if a connector is in good condition through visual inspection alone. The following is a list of common bugs, ranked loosely in descending order of popularity.

1. **Bad solder joint.** This includes cold solder joints, bridges, and forgotten joints. Careful visual inspection can catch many

instances of bad joints. The solder between all joints should appear to be smooth and shiny, and the solder should exhibit a wet-looking meniscus over circuit board pads and component leads. Pictures of good and bad solder joints can be found in the Appendix on Soldering Techniques. Poor solder joints can also be quickly identified on many surface mount packages by gently dragging a stiff wire, such as the tip of a tweezer or a paperclip, over the pins along the length of the package. Poorly connected pins will bend slightly. Flexing the board can also help reveal poor solder joints. In other cases, you may have to use an ohmmeter to verify the quality of a solder joint. If you had a messy experience soldering your components, clean the board with a mild solvent such as Isopropyl Alcohol using a cotton swab before inspection. Finally, remember that seeing is believing: use a magnifying lens to help your inspections. A medium-power microscope is preferred, but any mounted magnifying lens (like those found on drafter's lamps) or a ring loop like the kind used by jewelers will help enormously.

2. **Improper component values.** An improper component value can happen when a similar looking but different valued component is accidentally mounted on the circuit board. This is especially problematic with surface mount passives, which are often unlabeled or obscurely labeled. Keep in mind that the only way to properly test a component's value is to remove it from the board and then test it. Populating boards with wrong components can be avoided by being very careful and methodical about storing your components in clearly labeled bags or boxes during assembly.

3. **Bad connectors.** This includes connectors that have been installed backwards, or worse yet, designed with the wrong pin assignments. Pay attention to where pin 1 is, and the numbering system used by the connector. Some connectors use a zig-zag pin numbering system, while others use a circular pin numbering system. Wire-to-board connectors are also difficult to build by hand. Inspect all points where wires interface with connector contacts for poor crimps, excess insulation, or bad solder joints. In the worst case, use a voltmeter to verify the continuity of the connector.

4. **Configuration oversights as a result of not reading the data sheet.** Complex chips frequently support multiple operating modes that are selected by strapping a set of pins to high or low logic levels. Chips also frequently require external resistors to load or bias a pin for proper operation. Sometimes networks of capacitors, resistors and inductors are required by chips as well to stabilize internal functions. Keep in mind that unused inputs often require termination to a fixed voltage for proper operation, so do not ignore parts of a data sheet just because you do not use certain functions.

5. **Design problem or implementation problem.** Sometimes the bug is caused by at outright design error, or caused by a translation problem between a correct schematic and the board layout. Translation problems are frequently caused by typos when specifying the names of schematic nets, or by implicit power names on schematic symbols. Implicit power names are frequently used on digital components as a matter of convenience, but it can cause significant problems in designs that use multiple power supply voltages. These kinds of problems can be caught before going to layout with a heuristic netlist checking program, as described in Appendix C. Another kind of implementation problem are high speed design rule violations. Circuits that operate at high frequencies (25+ MHz) or have fast edge rates (< 5 ns) require special attention to electrical impedance and transmission line termination.

6. **Power supply is out of specification**. Test power supply voltages as close to the point of use as possible, as wires can reduce the actual delivered voltage. In some cases, there is nothing wrong with the circuit and the power supply is just incapable of providing enough juice to run your design. Also check for variations of the power supply voltage with time. Excess noise on a power supply can cause problems, and systems that use large amounts of high speed CMOS logic can have very demanding shifts in current consumption that can lead to short dips and spikes in the power supply voltage.

7. **Broken or damaged PC board traces.** This can be a problem if you hand-assembled a board and you were having troubles attaching a component. Excess heat during assembly can cause traces to lift off of the circuit board. Also, know your board vendor. Some board vendors (especially quick-turn discount prototype vendors) will not perform a full netlist electrical test of your circuit board. Look for over-etched traces that have thinned out of tolerance, and also check that every via hole has a silvery annulus around the hole. Sometimes the drill bits are misaligned or angled during board drilling, and the mis-drilled hole will end up breaking electrical connections.

8. **Latch-up or power-sequencing problem.** Latch-up is a potentially disastrous phenomenon where a parasitic short is created between power and ground within a chip's substrate. Latch-up is triggered by injecting current into the substrate. This can happen in mixed-voltage systems where input voltages are applied that are higher than a chip's power supply voltage. In many cases, latch-up is accompanied by chip overheating that can lead to permanent chip damage. A recommended practice when powering up a system for the first time is to use an ammeter to monitor how much current the system is drawing, and touch all the components to see if any are getting excessively hot. If a component has gone into latch-

up, you will typically observe excess current consumption on the order of hundreds of milliamps.

9. **Thermal problem.** This is a problem primarily with linear voltage regulators and high power digital circuitry. Verify that all high power components are properly heat sinked, and that the heat sinks are properly isolated in the case that they contact an electrically active part of the chip package.

10. **Unintentional short to bare copper.** This is a problem with connectors and chips that have exposed regions of metal on their undersides that can short across exposed regions of the board, such as vias. This is also a problem around areas where screws are used to hold a board in place. The head of a metal screw can inadvertently come in contact with a via that has been placed too close to the screw hole.

11. **Contamination of the board.** This problem is caused by solder flux residue or other process residue on the board causing low-current leakage paths. Some flux residues have a non-negligible (less than one mega-ohm) resistance and this can cause problems with high-impedance circuits, such as slow time constant R-C networks.

12. **Faulty test equipment.** This is especially a problem if you use second-hand or old test equipment. Test probes develop kinks and calibration faults over time, so sometimes the crummy signal you are seeing on the oscilloscope is actually a result of a bad test probe or a poor choice of probe ground. Calibrate your test equipment to a known good signal to eliminate test equipment problems.

13. The least likely problem is a **bad chip or a faulty component**. Component manufacturers go to great lengths to ensure that the parts shipped to you are functional. Typical failure rates are measured in the single-digit parts per million for simple to moderately complex parts. Frequently, we like to imagine that the cause of our problem is a bad chip from the manufacturer, but that is almost never the case. Usually, if a bad part is found, the part was damaged either by a processing problem (rough handling or assembly issues) or a design problem elsewhere in the circuit that induces the observed failure.

Recovering from a Lifted Trace or Pad

The lifting or tearing of the copper traces on a circuit board is a common problem encountered by people trying to install after-market modifications using flying wires. This delamination of the copper foil traces is usually caused by excessive heat from the soldering iron. Another common cause is pulling on the attached modification wire, as one might do while stripping the insulation off the end of a wire, after it has been soldered to the circuit board. Fortunately, it is usually fairly easy to recover from this problem.

Tip

The best solution is prevention. Do not use an over-powered soldering iron for working on circuit boards. A temperature-controlled iron is preferred, but an inexpensive low-wattage (15 watts) iron will also work. Also, if the solder does not seem to be sticking to the board, stop applying heat. Instead, put a touch of flux on the board and the wire, and clean the soldering iron tip with tip conditioner or a sponge damped with distilled water (tap water contains chemicals that can degrade soldering iron tips). This will enhance solderability so you do not need to apply as much heat or force to make the connection.

The first thing to do when you see a trace or pad lifting off of the circuit board is to STOP! Do not aggravate the problem further; the worst thing you can do is cause the entire trace to peel back by continuing to pull on the wire. Remove the wire, if it is still connected, by barely touching the soldering iron to the joint and letting the wire fall off. Figure E-1 illustrates such a disaster scene.

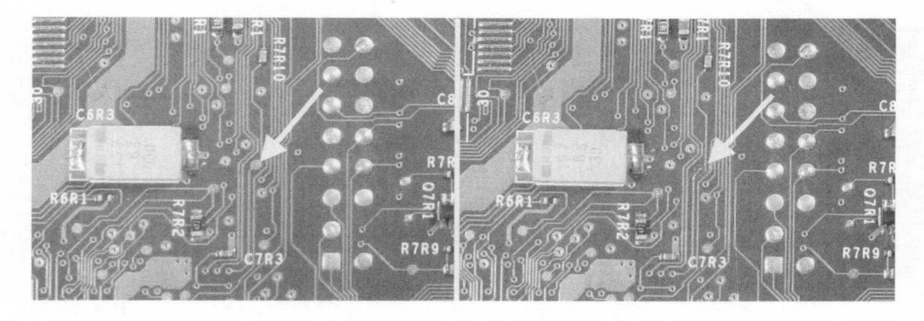

Figure E-1:
Left, arrow points to the original pad that is being soldered. Right, pad has been torn off through excess heat and force.

The strategy for recovering from a broken trace is to remove the soldermask, fix the trace with a jumper wire, and find an alternate point for soldering by following the trace to a nearby component or via.

Removing the soldermask reveals the underlying copper traces. A short jumper wire can be soldered to these bared traces to fix the discontinuity caused by the torn trace. The bare region also serves as a convenient starting point for using a continuity meter to find an alternate point for affixing the jumper wire. Remove the soldermask using either a fine-grit (200 or finer) sandpaper, or by scraping the surface with a sharp hobbyists knife. When removing the soldermask, be careful not to catch pieces of the broken trace and further tear the trace of the board. Once the soldermask has been removed, clean the region with a gentle solvent, such as rubbing alcohol, using a cotton swab. Then, apply a very thin layer of soldering flux to the region and rub a clean soldering iron tip along the exposed traces. Small amounts of solder sticking to the iron's tip will wick onto the circuitboard and coat the traces, preventing oxidation of the bare copper. If the iron's tip is too clean, apply a drop of solder to the iron's tip and lightly wipe the tip off in a wet sponge and try again. Do not attempt to tin the exposed traces with a ball of molten solder on the tip. Excess solder will be deposited that can lead to shorts. Note that the soldering flux is essential for getting a uniform, thin coating of solder on the traces. Do not skip the application of the solder flux. Figure E-2 illustrates what the traces will look like before and after the tinning process.

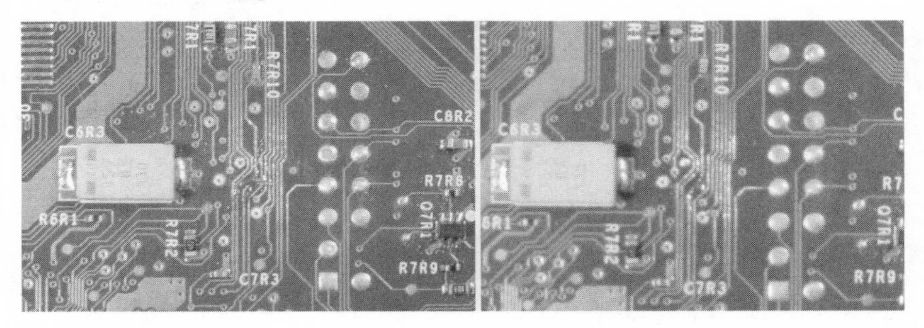

Figure E-2:
Left, region after soldermask has been removed with fine-grit sandpaper. Right, region after it has been tinned (reconditioned for soldering).

At this point, you may want to use a continuity meter to determine an alternate point for attaching your modification wire. Most voltmeters come with an audible continuity meter function. When selected, a tone is emitted from the voltmeter whenever the resistance between the probes is very low. Vias and component leads both make good alternate attachment points. If you decide to use a via, you must scrap the solder mask off and condition the via prior to attaching the modification wire. Figure E-3 illustrates using a continuity meter to find an alternate soldering point. Keep in mind that sometimes you will have to trace through several vias to find the best alternate attachment point.

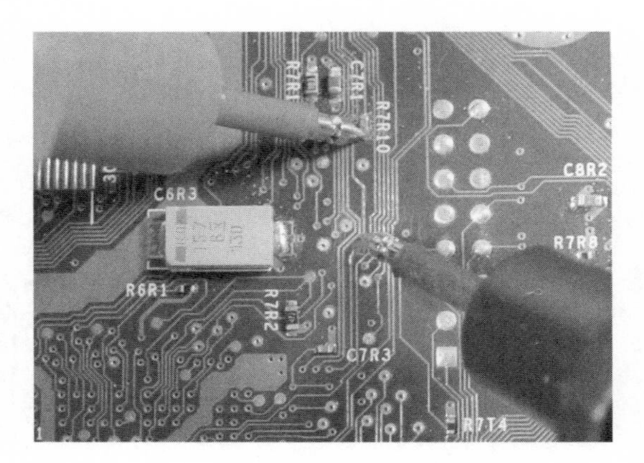

Figure E-3:
Using a continuity meter to find an alternate attachment point. In this case, R7R10 turns out to be a good alternate attachment point.

The next step is to attach a short jumper wire across the broken trace. Apply a touch more soldering flux over the region of the broken trace. Cut a piece of fine wire (about 30-gauge wire) that is about the length of the gap in question. Place the wire over the gap, using the stickiness of the soldering flux to aid the placement process. Hold the wire in place with a pair of tweezers, and apply heat with the soldering iron until both sides have bonded to the edges of the broken trace. Verify that the wire is in place by gently pushing on the wire with the tweezers; the wire should not move if a secure connection was made. Also inspect for shorts to neighboring traces using your continuity meter. If a short is discovered, simply heat the jumper until it falls off the board and try again. Figure E-4 illustrates what the repaired trace looks like.

Finally, attach the modification wire to the alternate soldering point that was discovered previously using the continuity meter.

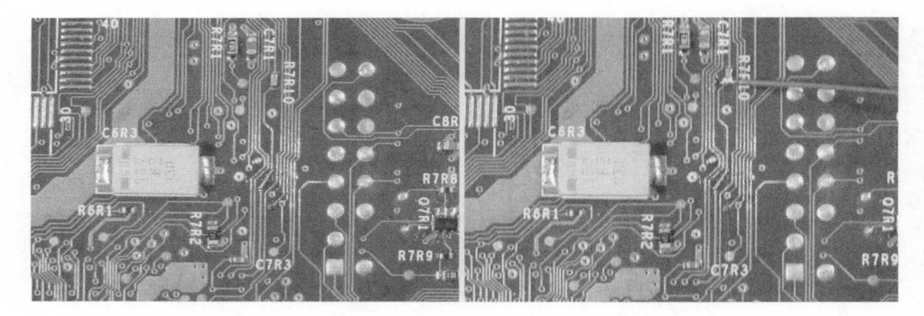

Figure E-4:

Left, a jumper has been installed over the damaged trace. Right, the modification wire has been successfully attached to the alternate soldering point.

APPENDIX F

Xbox Hardware Reference

This appendix summarizes the pinouts of the major connectors employed in the Xbox hardware.

Power Supply Pinout

The power supply used in the Xbox is a switcher rated at 96 watts maximum, with a peak pulse capability of 160 watts for less than 10 seconds. Microsoft buys this power supply from multiple vendors. Delta Electronics, Inc. (`www.deltaww.com`) is is one of these vendors. Their DPSN-96AP A is used in the United States Xboxes and you can find a datasheet for this part through their website or through a web search.

Pin	Description	Wire Color
1	+12V	Yellow
2	+5V	Red
3	+5V	Red
4	+5V	Red
5	+3.3V	Orange
6	+3.3V Standby	Brown
7	GND	Black
8	GND	Black
9	GND	Black
10	GND	Black
11	Power On	White
12	Power OK	Blue

Table G-1:
Main power connector pinouts. Wire colors may vary slightly depending upon the specific power supply model used in your Xbox. This table applies to the Delta DPSN-96AP A version power supply.

Description	Wire Color
+12V	Yellow
GND	Black
GND	Black
+5V	Red

Table G-2:
Hard disk power connector pinouts.

Video Connector Pinout

The video connector pinout is a little bit of a mystery because some of its signals show no obvious or recognizable signal patterns when probed, and because multiple display modes are supported by a single connector. There are a few websites that post pinouts for the video connector, but cross-checking the posted information with measurements reveals some discrepancies. I have done my best here to piece together and reconcile two separate postings from the XboxHacker BBS and the ucon64 web page at Sourceforge.net. The original postings can be found at `http://www.xboxhacker.net/index.php?do=article&id=10&page=1` and at `http://ucon64.sourceforge.net/ucon64misc/conn.html`. The definition of all eight video modes selectable by the MODE1-3 signals is listed on the XboxHacker BBS web page. My measurements indicate that all of the composite video and audio signal mappings are correct, but I was unable to verify the SDTV, HDTV and RGB mappings as given by the Xboxhacker BBS posting. I apologize in advance if any of these signals are incorrect.

Note that pins 12 and 24 have longer pins on the Xbox's connector, which indicate that they are used to supply power to peripherals attached to the video connector during hot-insertion events. The longer pins allow a peripheral's circuitry to power up before receiving signals in the event that the peripheral is connected while the Xbox is powered on. This helps prevent a potentially destructive situation inside the peripheral's chips called latch-up.

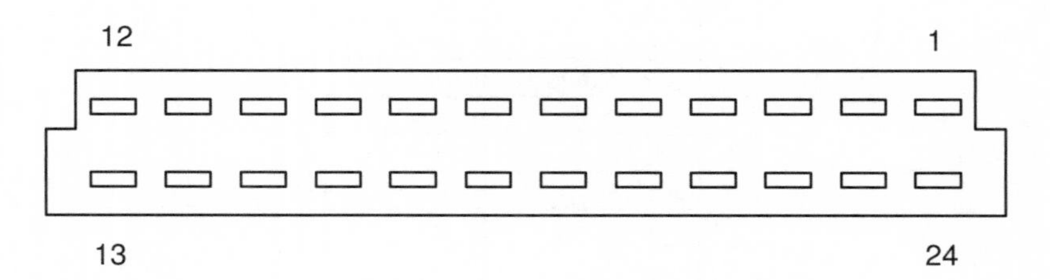

Figure G-1:
Xbox audio-video connector, as viewed while looking at the Xbox back panel from the outside.

Pin	Signal Name	I/O	Comment
1	Right Audio	Out	Audio out, right channel
2	GND	Power	
3	SPDIF	Out	Sony/Philips Digital Interface (S/PDIF) audio output
4	VSYNC	Out	Vertical Sync (VGA output mode)
5	GND	Power	
6	GND	Power	
7	GND	Power	
8	GND	Power	
9	Pb / B	Out	Pb for HDTV mode, Blue for RGB mode
10	GND	Power	
11	Y / G	Out	Y in SDTV and HDTV modes, Green in RGB mode
12	GND	Power	Has longer pins for hot-insertion
13	CVIDEO	Out	Composite video out.
14	GND	Power	
15	C / Pr / R	Out	C in SDTV, Pr in HDTV, Red in RGB mode
16	GND	Power	
17	STATUS	Out	SCART (Syndicat des Constructeurs d'Appareils Radio Récepteurs et Téléviseurs) status pin
18	MODE3	In	Video output mode select pin 3
19	MODE2	In	Video output mode select pin 2
20	MODE1	In	Video output mode select pin 1
21	HSYNC	Out	Horizontal Sync (VGA output mode)
22	GND	Power	Left channel audio cable shield
23	Left Audio	Out	Audio out, left channel
24	+5V	Power	+5V power, has longer pins for hot-insertion

Table G-3:
Video connector pinouts.

The pin numbering used by Table G-3 for the Xbox video connector is illustrated in Figure G-1. Both the Xboxhacker-derived pinout and the ucon64-derived pinouts disagree in terms of their numbering scheme, so I chose a number scheme that is somewhere in between the two schemes. Interestingly, pin 24 in Figure G-1 is mapped to a square pad on the Xbox video connector, indicating that the numbering scheme I chose to give the connector here is not consistent with the manufacturer's numbering scheme (square pads typically indicate pin 1, while round pads indicate all other pins). This should not have an effect on the correctness of the table, as pin numbering schemes are arbitrary and only need to be consistent with the pin definition table for correctness.

USB Connector Pinout

The Xbox uses a USB derivative for the game controller ports. There are four game controller ports on the front of the Xbox, and all of them have an identical pinout, depicted in Figure G-2.

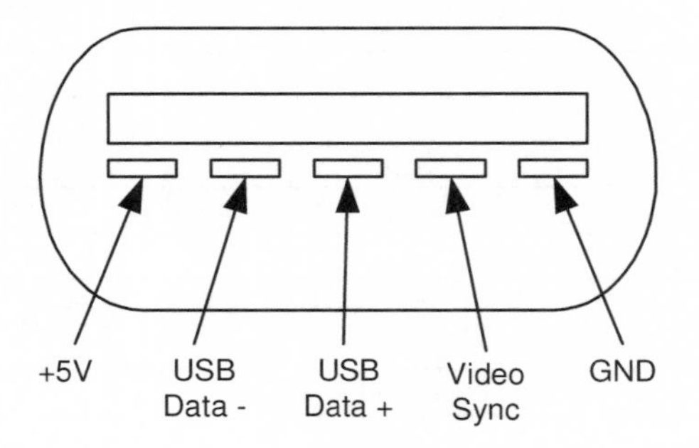

Figure G-2:
Game controller pinout, as viewed from outside the Xbox case looking at the connector.

The "video sync" signal is a 3.3V CMOS or TTL-compatible signal. It is a basic 15.734 kHz positive polarity pulse train synchronized to the horizontal line time of the composite video output, with a single longer pulse at the beginning of every video field. This signal enables peripherals, such as a light pen or a light gun for shooting games, that are pointed at the TV screen to derive position information.

The game controllers are connected to the Xbox via an intermediate break-away connector. The purpose of this break-away connector is to prevent console damage (particularly hard drive damage) by dragging or jerking in the event that a cord becomes entangled around a user's foot. The pinout of this break-away connector is depicted in Figure G-3.

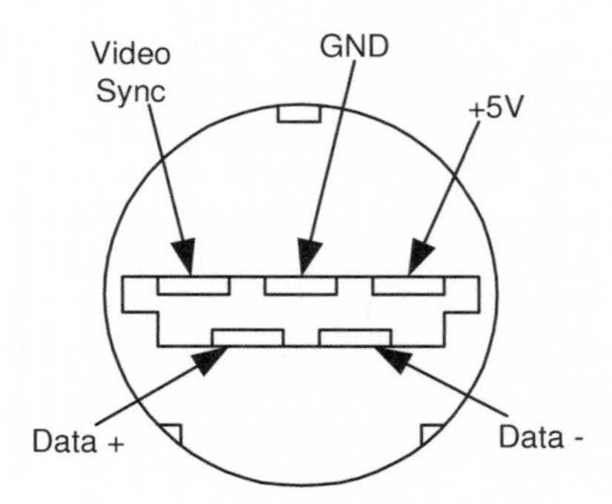

Figure G-3:
Game controller break-away pinout, as viewed looking head-on into the connector closer to the Xbox.

The Xbox game controller features two expansion slots for memory cards, microphones and other peripherals. These slots also provide a USB-compliant interface. The game controller contains a USB hub (an Atmel AT43USB401 hub chip) that repeats the incoming USB signal to the expansion slots. The pinout of the expansion connector is illustrated in Figure G-4.

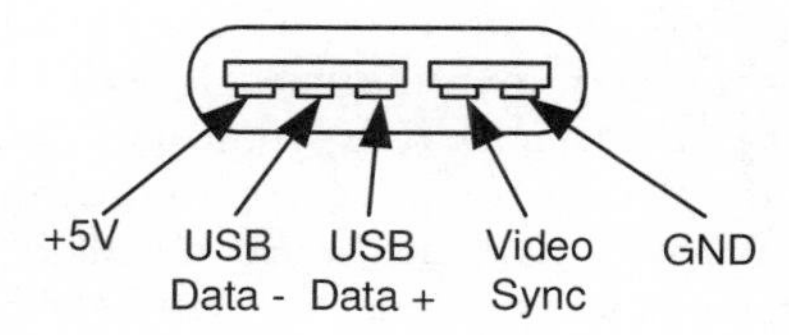

Figure G-4:
Game controller expansion slot pinout, as viewed looking into the game controller slot with the buttons facing up.

Ethernet Connector Pinout

The Ethernet port on the Xbox is a standard 10/100 base-TX twisted pair RJ-45 connector. The pinouts and colors of Table G-4 are based on the EIA/TIA 568B standard. Figure G-5 illustrates the pin numbering of the connector.

Pin	*Description*	*Wire Color*
1	Transmit +	Orange stripe
2	Transmit -	Orange
3	Receive +	Green stripe
4	*Not connected*	Blue
5	*Not connected*	Blue stripe
6	Receive -	Green
7	*Not connected*	Brown stripe
8	*Not connected*	Brown

Table G-4:
Ethernet 10/100 RJ-45 pinout.

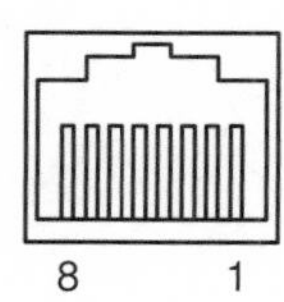

Figure G-5:
Pinout of the Xbox ethernet connector, seen looking from the outside toward the back panel of the Xbox.

ATA Connector Pinout

The Xbox uses the standard Advanced Technology Attachment (ATA) bus to communicate with its hard drive and DVD drive. The ATA bus is popularly (but technically improperly) referred to as the IDE (Integrated Drive Electronics) bus. Most drives today qualify as IDE-style drives; for example, SCSI drives also feature integrated drive electronics. However, years of (mis-) use has made the term IDE synonymous with the ATA bus. Table G-5 gives the pinout of the ATA connector, as viewed on the Xbox motherboard looking down on the connector with the back of the Xbox toward the viewer (connector should be on the right hand side). Note how the pin numbering zig-zags with all the odd pins on one side and the even pins on the other.

Pin	Name	Comment		Pin	Name	Comment
1	Reset			2	Ground	
3	Data 7			4	Data 8	
5	Data 6			6	Data 9	
7	Data 5			8	Data 10	
9	Data 4			10	Data 11	
11	Data 3			12	Data 12	
13	Data 2			14	Data 13	
15	Data 1			16	Data 14	
17	Data 0			18	Data 15	
19	Ground			20	Key	Blank pin for polarizing
21	DMARQ	DMA Request		22	Ground	
23	DIOW-	I/O Write		24	Ground	
25	DIOR-	I/O Read		26	Ground	
27	IORDY	I/O Ready		28	CSEL	Cable Select
29	DMACK-	DMA Acknowledge		30	Ground	
31	INTRQ	Interrupt Request		32	IOCS16-	16 bit I/O
33	DA1	Device Address Bit 1		34	PDIAG-	Passed Diagnostics
35	DA0	Device Address Bit 0		36	DA2	Device Address Bit 2
37	CS0-	Chip Select 0		38	CS1-	Chip Select 1
39	DASP-	Dev. Active/Slave Present		40	Ground	

Table G-5:
ATA connector pinout.

DVD-ROM Power Connector

The Xbox uses a proprietary DVD-ROM power connector. This connector not only brings power, but it also carries a few control and status signals. These signals convey information about the state of the drive and the drive tray. The pinouts given here are from the Xboxhacker BBS, and the original post by Ken Gasper that this pinout is based on can be found at
`http://www.xboxhacker.net/forums/`
`index.php?act=ST&f=5&t=1025&s=0755f2b600975b776552f93d0730e4b1`

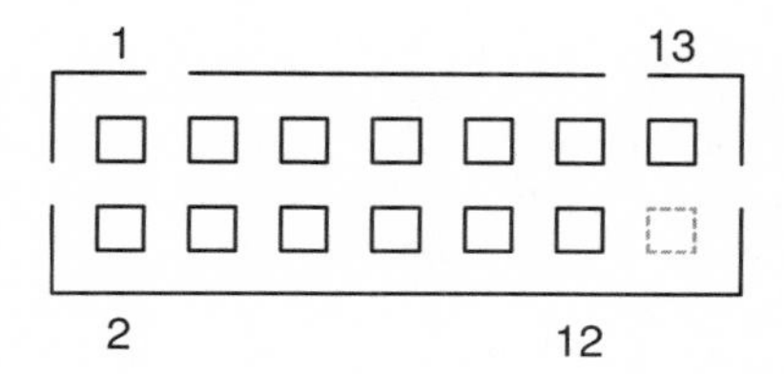

Figure G-6:
DVD-ROM power connector pin numbering, as viewed looking down at the Xbox motherboard.

The connector pin numbering, as viewed looking down at the Xbox motherboard, can be found in Figure G-6, and the pinout in Table G-6.

Pin	Name	Comment	Pin	Name	Comment
1	12VDC	+12 Volts power	2	5VDC	+5 Volts power
3	GND	Current return, reference	4	EJECT-	Active low tray eject
5	TS0	Traystate status 0	6	TS1	Traystate status 1
7	TS2	Traystate status 2	8	ACTIVITY-	Disk seek/data transfer
9	12VDC	+12 Volts power	10	5VDC	+5 Volts power
11	GND	Current return, reference	12	GND	Current return, reference
13	Key	Not connected			Blank for polarizing

Table G-6:
DVD power connector pinout (viewed on motherboard).

LPC Connector

The Xbox features a debug and test port based on the LPC (Low Pin Count) bus. This bus was originally defined by Intel for use with Southbridge chipsets to reduce pin count, thus saving on cost, while maintaining support for legacy PC I/O functions. These legacy I/O functions used to sit on the nearly extinct ISA bus, and they include the keyboard, mouse, serial port, parallel port, and boot ROM. Intel's specification for the LPC bus can be found at `http://www.intel.com/design/chipsets/industry/25128901.pdf`.

The LPC debug connector is particularly significant because it can be used to supply an alternate ROM image to the Xbox in the case that the built-in ROM is absent or corrupted in a fashion that makes the ROM seem absent or blank. This feature can be and has been used to make an easy to install alternate boot ROM for the Xbox.

The pinout for the Xbox LPC debug connector seems to be based on the Installable LPC Debug Module Design Guide by Intel, `http://www.intel.com/technology/easeofuse/LPC_mod_spec72.pdf`, with some minor modifications as noted in Table G-7. In particular, the function of pin 16 is unclear, as its companion pin 15 was re-assigned to be a power pin on the Xbox motherboard. The allocation of pin 15 as a power pin is deduced by the fat trace and nearby decoupling capacitor allocated to the pin. If pin 15 were intended for use as a permanently high SPDA1 signal, then a narrower trace without the power conditioning would have been used.

Pin	*Name*	*Comment*	*Pin*	*Name*	*Comment*
1	LCLK	33 MHz clock	2	VSS	Current return
3	LFRAME#	Start, end of LPC transactions	4	KEYWAY	Blank for polarizing
5	LRST#	LPC Reset	6	VCC5	+5V power
7	LAD3#	Muxed Address/Data	8	LAD2#	Muxed Address/Data
9	VCC3	+3.3V power	10	LAD1#	Muxed Address/Data
11	LAD0#	Muxed Address/Data	12	VSS	Current return
13	SCL	I2C serial clock	14	SDA	I2C serial data
15	VCC3	+3.3V power (was SPDA1 in Intel spec.)	16	SPDA0	Address select for serial EEPROM device (?).

Table G-7:
LPC connector pinout (as viewed on motherboard).

Fan Connector

The fan connector in the Xbox is a three-pin header, where pins 1 and 3 are connected to a temperature-regulating pulse-width-modulation (PWM) fan speed controller, and pin 2 is connected to the +12 volt power supply.

Front Panel Connector

The Xbox's front panel functions, namely the flashing LED, power switch and eject switch, are connected to the Xbox motherboard through the front panel connector. The pinout of this connector is given in Table G-8. The pinout reflects the pin numbering of the connector on the Xbox motherboard, as seen looking at the connector from above.

Pin	Comment	Pin	Comment
1	Ground	2	Power switch
3	Ground	4	Eject switch
5	Green LED	6	Red LED
7	Red LED	8	Green LED
9	Not connected but wired	10	No pin (polarization)

Table G-8:
Front panel connector (as viewed on motherboard).

Index of Chapters

D

E

F

G

H

I

J

K

L

M

N

O

P

R

S

T

U

V

W

X

Z